영어 오답의 모든 것 4

영끌극복 심화독해

꿈구두

독해 심화편 교재 소개하기

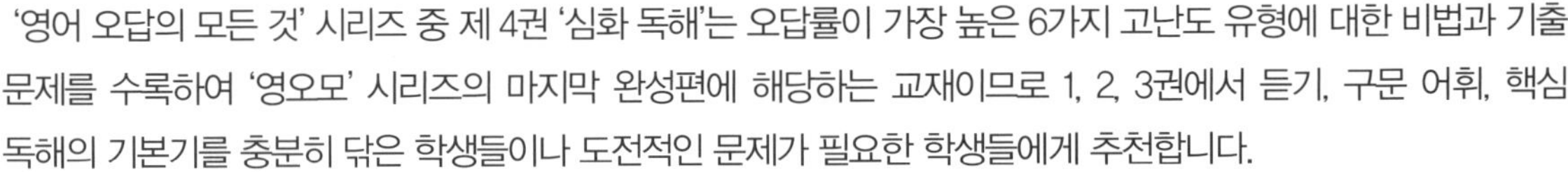

이 책의 특징

'영어 오답의 모든 것' 시리즈 중 제 4권 '심화 독해'는 오답률이 가장 높은 6가지 고난도 유형에 대한 비법과 기출 문제를 수록하여 '영오모' 시리즈의 마지막 완성편에 해당하는 교재이므로 1, 2, 3권에서 듣기, 구문 어휘, 핵심 독해의 기본기를 충분히 닦은 학생들이나 도전적인 문제가 필요한 학생들에게 추천합니다.

한국 교육 과정 평가원의 출제 원리에 따라 유형별 비법 소개, 비법 적용 방법, 오답인 이유 등을 철저히 분석하여 학생들 스스로가 혼자 공부할 수 있도록 구성하였습니다. 『글의 순서』와 『문장 삽입』 편에서는 논리적인 글의 흐름에 관련된 훈련을, 『빈칸 추론』과 『무관한 문장』 편에서는 논리적인 추론과 판단에 관련된 훈련을, 마지막으로 『어휘』와 『어법』 편에서는 글의 흐름상 적합한 것을 고를 수 있는 단계별 훈련이 가능한 교재입니다.

'심화 독해' 교재에 수록된 비법을 숙지하여 까다로운 유형에 대한 문제 풀이 감각을 기르고, 실전 연습 문제를 통해 응용력을 키우면, 학년별 학력평가와 대학수학능력 시험에서 향상된 자신의 실력을 확인할 수 있을 것입니다.

이 책의 구성 및 학습 활용법

1. Part OT

1 이 챕터는?

본격적인 독해 유형 학습 이전에, 반드시 알아야 할 연결사 7가지와 활용법을 알려 주는 챕터

2 학습 활용법 : 3단계 학습 구성

① 개념 학습

다양한 연결사의 의미와 종류에 대한 개념을 학습하는 단계

연결사를 활용한 글의 흐름 파악하기

1 「역접(대조)」 연결사

(1) A와 B는 서로 상반된 내용

연결사 앞 내용	역접(대조)의 연결사		연결사 뒤 내용
	의미	형태 및 종류	
A	그러나	but, yet, still, however	B (A의 반대)
	그럼에도 불구하고	nonetheless, nevertheless	
	대조적으로	in contrast, contrastingly, on the contrary	
그 외 역접(대조)의 표현들			
A	반면에	while, whereas, on the other hand	B (A의 반대)
	~임에도 불구하고	in spite of, despite, though, although, while, even if, even though	

② 비법 학습

다양한 실전 유형에 적용되는 구체적인 연결사의 핵심 비법을 학습하는 단계

(2) 연결사 핵심 비법

문제 유형	글의 흐름 파악
문장 삽입	주어진 문장에 '역접(대조)'의 연결사가 있을 경우, 주어진 문장이 들어갈 앞 부분에는 상반된 내용이 제시되어야 함.
글의 순서	글의 순서에서 '역접(대조)'의 연결사가 포함된 문단 앞에는 상반된 내용이 앞에 위치해야 함.
빈칸추론	빈칸에 해당하는 문장에 '역접(대조)'의 연결사가 있을 경우, 빈칸의 내용에는 앞 내용과 상반된 내용이 들어가야 함을 추론할 수 있음.

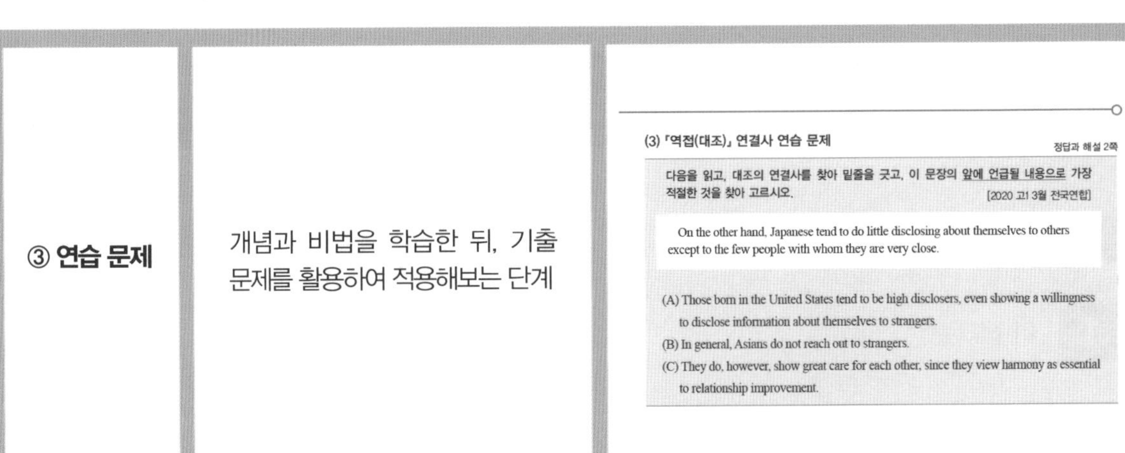

③ 연습 문제	개념과 비법을 학습한 뒤, 기출 문제를 활용하여 적용해보는 단계

(3) 「역접(대조)」 연결사 연습 문제 정답과 해설 2쪽

다음을 읽고, 대조의 연결사를 찾아 밑줄을 긋고, 이 문장의 앞에 언급될 내용으로 가장 적절한 것을 찾아 고르시오. [2020 고1 3월 전국연합]

On the other hand, Japanese tend to do little disclosing about themselves to others except to the few people with whom they are very close.

(A) Those born in the United States tend to be high disclosers, even showing a willingness to disclose information about themselves to strangers.
(B) In general, Asians do not reach out to strangers.
(C) They do, however, show great care for each other, since they view harmony as essential to relationship improvement.

2. Part I,II, III 독해 유형 학습

1 이 챕터는?

OT에서 학습한 내용을 바탕으로, 수능 영어 영역의 유형을 크게 '논리흐름/논리추론&판단/적합한 표현' 의 3가지로 나누어 각 유형의 실전 비법을 알려주는 챕터

2 학습 활용법 : 자기 주도 학습이 가능한 최적의 단계 구성

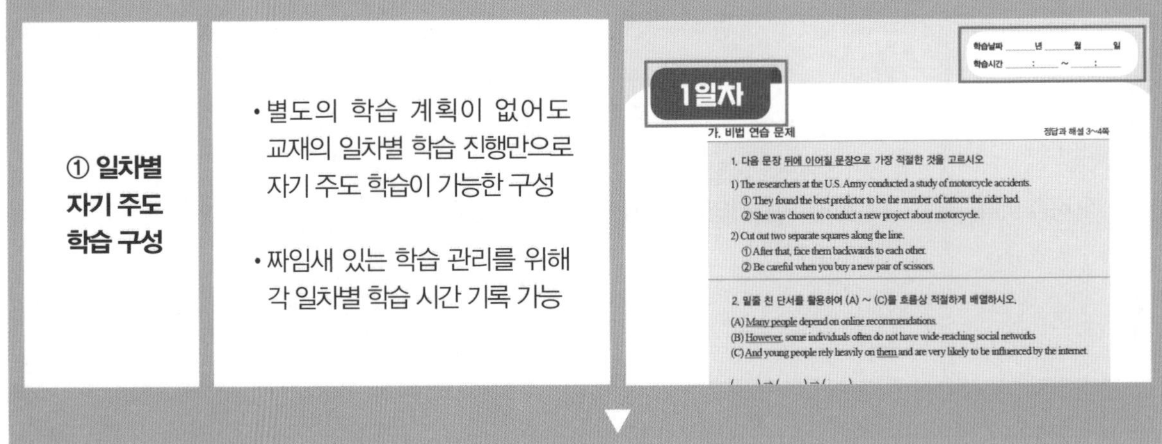

① 일차별 자기 주도 학습 구성	• 별도의 학습 계획이 없어도 교재의 일차별 학습 진행만으로 자기 주도 학습이 가능한 구성 • 짜임새 있는 학습 관리를 위해 각 일차별 학습 시간 기록 가능

학습날짜 ____년 ____월 ____일
학습시간 ____:____ ~ ____:____

1일차

가. 비법 연습 문제 정답과 해설 3~4쪽

1. 다음 문장 뒤에 이어질 문장으로 가장 적절한 것을 고르시오.

1) The researchers at the U.S. Army conducted a study of motorcycle accidents.
① They found the best predictor to be the number of tattoos the rider had.
② She was chosen to conduct a new project about motorcycle.

2) Cut out two separate squares along the line.
① After that, face them backwards to each other.
② Be careful when you buy a new pair of scissors.

2. 밑줄 친 단서를 활용하여 (A) ~ (C)를 흐름상 적절하게 배열하시오.

(A) Many people depend on online recommendations.
(B) However, some individuals often do not have wide-reaching social networks
(C) And young people rely heavily on them and are very likely to be influenced by the internet.

② 유형별 풀이 비법 학습

- 차원이 다른 유형별 비법
- 이보다 더 자세할 수 없을 만큼 친절하고 구체적인 안내 수록
- 가끔 등장하는 예외 사례까지 전부 포함

❶ 『글의 순서』

유형 풀이 비법 각 단락의 첫 문장과 마지막 문장에서 단서를 찾아라!

1) 특징 : 필자가 말하고자 하는 특정 소재의 특성을 나열함.

☞ 연결사, 대명사, 명사 앞 한정사 등의 단서를 통해 글의 연결고리를 찾을 수 있다.

단서의 종류	단서의 예	활용 방법 및 단락의 순서
연결사	역접, 인과, 예시 등	역접(however, still, yet 등) 연결사의 앞과 뒤는 서로 상반된 내용임. 인과(so, as a result 등) 연결사의 앞과 뒤는 서로 인과 관계의 내용임. 예시(for example, for instance)의 연결사 앞은 일반적인(general) 내용이며, 뒤에는 그에 대한 구체적인(specific) 내용이 나옴.
대명사	it/they/ them/their, he/his/him, she/her 등	구체적인 명사가 먼저 언급된 후 대명사로 표현됨. 대명사의 종류에 따라 성별/수일치에 유의해야 함.
명사 앞 한정사	the, such, this(these) that(those), another, +명사	'한정사+명사'에서 '명사'에 해당하는 말이 먼저 앞에서 나와야 함. *단, 명사에 해당하는 말이 추상적인 경우는 문맥상 내용의 연관성을 확인해야 함. ex) To prepare for the exams, you have to study hard on a regular basis. Through this process, you can get a high score. ☞여기서, this process는 앞 문장의 '규칙적인 학습'을 의미

③ 단계별 연습 문제

- 학습한 비법을 연습 문제를 통해 확인할 수 있도록 단계별 문제 제공

가. 비법 연습 문제

정답과 해설 3~4쪽

1. 다음 문장 뒤에 이어질 문장으로 가장 적절한 것을 고르시오

1) The researchers at the U.S. Army conducted a study of motorcycle accidents.
① They found the best predictor to be the number of tattoos the rider had.
② She was chosen to conduct a new project about motorcycle.

2) Cut out two separate squares along the line.
① After that, face them backwards to each other.
② Be careful when you buy a new pair of scissors.

2. 밑줄 친 단서를 활용하여 (A) ~ (C)를 흐름상 적절하게 배열하시오.

(A) Many people depend on online recommendations.
(B) However, some individuals often do not have wide-reaching social networks
(C) And young people rely heavily on them and are very likely to be influenced by the internet.

(　　) ⇒ (　　) ⇒ (　　)

④ 비법 적용

- 문제 풀이에서 자신이 적용한 비법과 적용하지 못 한 비법을 해설에서 직접 확인하고 비교 가능함

비법 적용

Suppose
☞ 바쁜 당신을 위하여 친구가 샌드위치를 사다 주겠다고 제안한 상황을 가정하고 있다.

(A) these two cases
☞ (these+명사) 'these two cases'를 의미하는 것이 먼저 제시되어야 하므로, 두 가지 상황이 이미 앞에서 펼쳐졌음을 예상할 수 있다.

(B) He
☞ (대명사) 'he' 에 해당하는 구체적인 명사가 앞에 등장하여야 하며, 'He'는 문맥상 당신에게 샌드위치를 사다 주겠다는 인물임을 알 수 있다.

(C) However, the same sandwich
☞ (역접, the+명사) 역접 연결사 'however'는 앞에 나온 내용에 상반되는 내용이 등장할 것임을 알려준다. 또한 'the same sandwich'는 앞에 어떤 샌드위치가 언급되었음을 의미한다. 낯선 사람이 샌드위치를 사다 주겠다고 제안한다면 당신은 혼란을 느낄 것이라 이야기하고 있다.
☞ 따라서 정답은 ③ (B)-(C)-(A)이다.

⑤ 오답의 모든 것	• 혹시 틀린 오답이 있더라도 정성껏 분석하고 피드백을 제공하여 똑같은 실수와 오답을 방지하도록 함	오답의 모든 것 (1) 첫 번째 문단 찾기 ▶ **친구가 샌드위치를 사다주겠다고 제안한 상황에서 대명사 'He'는 주어진 문장의 '당신의 친구(your best friend)'를 의미하므로 (B)가 먼저 오는 것이 정답** ▶ '이 두 경우(these two)'가 가리키는 것이 주어진 문장에 없으므로 (A)는 오답 ▶ 주어진 문장에 나온 친구에 대한 부연 설명 없이 'however'와 함께 '낯선 사람이 샌드위치를 사다 주겠다고 제안하는 상황'은 어색하므로 (C)는 오답 (2) 두 번째 문단 찾기 ▶ **친구가 샌드위치를 사다주겠다고 한다면, 고마움을 느낄 것이라는 (B)의 뒤에서, 낯선 사람이 같은 제안을 한다면, 고마움을 느끼지 않을 것이라는 내용이 'however'를 이용해 자연스럽게 이어지므로 (C)는 정답** ▶ '이 두 경우(these two)'가 가리키는 것을 (B)까지의 내용에서는 찾을 수 없으므로 (A)는 오답 (3) 세 번째 문단 찾기 ▶ **'이 두 경우(these two cases)'는 (B)와 (C)의 '친한 친구가 제안할 때'와 '낯선 사람이 제안할 때'의 두 가지 경우를 의미하므로 (A)는 정답**

3. Part Ⅳ 파이널 모의고사 2회

1 이 챕터는?

Part Ⅰ, Ⅱ, Ⅲ에서 학습한 비법을 마지막으로 최종 점검하고 확인할 수 있도록 6개의 유형별 문제를 각 2문항씩 12문항으로 구성한 모의고사 2회

2 학습 활용법 : 앞의 유형별, 단계별 학습이 완료된 후의 실력 점검

주의사항

① 앞에서 비법을 충분히 익힌 뒤 도전할 것

② 최대한 해설지에 의존하지 않고 자신의 힘만으로 해결하도록 할 것

③ 채점 후 반드시 모든 문항에 대한 비법 적용과 오답의 모든 것을 확인하여 자신의 것과 비교해 볼 것

④ 복습은 반드시 5회 이상하여 체화할 수 있도록 권장함

영끌극복
심화독해

영어 오답의 모든것

영끌극복 심화독해

OT 연결사를 활용한 글의 흐름 파악하기

I 글의 논리 흐름 관련 독해 유형

II 논리 추론 및 논리 판단 관련 독해 유형

III 글의 흐름상 적합한 표현 관련 독해 유형

IV 파이널 모의고사

OT

연결사를 활용한 글의 흐름 파악하기

영어
오답의
모든것

연결사를 활용한 글의 흐름 파악하기

1 『역접(대조)』 연결사

(1) A와 B는 서로 상반된 내용

연결사 앞 내용	역접(대조)의 연결사		연결사 뒤 내용
	의미	형태 및 종류	
A	그러나	but, yet, still, however	B (A의 반대)
	그럼에도 불구하고	nonetheless, nevertheless	
	대조적으로	in contrast, contrastingly, on the contrary	
그 외 역접(대조)의 표현들			
A	반면에	while, whereas, on the other hand	B (A의 반대)
	~임에도 불구하고	in spite of, despite, though, although, while, even if, even though	

(2) 연결사 핵심 비법

문제 유형	글의 흐름 파악
문장 삽입	주어진 문장에 '역접(대조)'의 연결사가 있을 경우, 주어진 문장이 들어갈 앞 부분에는 상반된 내용이 제시되어야 함.
글의 순서	글의 순서에서 '역접(대조)'의 연결사가 포함된 문단 앞에는 상반된 내용이 앞에 위치해야 함.
빈칸추론	빈칸에 해당하는 문장에 '역접(대조)'의 연결사가 있을 경우, 빈칸의 내용에는 앞 내용과 상반된 내용이 들어가야 함을 추론할 수 있음.

(3) 『역접(대조)』 연결사 연습 문제

정답과 해설 2쪽

다음을 읽고, 대조의 연결사를 찾아 밑줄을 긋고, 이 문장의 앞에 언급될 내용으로 가장 적절한 것을 찾아 고르시오. [2020 고1 3월 전국연합]

On the other hand, Japanese tend to do little disclosing about themselves to others except to the few people with whom they are very close.

(A) Those born in the United States tend to be high disclosers, even showing a willingness to disclose information about themselves to strangers.

(B) In general, Asians do not reach out to strangers.

(C) They do, however, show great care for each other, since they view harmony as essential to relationship improvement.

2 『예시』 연결사 학습하기

(1) 특징 : A는 B의 일반적인(general) 진술이며, B는 A에 대한 구체적(specific)인 부연 설명

연결사 앞 내용	예시의 연결사		연결사 뒤 내용
	의미	형태 및 종류	
A (general statement)	예를 들면	for example, for instance	B (specific statement)
	~의 예로	as an illustration of	
그 외 예시의 표현들			
A (general statement)	예를 들어보자	Suppose (that) Imagine (that) Let's say (that)	B (specific statement)

(2) 연결사 핵심 비법

문제 유형	글의 흐름 파악
주제, 제목, 요지	예시의 연결사가 있는 문장의 앞 내용이 글 전체의 주제가 됨.
빈칸 추론	빈칸 문장 뒤에 '예시'의 연결사가 있을 경우, 예시의 내용을 일반화하여 주제문을 완성하라는 뜻.
글의 순서	글의 순서 상, '예시'의 연결사가 포함된 문장 앞에는 예시를 포괄하는 일반적 진술의 문장이 먼저 와야 함.

(3) 『예시』 연결사 연습 문제

정답과 해설 2쪽

다음을 읽고, 예시의 연결사를 찾아 밑줄을 긋고, 이 문장의 앞에 올 수 있는 내용으로 가장 적절한 것을 고르시오. [2018 고1 6월 전국연합]

For example, if you are motivated to buy a good car, you will research vehicles online, look at ads, visit dealerships, and so on.

(A) Likewise, if you are motivated to lose weight, you will buy low-fat foods, eat smaller portions, and exercise.

(B) One outcome of motivation is behavior that takes considerable effort.

(C) Thus, someone motivated to buy a new smartphone may earn extra money for it, drive through a storm to reach the store, and then wait in line to buy it.

3 『인과(원인과 결과)』 연결사 학습하기

(1) 특징 : A는 B의 원인이며, B는 A로 인한 결과임. 즉 서로에 대해 영향을 주고받는 내용

연결사 앞 내용	인과의 연결사		연결사 뒤 내용
	의미	형태 및 종류	
A (원인)	따라서, 그래서	accordingly, and so, thus, therefore, hence	B (결과)
	결국, 그 결과	as a result, consequently, finally, at last, in consequence, in the end, in the long run, in conclusion	
그 외 인과의 표현들			
B (결과)	~ 때문에	because, since, because of, on account of, owing to, due to	A (원인)

(2) 연결사 핵심 비법

문제 유형	글의 흐름 파악
문장 삽입	주어진 문장에 '인과'의 연결사가 포함되어 있을 경우, 주어진 문장과 그 앞의 내용은 인과 관계가 성립해야 함.
글의 순서	'인과'의 연결사가 포함된 문장인 경우, 앞에 오는 내용은 인과 관계가 성립해야 함.
빈칸 추론	빈칸 문장이 '인과'의 연결사로 시작하는 경우, 빈칸 문장과 그 앞의 내용은 인과 관계가 성립해야 함.

(3) 『인과(원인과 결과)』 연결사 연습 문제

정답과 해설 2쪽

다음 문장에서 인과의 연결사 찾아 밑줄을 긋고, 이 문장의 앞에 올 수 있는 내용으로 가장 적절한 것을 고르시오.

[2018 고1 9월 전국연합]

As a result, we didn't have much of a relationship when I was young other than him constantly nagging me to take care of chores like mowing the lawn and cutting the hedges, which I hated.

(A) He was a responsible man dealing with an irresponsible kid.

(B) Memories of how we interacted seems funny to me today.

(C) My dad worked very late hours as a musician—until about three in the morning—so he slept late on weekends.

『비교』 연결사 학습하기

(1) 특징 : A와 B의 내용은 서로 유사하거나 같은 원리의 내용

예시 앞 내용	비교의 연결사		연결사 뒤 내용
	의미	형태 및 종류	
A	마찬가지로	similarly, likewise, in the same way, by the same token	B (A와 유사한 원리)
그 외 비교의 표현들			
A	~와 비교하여	compared with[to], in comparison to	B (A와 유사한 원리)

(2) 연결사 핵심 비법

문제 유형	글의 흐름 파악
문장 삽입	지문 속이나 주어진 문장에 '비교'의 연결사가 있을 경우, 비교 연결사가 있는 앞 • 뒤 내용의 속성은 서로 유사함.
글의 순서	글의 순서 상, '비교'의 연결사가 포함된 문장 앞 • 뒤에는 서로 유사한 속성의 내용이 배치되어야 함.
빈칸 추론	빈칸 앞이나 뒤에 '비교'의 연결사가 있을 경우, 서로 유사한 속성이거나 같은 원리의 내용을 빈칸에 적용해야 함.
어휘 추론	밑줄 친 어휘의 앞이나 뒤에 '비교' 연결사가 있을 경우, 연결사 앞 • 뒤의 내용을 유사한 의미로 만들어주는 어휘를 선택해야 함.

(3) 『비교』 연결사 연습 문제

정답과 해설 2쪽

다음을 읽고, 비교 연결사를 찾아 밑줄을 긋고, 각 문장의 앞에 올 수 있는 문장을 〈보기〉에서 고르시오.

〈보기〉

(A) If you are motivated to buy a good car, you will research vehicles online, look at ads, visit dealerships, and so on.

[2018 고1 6월 전국연합]

(B) One study of 137 instant messaging users revealed that emoticons allowed users to correctly understand the level and direction of emotion, attitude, and attention expression and that emoticons were a definite advantage in non-verbal communication.

[2020 고1 6월 전국연합]

(C) If a library has a long tradition of heavily collecting materials published in Mexico, its Mexican collection will still be large and impressive for several years to come unless they start withdrawing books.

[2020 고3 9월 평가원]

① Likewise, if a library has not collected much in a subject, and then decides to start collecting heavily in that area, it will take several years for the collection to be large enough and rich enough to be considered an important research tool. ( )

② Likewise, if you are motivated to lose weight, you will buy low-fat foods, eat smaller portions, and exercise. ( )

③ Similarly, another study showed that emoticons were useful in strengthening the intensity of a verbal message, as well as in the expression of sarcasm. ( )

5 『재진술(부연)』 연결사 학습하기

(1) 특징 : A와 B의 내용은 서로 동일한 의미

연결사 앞 내용	재진술(부연)의 연결사		연결사 뒤 내용
	의미	형태 및 종류	
A	즉, 다시 말해서	namely, or, in other words, that is (to say), so to speak, to put it another way	B (A와 동일한 의미)

(2) 연결사 핵심 비법

문제 유형	글의 흐름 파악
문장 삽입	주어진 문장이나 지문 속에 '재진술'의 연결사가 있을 경우, 재진술의 문장과 앞 문장이 서로 동일한 의미인지 확인해야 함.
글의 순서	글의 순서 상, '재진술'의 연결사가 포함된 문장 앞에는 동일한 의미의 문장이 제시되어야 함.
빈칸 추론	빈칸 뒤 또는 앞에 '재진술'의 연결사가 있을 경우, 앞 • 뒤 문장에는 서로 동일한 내용이 들어가야 함.
어휘 추론	밑줄 친 어휘의 앞이나 뒤에 '재진술' 연결사가 있을 경우, 연결사 앞 • 뒤의 내용을 동일한 의미로 만들어주는 어휘를 선택해야 함.
글의 흐름	지문에 '재진술'의 연결사가 있을 경우, 앞 • 뒤 문장이 서로 동일한 의미인지 확인해야 함.

(3) 『재진술(부연)』 연결사 연습 문제

정답과 해설 2쪽

다음을 읽고, 재진술의 연결사를 찾아 밑줄을 긋고, 이 문장의 앞에 언급될 내용으로 가장 적절한 것을 고르시오.

[2020 고3 6월 전국연합]

In other words, the adaptation process initiated by stress can lead to personal changes for the better.

(A) Having to deal with a moderate amount of stress may build resilience in the face of future stress.

(B) A follow-up study found a similar link between the amount of lifetime adversity and subjects' responses to laboratory stressors.

(C) Stressful events sometimes force people to develop new skills, reevaluate priorities, learn new insights, and acquire new strengths.

6 『나열(순서)』 연결사 학습하기

(1) 특징 : 필자가 말하고자 하는 특정 소재의 특성을 나열함.

나열(순서)의 연결사	
의미	형태 및 종류
우선, 먼저	first of all, in the first step, for one thing
~후에	then, next, later, after, that, afterwards, subsequently

(2) 연결사 핵심 비법

문제 유형	글의 흐름 파악
요약문 지칭 추론	실험과 관련된 지문에서 과정이나 절차가 순서대로 나열되거나, 어떤 대상을 소개하는 지문에서 세부 요소나 항목이 나열될 수 있다.
글의 순서	글의 순서에서 '나열'의 연결사가 포함된 문단은 앞의 내용에 뒤이어 나오는 이야기가 전개되어야 함.

(3) 『나열』 연결사 연습 문제

정답과 해설 2쪽

다음을 읽고, 나열의 연결사를 찾아 밑줄을 긋고, 이 문장의 앞에 올 수 있는 문장으로 가장 적절한 것을 고르시오.

[2019 고1 3월 전국연합]

Later, he regrets this, in case God was enjoying listening to the sound of the frog. I invite children to think of different animals for the saint to meet and different places for him to meet them.

(A) Some snakes and birds lives on frogs, mice, and rats.
(B) When the young frog hatches out of the eggs, it looks like fish.
(C) The saint meets a frog in a marsh and tells it to be quiet in case it disturbs his prayers.

7 『첨가』 연결사 학습하기

(1) 특징 : 동일한 소재에 대한 추가적 설명이 연결사 뒤에서 이어짐.

연결사 앞 내용	첨가의 연결사		연결사 뒤 내용
	의미	형태 및 종류	
A	게다가	besides, what is more furthermore, moreover into the bargain	B (추가 설명)
	덧붙여	in addition, additionally	
	또한	also, too, as well	

(2) 연결사 핵심 비법

문제 유형	글의 흐름 파악
글의 순서	글의 순서에 제시되는 (A), (B), (C) 중 '첨가'의 연결사가 포함되어 있을 경우, 동일한 소재에 대한 설명을 제공하는 내용 뒤에 배치되어야 함.
문장 삽입	주어진 문장에 '첨가'의 연결사가 있을 경우, 앞 내용과 동일한 소재에 대한 추가 설명이 이어지는 부분에 위치해야 함.

(3) 『첨가』 연결사 연습 문제

정답과 해설 2쪽

다음 문장을 읽고, '첨가'의 연결사를 찾아 밑줄을 긋고, 이 문장의 앞에 올 수 있는 내용으로 가장 적절한 것을 고르시오.

[2018 고1 3월 전국연합]

Moreover, the experience would be ruined if people were to behave in such a way.

(A) Rather, one person cooks dinner, another sets up the tent and the other purifies the water.

(B) Camping trip can be used as a metaphor for the ideal society.

(C) A camping trip where each person attempted to take advantages of others would quickly end in disaster and unhappiness.

check list

✓	영 • 오 • 모 1일차 공부하기

I

1~4일차 학습하기

글의 논리 흐름 관련 독해 유형

영어
오답의
모든것

I 글의 논리 흐름 관련 독해 유형

1~2일차 학습하기

1 『글의 순서』

유형 풀이 비법 각 단락의 첫 문장과 마지막 문장에서 단서를 찾아라!

1) 특징 : 필자가 말하고자 하는 특정 소재의 특성을 나열함.

☞ 연결사, 대명사, 명사 앞 한정사 등의 단서를 통해 글의 연결고리를 찾을 수 있다.

단서의 종류	단서의 예	활용 방법 및 단락의 순서
연결사	역접, 인과, 예시 등	✎ 역접(however, still, yet 등) 연결사의 앞과 뒤는 서로 상반된 내용임. ✎ 인과(so, as a result 등) 연결사의 앞과 뒤는 서로 인과 관계의 내용임. ✎ 예시(for example, for instance)의 연결사 앞은 일반적인(general) 내용이며, 뒤에는 그에 대한 구체적인(specific) 내용이 나옴.
대명사	it/they/them/their, he/his/him, she/her 등	✎ 구체적인 명사가 먼저 언급된 후 대명사로 표현됨. ✎ 대명사의 종류에 따라 성별/수일치에 유의해야 함.
명사 앞 한정사	the, such, this(these) that(those), another, +명사	✎ '한정사+명사'에서 '명사'에 해당하는 말이 먼저 앞에서 나와야 함. *단, 명사에 해당하는 말이 추상적인 경우는 문맥상 내용의 연관성을 확인해야 함. ex) To prepare for the exams, you have to study hard on a regular basis. Through this process, you can get a high score. ☞여기서, this process는 앞 문장의 '규칙적인 학습'을 의미

2) (A), (B), (C) 각 단락에 단서가 없는 경우

☞ 시간의 흐름, 논리적 관계 등을 통해 글의 연결고리를 찾을 수 있다. 사건이 자연스럽게 전개되는 과정을 생각해 본다. 장문 독해 유형에 자주 등장한다.

주어진 문장	도랑에 차가 빠졌다.
(A)	빠진 차를 꺼내기 위해 주변 사람에게 도움을 요청했다.
(B)	사람들이 도와주러 왔다.
(C)	도움을 받아 곤경에서 빠져 나왔다.

학습날짜 ______ 년 ______ 월 ______ 일

학습시간 ____ : ____ ~ ____ : ____

1일차

가. 비법 연습 문제

정답과 해설 3~4쪽

1. 다음 문장 뒤에 이어질 문장으로 가장 적절한 것을 고르시오

1) The researchers at the U.S. Army conducted a study of motorcycle accidents.

① They found the best predictor to be the number of tattoos the rider had.

② She was chosen to conduct a new project about motorcycle.

2) Cut out two separate squares along the line.

① After that, face them backwards to each other.

② Be careful when you buy a new pair of scissors.

2. 밑줄 친 단서를 활용하여 (A) ~ (C)를 흐름상 적절하게 배열하시오.

(A) Many people depend on online recommendations.

(B) However, some individuals often do not have wide-reaching social networks

(C) And young people rely heavily on them and are very likely to be influenced by the internet.

(　　) ⇒ (　　) ⇒ (　　)

나. 기출 연습 문제

주어진 글 뒤에 이어질 글의 순서로 가장 적절한 것을 고르시오.

[2019 고1 3월 전국연합 35번]

Suppose that you are busy working on a project one day and you have no time to buy lunch. All of a sudden your best friend shows up with your favorite sandwich.

(A) The key difference between these two cases is the level of trust. You trust your best friend so much that you won't worry about him knowing you too well, but you certainly would not give the same level of trust to a stranger.

(B) He tells you that he knows you are busy and he wants to help you out by buying you the sandwich. In this case, you are very likely to appreciate your friend's help.

(C) However, if a stranger shows up with the same sandwich and offers it to you, you won't appreciate it. Instead, you would be confused. You would likely think "Who are you, and how do you know what kind of sandwich I like to eat?"

① (A) - (C) - (B)　② (B) - (A) - (C)　③ (B) - (C) - (A)
④ (C) - (A) - (B)　⑤ (C) - (B) - (A)

비법 적용

Suppose
☞ 바쁜 당신을 위하여 친구가 샌드위치를 사다 주겠다고 제안한 상황을 가정하고 있다.

(A) these two cases
☞ (these+명사) 'these two cases'를 의미하는 것이 먼저 제시되어야 하므로, 두 가지 상황이 이미 앞에서 펼쳐졌음을 예상할 수 있다.

(B) He
☞ (대명사) 'he' 에 해당하는 구체적인 명사가 앞에 등장하여야 하며, 'He'는 문맥상 당신에게 샌드위치를 사다 주겠다는 인물임을 알 수 있다.

(C) However, the same sandwich
☞ (역접, the+명사) 역접 연결사 'however'는 앞에 나온 내용에 상반되는 내용이 등장할 것임을 알려준다. 또한 'the same sandwich'는 앞에 어떤 샌드위치가 언급되었음을 의미한다. 낯선 사람이 샌드위치를 사다 주겠다고 제안한다면 당신은 혼란을 느낄 것이라 이야기하고 있다.
☞ 따라서 정답은 ③ (B)-(C)-(A)이다.

오답의 모든 것

(1) 첫 번째 문단 찾기
▶ **친구가 샌드위치를 사다주겠다고 제안한 상황에서 대명사 'He'는 주어진 문장의 '당신의 친구(your best friend)'를 의미하므로 (B)가 먼저 오는 것이 정답**
▶ '이 두 경우(these two)'가 가리키는 것이 주어진 문장에 없으므로 (A)는 오답
▶ 주어진 문장에 나온 친구에 대한 부연 설명 없이 'however'와 함께 '낯선 사람이 샌드위치를 사다 주겠다고 제안하는 상황'은 어색하므로 (C)는 오답

(2) 두 번째 문단 찾기
▶ **친구가 샌드위치를 사다주겠다고 한다면, 고마움을 느낄 것이라는 (B)의 뒤에서, 낯선 사람이 같은 제안을 한다면, 고마움을 느끼지 않을 것이라는 내용이 'however'를 이용해 자연스럽게 이어지므로 (C)는 정답**
▶ '이 두 경우(these two)'가 가리키는 것을 (B)까지의 내용에서는 찾을 수 없으므로 (A)는 오답

(3) 세 번째 문단 찾기
▶ **'이 두 경우(these two cases)'는 (B)와 (C)의 '친한 친구가 제안할 때'와 '낯선 사람이 제안할 때'의 두 가지 경우를 의미하므로 (A)는 정답**

학습날짜 ______년 ______월 ______일

학습시간 ______:______ ~ ______:______

다. 실전 연습 문제

정답과 해설 4~5쪽

1. 주어진 글 다음에 이어질 글의 순서로 가장 적절한 것을 고르시오.

[2018 고1 6월 전국연합 36번]

In 1824, Peru won its freedom from Spain. Soon after, Simón Bolívar, the general who had led the liberating forces, called a meeting to write the first version of the constitution for the new country.

(A) "Then," said Bolívar, "I'll add whatever is necessary to this million pesos you have given me and I will buy all the slaves in Peru and set them free. It makes no sense to free a nation, unless all its citizens enjoy freedom as well."

(B) Bolívar accepted the gift and then asked, "How many slaves are there in Peru?" He was told there were about three thousand. "And how much does a slave sell for?" he wanted to know. "About 350 pesos for a man," was the answer.

(C) After the meeting, the people wanted to do something special for Bolívar to show their appreciation for all he had done for them, so they offered him a gift of one million pesos, a very large amount of money in those days.

① (A) - (C) - (B)　② (B) - (A) - (C)　③ (B) - (C) - (A)
④ (C) - (A) - (B)　⑤ (C) - (B) - (A)

✐ **어휘 Box** (모르는 어휘와 표현을 아래에 정리하고 해설을 통해 복습하세요.)

✐ **비법 적용 Box** (앞에서 배운 비법을 스스로 문장에 적용하고 해설과 비교해 보세요.)

2. 주어진 글 다음에 이어질 글의 순서로 가장 적절한 것을 고르시오.

[2019 고1 3월 전국연합 36번]

The basic difference between an AI robot and a normal robot is the ability of the robot and its software to make decisions, and learn and adapt to its environment based on data from its sensors.

(A) For instance, if faced with the same situation, such as running into an obstacle, then the robot will always do the same thing, such as go around the obstacle to the left. An AI robot, however, can do two things the normal robot cannot: make decisions and learn from experience.

(B) It will adapt to circumstances, and may do something different each time a situation is faced. The AI robot may try to push the obstacle out of the way, or make up a new route, or change goals.

(C) To be a bit more specific, the normal robot shows deterministic behaviors. That is, for a set of inputs, the robot will always produce the same output.

* deterministic: 결정론적인

① (A) - (C) - (B)
② (B) - (A) - (C)
③ (B) - (C) - (A)
④ (C) - (A) - (B)
⑤ (C) - (B) - (A)

어휘 Box (모르는 어휘와 표현을 아래에 정리하고 해설을 통해 복습하세요.)

비법 적용 Box (앞에서 배운 비법을 스스로 문장에 적용하고 해설과 비교해 보세요.)

3. 주어진 글 다음에 이어질 글의 순서로 가장 적절한 것을 고르시오.

[2019 고2 3월 전국연합 36번]

One of the first things I did in each classroom in South Milwaukee was to draw a diagram of the students' desks, labelled with their names, as an aid to recognizing them.

(A) One said, "Where's your name?" and was not satisfied until I included a sketch of the chair by the bookcase where I was sitting, labelled with my name. It had not occurred to me that I needed to be included: after all, I knew where I was sitting, and knew my name.

(B) At lunch in the first grade classroom the first day I was present, a group of students came over, saw the diagram, and began finding their names on my picture.

(C) But to her, my presence in the classroom was the newest, most noteworthy thing that had occurred that day, and it was logical to include me. Her point of view was different from mine, and resulted in a different diagram of the classroom.

① (A) - (C) - (B)　② (B) - (A) - (C)　③ (B) - (C) - (A)
④ (C) - (A) - (B)　⑤ (C) - (B) - (A)

✐ **어휘 Box** (모르는 어휘와 표현을 아래에 정리하고 해설을 통해 복습하세요.)

✐ **비법 적용 Box** (앞에서 배운 비법을 스스로 문장에 적용하고 해설과 비교해 보세요.)

4. 주어진 글 다음에 이어질 글의 순서로 가장 적절한 것을 고르시오.

[2019 고2 6월 전국연합 36번]

Without money, people could only barter. Many of us barter to a small extent, when we return favors.

(A) There is no need to find someone who wants what you have to trade; you simply pay for your goods with money. The seller can then take the money and buy from someone else. Money is transferable and deferrable — the seller can hold on to it and buy when the time is right.

(B) What would happen if you wanted a loaf of bread and all you had to trade was your new car? Barter depends on the double coincidence of wants, where not only does the other person happen to have what I want, but I also have what he wants. Money solves all these problems.

(C) A man might offer to mend his neighbor's broken door in return for a few hours of babysitting, for instance. Yet it is hard to imagine these personal exchanges working on a larger scale.

* barter: 물물 교환(하다)

① (A) - (C) - (B)　　② (B) - (A) - (C)　　③ (B) - (C) - (A)
④ (C) - (A) - (B)　　⑤ (C) - (B) - (A)

어휘 Box (모르는 어휘와 표현을 아래에 정리하고 해설을 통해 복습하세요.)

비법 적용 Box (앞에서 배운 비법을 스스로 문장에 적용하고 해설과 비교해 보세요.)

라. 고난도 실전 문제

정답과 해설 11~12쪽

1. 주어진 글 다음에 이어질 글의 순서로 가장 적절한 것을 고르시오.

[2020 고3 3월 전국연합 36번]

Many people cannot understand what there is about birds to become obsessed about. What are birdwatchers actually doing out there in the woods, swamps, and fields?

(A) And because birders are human, these birding memories—like most human memories improve over time. The colors of the plumages become richer, the songs sweeter, and those elusive field marks more vivid and distinct in retrospect.

(B) The key to comprehending the passion of birding is to realize that birdwatching is really a hunt. But unlike hunting, the trophies you accumulate are in your mind.

(C) Of course, your mind is a great place to populate with them because you carry them around with you wherever you go. You don't leave them to gather dust on a wall or up in the attic. Your birding experiences become part of your life, part of who you are.

* plumage: 깃털 ** in retrospect: 돌이켜 생각해 보면

① (A) - (C) - (B)　② (B) - (A) - (C)　③ (B) - (C) - (A)
④ (C) - (A) - (B)　⑤ (C) - (B) - (A)

✐ **어휘 Box** (모르는 어휘와 표현을 아래에 정리하고 해설을 통해 복습하세요.)

✐ **비법 적용 Box** (앞에서 배운 비법을 스스로 문장에 적용하고 해설과 비교해 보세요.)

2. 주어진 글 다음에 이어질 글의 순서로 가장 적절한 것을 고르시오.

[2019 고3 4월 전국연합 36번]

Because humans are now the most abundant mammal on the planet, it is somewhat hard to imagine us ever going extinct.

(A) Many branches broke off from each other and developed branches of their own, instead. There were at least three or four different species of hominids living simultaneously for most of the past five million years. Of all these branches, only one survived until today: ours.

(B) However, that is exactly what almost happened—many times, in fact. From the fossil record and from DNA analysis, we can tell that our ancestors nearly went extinct, and their population shrunk to very small numbers countless times.

(C) In addition, there are many lineages of hominids that did go extinct. Since the split between our ancestors and those of the chimps, our lineage has not been a single line of gradual change. Evolution never works that way.

* hominid: 진화 인류의 모체가 된 사람이나 동물 ** lineage: 혈통

① (A) - (C) - (B)　② (B) - (A) - (C)　③ (B) - (C) - (A)
④ (C) - (A) - (B)　⑤ (C) - (B) - (A)

어휘 Box (모르는 어휘와 표현을 아래에 정리하고 해설을 통해 복습하세요.)

비법 적용 Box (앞에서 배운 비법을 스스로 문장에 적용하고 해설과 비교해 보세요.)

2 『문장 삽입』

유형 풀이 비법 주어진 문장의 단서를 토대로 앞 또는 뒤 (혹은 앞과 뒤) 내용을 예상해 보자!

1) 주어진 문장에 단서가 있는 경우

단서의 종류	단서의 예	활용 방법
대명사	it/ they(them/ their), he/she 등	✎ 주어진 문장에 등장한 대명사는 앞 문장에서 '구체적인 명사' 형태로 이미 언급된 것임.
한정사 + 명사	the, such, this(these), that(those), another + 명사	✎ '한정사+명사'는 앞에서 이미 등장한 '명사'가 다시 언급되었음을 의미하므로 해당 '명사'를 확인해야 함. 대명사의 종류에 따라 성별/수일치에 유의해야 함. ✎ 단, 해당 명사가 추상 명사인 경우 유사한 의미의 단어로 대체되어 있을 수 있으니 문맥을 통해 확인함.
연결사	역접, 인과, rather/ instead 등	✎ 역접 (however, but, yet, nevertheless 등)의 연결사 앞 · 뒤에는 동일한 소재에 대한 상반된 설명이 각각 배치됨. (단, 의미를 강조하기 위해 역접을 쓰기도 함.) ✎ 인과 (So, As a result 등)의 연결사 앞 · 뒤에는 동일한 소재에 대한 인과 관계의 내용이 나옴. ✎ rather와 instead는 부정문이나 부정의 의미를 가진 문장 뒤에 나오며, 주어진 문장은 앞 내용에 대한 대체/대안의 내용임.

2) 주어진 문장에 단서가 없는 경우(지문 속 단서를 찾아라)

✎ 주어진 문장에 단서가 없고, 앞 • 뒤 예상이 어려운 경우에는 지문 속 단서에 유의하여 문장과 문장 사이에 논리적으로 어긋나는 부분을 찾는다.

✎ 답을 선택한 뒤에는 주어진 문장을 포함한 앞 • 뒤의 내용을 연결해서 해석해 보고 지문 속에 있는 단서들과 주어진 문장 사이에 오류가 없는지 검증해야 한다.

* 문장 삽입의 출제 원리

1) 주어진 문장의 위치를 묻는 유형은 원래 완벽한 지문에서 출제가 된다.
2) 그 완벽한 지문에서 주변에 단서를 이용해 위치를 추론할 수 있는 '주어진 문장'을 뽑아낸다.
3) '주어진 문장'이 되기 위해서는 다음과 같은 조건이 필요하다.

☞ 주어진 문장이 지문에서 빠져나왔을 때, 지문의 흐름에 논리적인 어색함이 발생하게 된다.
만일, 주어진 문장이 빠져나온 후에도 지문의 내용이나 흐름에 변화가 없으면 주어진 문장이 없어도 된다는 결론(정답 없음) 혹은 아무 곳에나 넣어도 된다는 결론(복수 정답)이 나와서 문제 자체에 오류가 발생하게 된다.

3 일차

가. 비법 연습 문제

정답과 해설 15쪽

다음을 읽고 흐름이 어색한 부분에 √표시를 하고, 들어갈 적절한 문장을 (A), (B), (C)에서 고르시오.

(A) Unfortunately, she was sick yesterday.
(B) Instead, he focused more on composing.
(C) The doctor cured me of it.

1) My brother was so interested in science in his early days. (①) However, he did not study science in high school at all. (②) As a result of it, he became a famous composer later.

2) Jane was supposed to come to the party. (①) So she couldn't come to the party. (②) Everyone was waiting for her to come to the party.

3) When young, I was diagnosed as heart disease. (①) One day, one of my friends introduced a capable doctor to me. (②) I owed him my life.

나. 기출 연습 문제

글의 흐름으로 보아, 주어진 문장이 들어가기에 가장 적절한 곳을 고르시오.

[2017학년도 고3 수능 39번]

Rather, they will happen only through state intervention, based on parliamentary decision.

I expect that global society will increase annual investments from 24% today to 36% of the GDP in 2052. Much of this investment will be in energy-efficient goods that are more expensive than old-fashioned stuff designed for an era of cheap energy. (①) Another share will be invested in the shift from coal to more expensive fuels, like conventional gas. (②) Some will go into the construction of new renewable energy supply, even during the years before it becomes competitive. (③) And a lot will go into repair of climate damage or adaptation to future climate damage — for example, investing in new protective walls along the coast to keep the rising ocean back. (④) These huge increases in investment would not come about if investment was left to the market. (⑤) It will be either direct, when the government invests the tax dollars in whatever capacity it considers to be most necessary, or indirect, when the government passes legislation that makes the desired activity more profitable.

비법 적용

Rather, they will happen only through state intervention, based on parliamentary decision.

☞ **주어진 문장의 단서인 연결사 'Rather'를 통해 앞 문장이 부정문임을 예상한다.**

☞ **복수 대명사 'they'를 통해 앞 문장에 복수 형태의 명사가 나왔음을 예상한다.**

I expect that global society will increase annual investments from 24% today to 36% of the GDP in 2052. Much of this investment will be in energy-efficient goods that are more expensive than old-fashioned stuff designed for an era of cheap energy.

☞ 국제 사회의 연간 투자율 증가의 첫 번째 항목으로 에너지 효율이 높은 제품을 예로 들고 있다.

(①) **Another share**

☞ 'Another share(한정사+명사)'는 앞에서 'share(몫)'에 해당하는 말이 언급되었음을 의미하므로, 'share' 단어 자체 또는 'share'에 해당하는 내용이 앞 문장에 있는지 확인하며 읽는다.

(②) **Some**

☞ 'Some(대명사)'으로 나타낼 만한 것이 앞 문장에 있는지 확인한다.

(③) **And a lot**

☞ 'And a lot'의 'And'는 현재 나열되는 것의 마지막 내용임을 뜻한다. 'a lot'은 어떤 것의 '많은 부분'을 의미하므로, 해당하는 내용이 앞 문장에 있는지 확인한다.

(④) **These huge increases**

☞ 'these+명사'라는 단서를 통해 앞 내용에서 이에 해당하는 명사 표현 즉, '엄청난 투자의 증가'가 있었는지 확인해야 한다. 또한, 연결사 'rather'와 어울리는 부정어 'not'에 주목한다.

(⑤) **It, the government**

☞ 앞 문장에 대명사 'It'이 가리키는 대상이 있는지, '정부(the government)'라는 단어가 있는지 확인해야 한다. 만약, 이러한 단어가 없다면 논리적 흐름이 어색한 글이 된다.

오답의 모든 것

① Another share

▶ 국제사회가 투자하는 여러 항목 중 첫 번째인 'energy-efficient goods' 외의 또 다른 투자의 '몫, 지분(share)'을 의미하고 있으므로 오답

② 대명사 Some

▶ 대명사 'some'은 국제 사회가 투자하는 분야 중 또 다른 일부를 의미하므로 오답

③ And a lot

▶ 국제 사회의 투자 중 많은 부분을 의미한다는 어휘이므로 오답

④ These huge increases in investment와 부정어 not

▶ 'These huge increase'라는 '투자의 증가'가 앞에서 이미 나왔음을 의미하며, 문맥상 ④번 앞까지 나열된 것들을 의미하는 올바른 표현이므로 오답

⑤ It, the government

▶ **문맥상 단수 대명사 'It'과 'the government'가 가리키는 말이 지문 속에 없으며, 'It'은 주어진 문장의 '국가 개입을 통한 투자'를, 'the government'는 주어진 문장의 'state'를 의미하기 때문에 정답**

4 일차

다. 실전 연습 문제

정답과 해설 16~17쪽

1. 글의 흐름으로 보아 주어진 문장이 들어가기에 가장 적절한 곳을 고르시오.

[2018 고1 11월 전국연합 38번]

However, as society becomes more diverse, the likelihood that people share assumptions and values diminishes.

The way we communicate influences our ability to build strong and healthy communities. Traditional ways of building communities have emphasized debate and argument. (①) For example, the United States has a strong tradition of using town hall meetings to deliberate important issues within communities. (②) In these settings, advocates for each side of the issue present arguments for their positions, and public issues have been discussed in such public forums. (③) Yet for debate and argument to work well, people need to come to such forums with similar assumptions and values. (④) The shared assumptions and values serve as a foundation for the discussion. (⑤) As a result, forms of communication such as argument and debate become polarized, which may drive communities apart as opposed to bringing them together.

✐ **어휘 Box** (모르는 어휘와 표현을 아래에 정리하고 해설을 통해 복습하세요.)

✐ **비법 적용 Box** (앞에서 배운 비법을 스스로 문장에 적용하고 해설과 비교해 보세요.)

학습날짜 ______년 ______월 ______일
학습시간 ____:____ ~ ____:____

정답과 해설 18~19쪽

2. 글의 흐름으로 보아, 주어진 문장이 들어가기에 가장 적절한 곳을 고르시오.

[2020 고1 6월 전국연합 38번]

Because of these obstacles, most research missions in space are accomplished through the use of spacecraft without crews aboard.

Currently, we cannot send humans to other planets. One obstacle is that such a trip would take years. (①) A spacecraft would need to carry enough air, water, and other supplies needed for survival on the long journey. (②) Another obstacle is the harsh conditions on other planets, such as extreme heat and cold. (③) Some planets do not even have surfaces to land on. (④) These explorations pose no risk to human life and are less expensive than ones involving astronauts. (⑤) The spacecraft carry instruments that test the compositions and characteristics of planets.

*composition: 구성 성분

✐ **어휘 Box** (모르는 어휘와 표현을 아래에 정리하고 해설을 통해 복습하세요.)

✐ **비법 적용 Box** (앞에서 배운 비법을 스스로 문장에 적용하고 해설과 비교해 보세요.)

3. 글의 흐름으로 보아 주어진 문장이 들어가기에 가장 적절한 곳을 고르시오.

[2020 고2 11월 전국연합 39번]

However, according to Christakis and Fowler, we cannot transmit ideas and behaviours much beyond our friends' friends' friends (in other words, across just three degrees of separation).

In the late twentieth century, researchers sought to measure how fast and how far news, rumours or innovations moved. (①) More recent research has shown that ideas—even emotional states and conditions—can be transmitted through a social network. (②) The evidence of this kind of contagion is clear: 'Students with studious roommates become more studious. Diners sitting next to heavy eaters eat more food.' (③) This is because the transmission and reception of an idea or behaviour requires a stronger connection than the relaying of a letter or the communication that a certain employment opportunity exists. (④) Merely knowing people is not the same as being able to influence them to study more or overeat. (⑤) Imitation is indeed the sincerest form of flattery, even when it is unconscious..

어휘 Box (모르는 어휘와 표현을 아래에 정리하고 해설을 통해 복습하세요.)

비법 적용 Box (앞에서 배운 비법을 스스로 문장에 적용하고 해설과 비교해 보세요.)

4. 글의 흐름으로 보아, 주어진 문장이 들어가기에 가장 적절한 곳을 고르시오.

[2019 고3 9월 모의평가 39번]

So, there was a social pressure for art to come up with some vocation that both distinguished it from science and, at the same time, made it equal in stature to science.

Representational theories of art treat the work of the artist as similar to that of the scientist. Both, so to speak, are involved in describing the external world. (①) But by the nineteenth century, any comparison between the scientist and the artist was bound to make the artist look like a poor relation in terms of making discoveries about the world or holding a mirror up to nature. (②) Here, science clearly had the edge. (③) The notion that art specialized in the expression of the emotions was particularly attractive in this light. (④) It rendered unto science its own — the exploration of the objective world — while saving something comparably important for art to do — to explore the inner world of feeling. (⑤) If science held the mirror up to nature, art turned a mirror at the self and its experiences.

*vocation: 소명 **stature: 수준 ***render: 주다

어휘 Box (모르는 어휘와 표현을 아래에 정리하고 해설을 통해 복습하세요.)

비법 적용 Box (앞에서 배운 비법을 스스로 문장에 적용하고 해설과 비교해 보세요.)

라. 고난도 실전 문제

정답과 해설 24~26쪽

1. 글의 흐름으로 보아 주어진 문장이 들어가기에 가장 적절한 곳을 고르시오.

[2020 고3 6월 모의평가 39번]

When the team painted fireflies' light organs dark, a new set of bats took twice as long to learn to avoid them.

Fireflies don't just light up their behinds to attract mates, they also glow to tell bats not to eat them. This twist in the tale of the trait that gives fireflies their name was discovered by Jesse Barber and his colleagues. The glow's warning role benefits both fireflies and bats, because these insects taste disgusting to the mammals. (①) When swallowed, chemicals released by fireflies cause bats to throw them back up. (②) The team placed eight bats in a dark room with three or four fireflies plus three times as many tasty insects, including beetles and moths, for four days. (③) During the first night, all the bats captured at least one firefly. (④) But by the fourth night, most bats had learned to avoid fireflies and catch all the other prey instead. (⑤) It had long been thought that firefly bioluminescence mainly acted as a mating signal, but the new finding explains why firefly larvae also glow despite being immature for mating.

*bioluminescence: 생물 발광(發光) **larvae: larva (애벌레)의 복수형

✐ **어휘 Box** (모르는 어휘와 표현을 아래에 정리하고 해설을 통해 복습하세요.)

✐ **비법 적용 Box** (앞에서 배운 비법을 스스로 문장에 적용하고 해설과 비교해 보세요.)

정답과 해설 26~28쪽

2. 글의 흐름으로 보아, 주어진 문장이 들어가기에 가장 적절한 곳을 고르시오.

[2021학년도 고3 수능 39번]

Note that copyright covers the expression of an idea and not the idea itself.

Designers draw on their experience of design when approaching a new project. This includes the use of previous designs that they know work — both designs that they have created themselves and those that others have created. (①) Others' creations often spark inspiration that also leads to new ideas and innovation. (②) This is well known and understood. (③) However, the expression of an idea is protected by copyright, and people who infringe on that copyright can be taken to court and prosecuted. (④) This means, for example, that while there are numerous smartphones all with similar functionality, this does not represent an infringement of copyright as the idea has been expressed in different ways and it is the expression that has been copyrighted. (⑤) Copyright is free and is automatically invested in the author, for instance, the writer of a book or a programmer who develops a program, unless they sign the copyright over to someone else.

*infringe: 침해하다 **prosecute: 기소하다

어휘 Box (모르는 어휘와 표현을 아래에 정리하고 해설을 통해 복습하세요.)

비법 적용 Box (앞에서 배운 비법을 스스로 문장에 적용하고 해설과 비교해 보세요.)

II

5~8일차 학습하기

논리 추론 및 논리 판단 관련 독해 유형

영어
오답의
모든것

II 논리 추론 및 논리 판단 관련 독해 유형 5~6일차 학습하기

1 『빈칸 추론』

유형 풀이 비법

1) 빈칸에서 묻고자 하는 것이 무엇인지 정확히 파악하여 주제와 연관지어 생각하라!

✎ 빈칸은 주로 글 전체의 주제문에 해당한다. 주제문 은 '소재 + 설명'으로 구성되어 있다.

주제문 : 인간의 시각은 다른 어떤 감각 기관보다 강하다.
소재 / 설명

✎ 빈칸 추론 유형은 빈칸을 채움으로써 하나의 주제문이 완성되는 식의 구조가 많으므로 빈칸에서 묻는 말이 소재인지, 그에 대한 설명인지, 주제 전체인지 정확히 파악할 필요가 있다. (아래의 예시 참조)

① Heritage is ____________________.

⇒ 본문에서 필자가 말하는 '유산(Heritage)'의 설명을 찾아 빈칸을 채우라는 의미

② Beware of ____________________.

⇒ 무엇을 조심해야 하는지에 대한 필자의 의견을 찾아 주제를 완성하라는 의미

2) 빈칸 문장과 빈칸 주변 문장이 주는 단서에 주목하라!

✎ 빈칸 앞 또는 뒤에 **예시**가 제시된 경우
: 예시 앞의 문장은 예시문을 포괄할 수 있는 일반적인(general) 문장이며, 예시문은 주제문에 대한 구체적인(specific) 설명이므로 예시 앞 · 뒤의 문장이 **서로 유사한 의미**가 되도록 빈칸을 완성함.

All of my friends like animals. For instance, Jane likes dogs, Tom cats, and Jim rabbits.

general sentence		specific sentence
all of my friends	≥	Jane, Tom, Jim
animals	≥	dogs, cats, rabbits

✎ 빈칸 문장이 **역접**의 연결사와 함께 제시된 경우
: 빈칸에 들어갈 말은 앞 내용보다 중요하거나, 앞 내용과 서로 상반된 내용이 되도록 빈칸을 완성함.

✎ 빈칸 문장이 **재진술**의 연결사와 함께 있거나 빈칸 문장 앞 · 뒤에 재진술의 연결사가 있는 경우
: 재진술 문장과 앞에 제시된 문장이 서로 유사한 의미가 되도록 빈칸을 완성함.

ex) In practice, their work and theoretical conclusions partly developed ______. In other words, they already knew the data when they decided upon an interpretation.

3) 빈칸 문장에 부정어가 포함되어 있을 때 주의하라.

✎ 빈칸은 주로 주제문인 경우가 많으나, 만약 빈칸 문장 속에 부정어나 부정의 의미가 포함되어 있으면 주제와 반대 의미가 들어가야 한다.

ex) It's **not** good to assume that a cultural product ________.
☞ 'a cultural product'를 빈칸이라 생각하지 말라는 의미이므로 주제의 반대 의미가 들어가야 함.

학습날짜 ______ 년 ______ 월 ______ 일

학습시간 ______ : ______ ~ ______ : ______

가. 비법 연습 문제

정답과 해설 29~30쪽

1. 다음 글을 읽고 밑줄 친 부분에 유의하여 빈칸에 들어갈 가장 적절한 말을 고르시오.

Most of us <u>are suspicious of rapid cognition.</u> We believe that the quality of the decision is directly related to the time and effort that went into making it. That's what we tell our children: "Haste makes waste." "Look before you leap." "Stop and think." "Don't judge a book by its cover." We believe that we are always better off gathering as much information as possible and spending as much time as possible in careful consideration. <u>But</u> there are moments, particularly in time-driven, critical situations, when ________________, when our snap judgments and first impressions can offer better means of making sense of the world.

① haste does not make waste
② it is never too late to learn
③ many hands make light work

2. 다음 글을 읽고 밑줄 친 부분에 유의하여 빈칸에 들어갈 가장 적절한 말을 고르시오.

1) People think identical twins are exactly alike in every way. <u>However</u>, identical twins are ______________ individuals. <u>For example</u>, my own children have always shown about a twenty-five percent difference in their weight. <u>Also</u>, they <u>don't act alike either</u>.

① active ② paired ③ unique ④ talented ⑤ thoughtful

2) The goal of the researchers was to determine <u>what high-achieving people had in common</u>. There was one thing they all had in common: the willingness to ________________. All of them agreed that <u>success wasn't something that had just happened to them</u>. It happened because they'd made it happen <u>through continuous effort</u>.

① take a risk ② make plans ahead ③ get rid of bad habits
④ work long, hard hours ⑤ respect others' opinions

나. 기출 연습 문제 A

정답과 해설 30쪽

다음 글을 읽고 빈칸에 들어갈 말로 가장 적절한 것을 고르시오.

[2019 고1 6월 모의평가 32번]

We are more likely to eat in a restaurant if we know that it is usually busy. Even when nobody tells us a restaurant is good, our herd behavior determines our decisionmaking. Let's suppose you walk toward two empty restaurants. You do not know which one to enter. However, you suddenly see a group of six people enter one of them. Which one are you more likely to enter, the empty one or the other one? Most people would go into the restaurant with people in it. Let's suppose you and a friend go into that restaurant. Now, it has eight people in it. Others see that one restaurant is empty and the other has eight people in it. So, ______________________________.

① both restaurants are getting busier
② you and your friend start hesitating
③ your decision has no impact on others'
④ they reject what lots of other people do
⑤ they decide to do the same as the other eight

비법 적용

〈빈칸에서 묻는 말 파악하기〉

So, ____ .

☞ **'So'를 이용해 앞 내용에 대한 결과이면서 주제를 요약해야 하는 부분이다.**

We are more likely to eat in a restaurant if we know that it is usually busy. Even when nobody tells us a restaurant is good, our herd behavior determines our decisionmaking.

☞ 구체적인 예시 앞에 오는 문장이므로 주제문임을 알 수 있다. '무리 행동(herd behavior)'이 우리의 '의사 결정(decisionmaking)'을 좌우한다는 내용이다.

Let's suppose you walk toward two empty restaurants. You do not know which one to enter. However, you suddenly see a group of six people enter one of them. Which one are you more likely to enter, the empty one or the other one? Most people would go into the restaurant with people in it.

☞ 'Let's suppose'를 이용해 '무리가 의사 결정(decisionmaking)에 미치는 영향'을 예시를 들어 설명하고 있다.

Let's suppose you and a friend go into that restaurant. Now, it has eight people in it. Others see that one restaurant is empty and the other has eight people in it. So, ______________ .

☞ 당신과 친구가 6명의 무리가 있는 식당에 들어가 식당 안에 8명이 되었고, 나머지 한 식당은 텅 빈 상황에 대한 결과를 추론해야 한다.

오답의 모든 것

① 두 개의 식당이 모두 더 바빠진다.
▶ 하나의 식당은 텅 비어 있다고 하였으므로 오답

② 당신과 당신의 친구는 망설이기 시작한다.
▶ 당신과 당신의 친구는 이미 6명의 사람들이 있는 식당을 선택했으므로 오답

③ 당신의 결정은 다른 사람들에게 아무런 영향력을 미치지 않는다.
▶ 당신을 포함한 8명이라는 무리가 다른 이의 의사 결정에 영향을 미친다는 내용이므로 오답

④ 많은 사람들이 하는 것을 거부한다.
▶ 무리가 의사 결정에 영향을 미친다는 것과 반대의 선택지이므로 오답

⑤ 나머지 8명이 한 것과 같은 결정을 한다.
▶ **무리의 행동이 의사 결정에 영향을 미친다는 주제와 일치하므로 정답**

나. 기출 연습 문제 B

정답과 해설 30~31쪽

다음 글을 읽고 빈칸에 들어갈 말로 가장 적절한 것을 고르시오.

[2018 고1 11월 모의평가 32번]

We have to recognize that there always exists in us the strongest need to utilize all our attention. And this is quite evident in the great amount of displeasure we feel any time the entirety of our capacity for attention is not being put to use. When this is the case, we will seek ____________________. If we are playing a chess game with a weaker opponent, we will seek to supplement this activity with another: such as watching TV, or listening to music, or playing another chess game at the same time. Very often this reveals itself in unconscious movements, such as playing with something in one's hands or pacing around the room; and if such an action also serves to increase pleasure or relieve displeasure, all the better.

*supplement : 보충하다

① to please others with what we are good at

② to pay more attention to the given task

③ to find outlets for our unused attention

④ to play with a stronger opponent

⑤ to give our brain a short break

비법 적용

〈빈칸에서 묻는 말 파악하기〉

When this is the case, we will seek ______________________ .

☞ 'this'는 앞내용을 의미하는 것으로, 앞의 사례가 사실일 때 우리가 무엇을 추구하는지 묻고 있다. 빈칸의 단서가 주로 빈칸 뒷부분에 나올 것이라 예상할 수 있다.

We have to recognize that there always exists in us the strongest need to utilize all our attention.

☞ 우리의 '모든' 주의력을 활용하려는 강렬한 우리 안의 욕구에 대한 글이다. 'have to'에서 필자의 의도를 파악할 수 있다.

And this is quite evident in the great amount of displeasure we feel any time the entirety of our capacity for attention is not being put to use.

☞ 'this is evident'라는 표현 뒤에 우리의 주의력 전체를 사용하지 못하면 '불쾌함(displeasure)'을 느낀다는 앞 문장에 대한 부연 설명이 이어지고 있다.

When this is the case, we will seek ______________________ .

☞ 앞에서 말한 불쾌함이라는 문제 상황에서 우리가 어떻게 행동하는가에 대해 묻고 있다. 빈칸 뒤에서 'a chess game'이라는 구체적인 사례가 등장하므로, 이 빈칸 문장은 주제문이라 볼 수 있다.

If we are playing a chess game with a weaker opponent, we will seek to supplement this activity with another: such as watching TV, or listening to music, or playing another chess game at the same time. Very often this reveals itself in unconscious movements, such as playing with something in one's hands or pacing around the room; and if such an action also serves to increase pleasure or relieve displeasure, all the better.

☞ 자신보다 못하는 사람과 체스 게임을 할 경우를 사례로 들고 있다. 즉, 빈칸 앞 내용과 연결지어 생각하면 우리의 주의력을 충분히 활용하지 못하는 불쾌한 상황이 제시되고 있으며 이 때의 우리의 행동이 빈칸에 들어갈 말이 된다. 따라서 예시에 언급된 TV 시청, 음악 감상 등과 같은 예시를 일반화한 문장이 정답이다.

오답의 모든 것

① 우리가 잘하는 것으로 다른 사람을 기쁘게 해주려
▶ 다른 사람의 기쁨이 아니라 나의 기쁨을 위한 행동에 대한 내용이므로 오답

② 주어진 일에 더욱더 집중하려
▶ 체스의 예시에서 체스가 아닌 다른 일에 집중력을 분산시킨다고 하였으므로 오답

③ 사용되지 않은 주의력의 배출구를 찾으려
▶ 체스에 온전히 집중하지 못하는 것은 '사용되지 않은 주의력(our unused attention)'을 의미하며, 이러한 상황에서 하는 'TV, 음악' 등의 행동은 불쾌함을 해소하려는 '배출구(outlet)'를 뜻하므로 정답

④ 더 강력한 상대와 게임을 하려
▶ 상대를 바꾼다는 것은 언급되지 않은 내용이며, '더 강한 상대와의 게임'은 예시를 활용한 오답

⑤ 우리 뇌에 짧은 휴식을 주려
▶ 핵심 소재 및 주제와 무관한 내용으로 'chess'라는 예시를 휴식으로 생각할 수 있는 매력적인 오답

6 일차

다. 실전 연습 문제

정답과 해설 31~32쪽

1. 다음 빈칸에 들어갈 말로 가장 적절한 것을 고르시오.

[2019 고1 3월 전국연합 34번]

It is difficult to know how to determine whether one culture is better than another. What is the cultural rank order of rock, jazz, and classical music? When it comes to public opinion polls about whether cultural changes are for the better or the worse, looking forward would lead to one answer and looking backward would lead to a very different answer. Our children would be horrified if they were told they had to go back to the culture of their grandparents. Our parents would be horrified if they were told they had to participate in the culture of their grandchildren. Humans tend to __________________________. After a certain age, anxieties arise when sudden cultural changes are coming. Our culture is part of who we are and where we stand, and we don't like to think that who we are and where we stand are shortlived.

① seek cooperation between generations
② be forgetful of what they experienced
③ adjust quickly to the new environment
④ make efforts to remember what their ancestors did
⑤ like what they have grown up in and gotten used to

✐ **어휘 Box** (모르는 어휘와 표현을 아래에 정리하고 해설을 통해 복습하세요.)

✐ **비법 적용 Box** (앞에서 배운 비법을 스스로 문장에 적용하고 해설과 비교해 보세요.)

정답과 해설 33~34쪽

2. 다음 빈칸에 들어갈 말로 가장 적절한 것을 고르시오.

[2018 고1 9월 전국연합 34번]

One CEO in one of Silicon Valley's most innovative companies has what would seem like a boring, creativitykilling routine. He holds a threehour meeting that starts at 9:00 A.M. one day a week. It is never missed or rescheduled at a different time. It is mandatory—so much so that even in this global firm all the executives know never to schedule any travel that will conflict with the meeting. At first glance there is nothing particularly unique about this. But what is unique is the quality of ideas that come out of ______________. Because the CEO has eliminated the mental cost involved in planning the meeting or thinking about who will or won't be there, people can focus on creative problem solving.

① consumer complaints
② the regular meetings
③ traveling experiences
④ flexible working hours
⑤ the financial incentives

어휘 Box (모르는 어휘와 표현을 아래에 정리하고 해설을 통해 복습하세요.)

비법 적용 Box (앞에서 배운 비법을 스스로 문장에 적용하고 해설과 비교해 보세요.)

3. 다음 빈칸에 들어갈 말로 가장 적절한 것을 고르시오.

[2020 고2 3월 전국연합 31번]

When he was dying, the contemporary Buddhist teacher Dainin Katagiri wrote a remarkable book called Returning to Silence. Life, he wrote, "is a dangerous situation." It is the weakness of life that makes it precious; his words are filled with the very fact of his own life passing away. "The china bowl is beautiful because sooner or later it will break.... The life of the bowl is always existing in a dangerous situation." Such is our struggle: this unstable beauty. This inevitable wound. We forget—how easily we forget—that love and loss are intimate companions, that we love the real flower so much more than the plastic one and love the cast of twilight across a mountainside lasting only a moment. It is this very ____________________ that opens our hearts.

① fragility ② stability ③ harmony
④ satisfaction ⑤ diversity

✐ **어휘 Box** (모르는 어휘와 표현을 아래에 정리하고 해설을 통해 복습하세요.)

✐ **비법 적용 Box** (앞에서 배운 비법을 스스로 문장에 적용하고 해설과 비교해 보세요.)

4. 다음 빈칸에 들어갈 말로 가장 적절한 것을 고르시오.

[2018 고1 9월 전국연합 34번]

Sociologists have proven that people bring their own views and values to the culture they encounter; books, TV programs, movies, and music may affect everyone, but they affect different people in different ways. In a study, Neil Vidmar and Milton Rokeach showed episodes of the sitcom All in the Family to viewers with a range of different views on race. The show centers on a character named Archie Bunker, an intolerant bigot who often gets into fights with his more progressive family members. Vidmar and Rokeach found that viewers who didn't share Archie Bunker's views thought the show was very funny in the way it made fun of Archie's absurd racism—in fact, this was the producers' intention. On the other hand, though, viewers who were themselves bigots thought Archie Bunker was the hero of the show and that the producers meant to make fun of his foolish family! This demonstrates why it's a mistake to assume that a certain cultural product ________________________ .

*bigot : 고집쟁이

① can provide many valuable views
② reflects the idea of the sociologists
③ forms prejudices to certain characters
④ will have the same effect on everyone
⑤ might resolve social conflicts among people

어휘 Box (모르는 어휘와 표현을 아래에 정리하고 해설을 통해 복습하세요.)

비법 적용 Box (앞에서 배운 비법을 스스로 문장에 적용하고 해설과 비교해 보세요.)

1. 다음 빈칸에 들어갈 말로 가장 적절한 것을 고르시오.

[2020 고3 3월 전국연합 31번]

A distinct emotional trait of human nature is to watch fellow humans closely, to learn their stories, and thereby to judge their character and dependability. And so it has ever been since the Pleistocene. The first bands classifiable to the genus Homo and their descendants were hunter-gatherers. Like the Kalahari Ju/'hoansi of today, they almost certainly depended on sophisticated cooperative behavior just to survive from one day to the next. That, in turn, required exact knowledge of the personal history and accomplishments of each of their groupmates, and equally they needed an empathetic sense of the feelings and propensities of others. It gives deep satisfaction — call it, if you will, a human instinct—not just to learn but also to share emotions stirred by the stories told by our companions. The whole of these performances pays off in survival and reproduction. ____________________ are Darwinian phenomena.

*the Pleistocene : 홍적세(洪積世) **propensity : (행동의) 성향

① Gossip and storytelling
② Planning and practicing
③ Executing and revising
④ Exhibition and jealousy
⑤ Competitions and rewards

✐ **어휘 Box** (모르는 어휘와 표현을 아래에 정리하고 해설을 통해 복습하세요.)

✐ **비법 적용 Box** (앞에서 배운 비법을 스스로 문장에 적용하고 해설과 비교해 보세요.)

2. 다음 빈칸에 들어갈 말로 가장 적절한 것을 고르시오.

[2020 고3 9월 전국연합 34번]

Protopia is a state of becoming, rather than a destination. It is a process. In the protopian mode, things are better today than they were yesterday, although only a little better. It is incremental improvement or mild progress. The "pro" in protopian stems from the notions of process and progress. This subtle progress is not dramatic, not exciting. It is easy to miss because a protopia generates almost as many new problems as new benefits. The problems of today were caused by yesterday's technological successes, and the technological solutions to today's problems will cause the problems of tomorrow. This circular expansion of both problems and solutions ________________________. Ever since the Enlightenment and the invention of science, we've managed to create a tiny bit more than we've destroyed each year. But that few percent positive difference is compounded over decades into what we might call civilization. Its benefits never star in movies.

*incremental : 증가의 **compound : 조합하다

① conceals the limits of innovations at the present time

② makes it difficult to predict the future with confidence

③ motivates us to quickly achieve a protopian civilization

④ hides a steady accumulation of small net benefits over time

⑤ produces a considerable change in technological successes

✐ **어휘 Box** (모르는 어휘와 표현을 아래에 정리하고 해설을 통해 복습하세요.)

✐ **비법 적용 Box** (앞에서 배운 비법을 스스로 문장에 적용하고 해설과 비교해 보세요.)

논리 추론 및 논리 판단 관련 독해 유형 7~8일차 학습하기

2 『무관한 문장』

유형 풀이 비법

무관한 문장을 고르는 유형의 지문은 일발적으로 두괄식 구조를 취한다.
선택지 ①번 앞에서 대부분 주제가 드러난다 → '핵심 소재' 파악!

정답의 핵심 포인트!	무관한 문장 확인 비법 3가지
첫 문장 을 꼼꼼히 읽고 주제와 소재 파악 ☞ 무관한 문장을 고른 뒤, 무관한 문장을 제외한 앞 · 뒤 내용이 자연스러운지 반드시 확인한다.	1) 핵심 소재와 관련된 소재가 등장하지 않음 2) 글의 주제와 일치하지 않음 3) 연결사나 지시어의 흐름이 부자연스러움

학습날짜 ______ 년 ______ 월 ______ 일

학습시간 ______ : ______ ~ ______ : ______

7일차

가. 비법 연습 문제

정답과 해설 41쪽

1. 다음 주어진 문장과 관련이 없는 무관한 문장을 아래 ①~④ 중에서 고르고, 그 근거를 〈보기〉의 비법에서 고르시오.

⇒ 주어진 문장과 무관한 문장 (　　　　) – 근거 (　　　　)

음식과 제품에 내포된 물은 '가상의 물(공산품 • 농축산물의 제조 • 재배에 드는 물)'이라고 불린다. 예를 들어 2파운드의 밀을 생산하기 위해서 약 265갤런의 물이 필요하다.

① 따라서 이 2파운드의 밀의 가상의 물은 265갤런이다.
② 하지만 건강을 유지하기 위해 가능한 한 많은 물을 마시는 것이 필요하다.
③ 이러한 가상의 물의 함유량은 제품에 따라 다르다.
④ 예를 들어, 2파운드의 고기를 생산하려면 2파운드의 채소를 생산하는 것의 약 5배에서 10배의 물이 필요하다

〈보기〉

a) 핵심 소재와 관련된 소재가 등장하지 않음
b) 글의 주제와 일치하지 않음
c) 연결사나 지시어의 흐름이 부자연스러움

나. 기출 연습 문제

다음 글에서 전체 흐름과 관계 없는 문장을 고르시오.

[2018 고1 3월 전국연합 39번]

In 2006, 81% of surveyed American shoppers said that they considered online customer ratings and reviews important when planning a purchase. Though an online comment — positive or negative — is not as powerful as a direct interpersonal exchange, it can be very important for a business. ② Many people depend on online recommendations. ① And young people rely heavily on them and are very likely to be influenced by the Internet when deciding what movie to see or what album to purchase. ③ These individuals often have widereaching social networks and communicate regularly with dozens of others — with the potential to reach thousands. ④ Experts suggest that young people stop wasting their money on unnecessary things and start saving it. ⑤ It has been reported that young people aged six to 24 influence about 50% of all spending in the US.

비법 적용

In 2006, 81% of surveyed American shoppers said that they considered online customer ratings and reviews important when planning a purchase. Though an online comment — positive or negative — is not as powerful as a direct interpersonal exchange, it can be very important for a business.

☞ 글의 주제 : 구매 계획시 온라인 고객 평점과 후기가 중요하다.
글의 핵심 소재 : online customer ratings and reviews

① Many people depend on online recommendations.
☞ '온라인 추천(online recommendations)'은 핵심 소재인 '온라인 고객 평점과 후기(online customer ratings and reviews)'와 같은 맥락의 표현이다.

② And young people rely heavily on them and are very likely to be influenced by the Internet when deciding what movie to see or what album to purchase.
☞ 대명사 'them'은 'online recommendations'을 가리키며, 젊은이들은 구매시 인터넷 즉, 온라인 평가의 영향을 받는다는 앞 내용과 일치하는 문장이다.

③ These individuals often have widereaching social networks and communicate regularly with dozens of others — with the potential to reach thousands.
☞ 'These individuals'은 앞 내용의 'young people'을 의미하며 '소셜 네크워크(social networks)'는 온라인 평가, 온라인 후기 등과 유사한 속성을 갖는다.

④ Experts suggest that young people stop wasting their money on unnecessary things and start saving it.
☞ 비법 1, 2 오류) '젊은이들은 불필요한 곳에 낭비하지 않고 저축해야 한다'는 주제와 무관한 내용이다.

⑤ It has been reported that young people aged six to 24 influence about 50% of all spending in the US.
☞ 'young people'은 ②, ③에 등장하는 인물과 동일인물이며 이들의 소비가 ③번의 소셜 네트워크 즉, 온라인 평가에 의해 영향을 받는다는 의미이다.

오답의 모든 것

①, ② online recommendations
▶ '온라인 평가'라는 핵심 소재와 주제가 유지되고 있으므로 오답

③ These individuals
▶ 온라인 평가'를 중요시하는 젊은이들에 관해 언급하는 관련된 문장이므로 오답

④ young people
▶ ②의 '온라인 평가'를 중요시하는 젊은이들이 아닌 일반적인 젊은이들에 관한 전문가의 충고이자 소비와 저축에 관한 내용을 언급하고 있는 무관한 문장이므로 정답

⑤ young people
▶ 미국 소비의 절반을 차지하는 영향력 있는 젊은이들은 '온라인 평가'를 중요시하는 ②번의 젊은이들을 의미하므로 오답

다. 실전 연습 문제

정답과 해설 42~43쪽

1. 다음 글에서 전체 흐름과 관계 없는 문장을 고르시오.

[2019 고1 3월 전국연합 35번]

Public speaking is audience centered because speakers "listen" to their audiences during speeches. They monitor audience feedback, the verbal and nonverbal signals an audience gives a speaker. ① Audience feedback often indicates whether listeners understand, have interest in, and are ready to accept the speaker's ideas. ② This feedback assists the speaker in many ways. ③ It helps the speaker know when to slow down, explain something more carefully, or even tell the audience that she or he will return to an issue in a questionandanswer session at the close of the speech. ④ It is important for the speaker to memorize his or her script to reduce onstage anxiety. ⑤ Audience feedback assists the speaker in creating a respectful connection with the audience.

* verbal : 언어적인

✐ **어휘 Box** (모르는 어휘와 표현을 아래에 정리하고 해설을 통해 복습하세요.)

✐ **비법 적용 Box** (앞에서 배운 비법을 스스로 문장에 적용하고 해설과 비교해 보세요.)

2. 다음 글에서 전체 흐름과 관계 없는 문장을 고르시오.

[2020 고1 6월 전국연합 35번]

Given the widespread use of emoticons in electronic communication, an important question is whether they help Internet users to understand emotions in online communication. ① Emoticons, particularly character–based ones, are much more ambiguous relative to face–to–face cues and may end up being interpreted very differently by different users. ② Nonetheless, research indicates that they are useful tools in online text–based communication. ③ One study of 137 instant messaging users revealed that emoticons allowed users to correctly understand the level and direction of emotion, attitude, and attention expression and that emoticons were a definite advantage in non–verbal communication. ④ In fact, there have been few studies on the relationships between verbal and nonverbal communication. ⑤ Similarly, another study showed that emoticons were useful in strengthening the intensity of a verbal message, as well as in the expression of sarcasm.

* ambiguous : 모호한 ** verbal : 언어적인 *** sarcasm: 풍자

어휘 Box (모르는 어휘와 표현을 아래에 정리하고 해설을 통해 복습하세요.)

비법 적용 Box (앞에서 배운 비법을 스스로 문장에 적용하고 해설과 비교해 보세요.)

3. 다음 글에서 전체 흐름과 관계 없는 문장을 고르시오.

[2019 고2 9월 전국연합 35번]

The first commercial train service began operating between Liverpool and Manchester in 1830. Ten years later, the first train timetable was issued. The trains were much faster than the old carriages, so the peculiar differences in local hours became a severe nuisance. ① In 1847, British train companies put their heads together and agreed that henceforth all train timetables would be adjusted to Greenwich Observatory time, rather than the local times of Liverpool, Manchester, or Glasgow. ② More and more institutions followed the lead of the train companies. ③ Railways faced infrastructurerelated challenges such as those related to stations, tracks, and other facilities. ④ Finally, in 1880, the British government took the unprecedented step of legislating that all timetables in Britain must follow Greenwich. ⑤ For the first time in history, a country adopted a national time and obliged its population to live according to an artificial clock rather than local ones or sunrisetosunset cycles.

* nuisance : 골칫거리

✐ **어휘 Box** (모르는 어휘와 표현을 아래에 정리하고 해설을 통해 복습하세요.)

✐ **비법 적용 Box** (앞에서 배운 비법을 스스로 문장에 적용하고 해설과 비교해 보세요.)

4. 다음 글에서 전체 흐름과 관계 없는 문장을 고르시오.

[2020 고2 6월 전국연합 35번]

Marketing management is concerned not only with finding and increasing demand but also with changing or even reducing it. For example, Uluru (Ayers Rock) might have too many tourists wanting to climb it, and Daintree National Park in North Queensland can become overcrowded in the tourist season. ① Power companies sometimes have trouble meeting demand during peak usage periods. ② In these and other cases of excess demand, the needed marketing task, called demarketing, is to reduce demand temporarily or permanently. ③ Efforts should be made to compensate for the losses caused by the increase in supply. ④ The aim of demarketing is not to completely destroy demand, but only to reduce or shift it to another time, or even another product. ⑤ Thus, marketing management seeks to affect the level, timing, and nature of demand in a way that helps the organisation achieve its objectives.

어휘 Box (모르는 어휘와 표현을 아래에 정리하고 해설을 통해 복습하세요.)

비법 적용 Box (앞에서 배운 비법을 스스로 문장에 적용하고 해설과 비교해 보세요.)

라. 고난도 실전 문제

정답과 해설 49~51쪽

1. 다음 글에서 전체 흐름과 관계 없는 문장을 고르시오.

[2019 고3 6월 모의평가 35번]

When a dog is trained to detect drugs, explosives, contraband, or other items, the trainer doesn't actually teach the dog how to smell; the dog already knows how to discriminate one scent from another. Rather, the dog is trained to become emotionally aroused by one smell versus another. ① In the step-by-step training process, the trainer attaches an "emotional charge" to a particular scent so that the dog is drawn to it above all others. ② And then the dog is trained to search out the desired item on cue, so that the trainer can control or release the behavior. ③ This emotional arousal is also why playing tug with a dog is a more powerful emotional reward in a training regime than just giving a dog a food treat, since the trainer invests more emotion into a game of tug. ④ As long as the trainer gives the dog a food reward regularly, the dog can understand its "good" behavior results in rewards. ⑤ From a dog's point of view, the tug toy is compelling because the trainer is "upset" by the toy.

* contraband : 밀수품 ** tug : 잡아당김

✐ **어휘 Box** (모르는 어휘와 표현을 아래에 정리하고 해설을 통해 복습하세요.)

✐ **비법 적용 Box** (앞에서 배운 비법을 스스로 문장에 적용하고 해설과 비교해 보세요.)

2. 다음 글에서 전체 흐름과 관계 없는 문장을 고르시오.

[2020 고3 9월 모의평가 35번]

In a highly commercialized setting such as the United States, it is not surprising that many landscapes are seen as commodities. In other words, they are valued because of their market potential. Residents develop an identity in part based on how the landscape can generate income for the community. ① This process involves more than the conversion of the natural elements into commodities. ② The landscape itself, including the people and their sense of self, takes on the form of a commodity. ③ Landscape protection in the US traditionally focuses on protecting areas of wilderness, typically in mountainous regions. ④ Over time, the landscape identity can evolve into a sort of "logo" that can be used to sell the stories of the landscape. ⑤ Thus, California's "Wine Country," Florida's "Sun Coast," or South Dakota's "Badlands" shape how both outsiders and residents perceive a place, and these labels build a set of expectations associated with the culture of those who live there.

✐ **어휘 Box** (모르는 어휘와 표현을 아래에 정리하고 해설을 통해 복습하세요.)

✐ **비법 적용 Box** (앞에서 배운 비법을 스스로 문장에 적용하고 해설과 비교해 보세요.)

check list

✓ 영 • 오 • 모 1일차 공부하기

III

9~12일차 학습하기

글의 흐름상 적합한 표현 관련 독해 유형

영어
오답의
모든것

글의 흐름상 적합한 표현 관련 독해 유형 9~10일차 학습하기

1 『어휘 추론』

유형 풀이 비법

주어진 문맥 안에서 해당 어휘를 포함한 문장과 그 문장의 앞・뒤의 논리 관계를 파악하는 것이 핵심!

1) 반의어를 공략하라.

정답의 핵심 포인트!	무관한 문장 확인 비법 3가지
두 단어 중 선택하는 유형 (예 : close/distant)	✎ 두 개의 단어 중 하나를 선택하는 문제는 서로 반의어일 가능성이 크다. 둘 중 하나의 단어 뜻만 안다면 나머지 하나는 반의어로 생각하고 푼다.
밑줄 유형 (예 : ② increase)	✎ 밑줄 친 어휘 중 어색한 것을 고르는 유형에서는 반의어가 있는 어휘가 답일 가능성이 높다. 따라서, 해당 어휘에 들어갈 것이 원래는 그 어휘의 반의어가 아닐지 의심해 본다. 예를 들어 'increase'는 'decrease'가 아닌지, 'easy'는 'difficult'가 아닌지 생각하며 읽는다.

2) 어휘 추론의 출제 방향은 크게 [순접] 과 [역접] 으로 나눌 수 있다.

논리 관계		오답 타파 해법	문장 구조
순접	병렬	A와 B의 속성이 유사(동일)함을 활용	① [A] and [B] (예: smart and clever) ② 역접의 단서가 없으면, 앞 내용과 동일한 의미로 읽어야 함.
	인과	인과 구조의 답의 근거는 A와 B의 속성이 인과 관계임을 활용	① [A] [so, therefore, because, if, when 등] [B] (예: Because I have more friends, I am happier.) ② the 비교급 A, the 비교급 B (예: The more, the better.)
	부연 설명	부연 설명의 답의 근거는 수식하는 말과 수식받는 말 사이의 속성이 유사(동일)함을 활용	① [A] [관계대명사/관계부사] [B] (예: They are my parent who gave me a life.) ② [A] [분사구문/콜론(:)/세미콜론(;)] [B] (예: It rained all day long, ruining my holiday.) (예: This need isn't simply learned; it is innate.)
역접		A나 B에 밑줄이 있는 경우, 두 어휘의 의미가 전체 문맥상 반대의 속성임을 활용	① [A] ⟺ but, however, yet, still 등 ⟺ [B] (예: smart but strong)

학습날짜 ______년 ______월 ______일

학습시간 ____:____ ~ ____:____

9일차

가. 비법 연습 문제

정답과 해설 54~55쪽

1. 다음 중 문맥상 적절한 단어를 고르고, 비법에서 제시된 논리 관계 중 어떤 것이 활용되었는지 쓰시오.

① [Distance/Friendliness] is seen as good if you have a hierarchical preference. (　　　　　　)

② Far from being static, the environment is constantly [changing/unchanging] and offering new challenges to evolving populations. ……………………………………………… (　　　　　　)

③ Even under ideal circumstances, hunting these fast animals with spear or bow and arrow is an uncertain task. The reindeer, however, had a [weakness/strength] that mankind would mercilessly exploit: it swam poorly. ……………………………………………… (　　　　　　)

나. 기출 연습 문제

다음 글의 밑줄 친 부분 중, 문맥상 낱말의 쓰임이 적절하지 않은 것을 고르시오.

[2017 고2 6월 전국연합 29번]

The overabundance of options in today's marketplace gives you more freedom of choice. However, there may be a price to pay in terms of happiness. According to research by psychologists David Myers and Robert Lane, all this choice often makes people ① depressed. Researchers gave some shoppers 24 choices of jams to taste and others only 6 choices. Those who had ② fewer choices were happier with the tasting. Even more surprisingly, the ones with a smaller selection purchased jam 31% of the time, while those with a wider range of choices only purchased jam 3% of the time. The ironic thing about this is that people nearly always say they want ③ more choices. Yet, the more options they have, the more ④ relieved they become. Savvy restaurant owners provide fewer choices. This allows customers to feel more relaxed, ⑤ prompting them to choose easily and leave more satisfied with their choices.

* savvy : 사리에 밝은

비법 적용

According to research by psychologists David Myers and Robert Lane, **all this choice** often makes people ① depressed.

☞ (병렬) 'all this choice'는 앞 내용의 풍부한 선택사항을 의미한다. 이러한 선택에는 치러야 할 대가가 있다고 하였으므로 해당 어휘가 포함된 문장이 앞 문장과 동일한 의미인지 확인한다.

Those who had ② fewer choices were happier with the tasting. Even more surprisingly, the ones with a smaller selection purchased jam 31% of the time, **while** those with a wider range of choices only purchased jam 3% of the time.

☞ (병렬) 역접의 연결사 없이 문장이 이어지고 있으므로 앞 문장과 같은 의미인지 확인한다.

☞ 더 적은 선택이 구매율 상승으로 이어졌다는 내용을 추가적으로 서술하였다. '더 적은 선택(a smaller selection)'과 '더 폭넓은 선택(a wider range of choices)'을 하였을 경우를 대조하고 있으므로 'while'은 '~반면에'라는 의미로 해석한다.

The ironic thing about this is that people nearly always say they want ③ more choices.

☞ (역접) '역설적인 것(The ironic thing)'을 언급하고 있으므로, 앞 문장과 반대의 상황이 제시되어야 한다.

Yet, the more options they have, the more ④ relieved they become.

☞ (역접) 역설적인 상황을 언급한 뒤에 이어지는 문장이므로, 필자의 원래 의도를 서술하는 의미가 되어야 한다.

This allows customers to feel more relaxed, ⑤ prompting them to choose easily and leave more satisfied with their choices.

☞ (부연 설명) 콤마 뒤에 오는 분사구문은 콤마 앞 내용에 대한 결과인 경우가 많다. 따라서, 고객들이 편안한(행복한) 감정을 느낀 후에 어떤 결과가 이어질지 생각해 본다.

오답의 모든 것

① depressed

▶ 앞 문장의 'a price to pay in terms of happiness'와 같은 의미의 올바른 어휘 (price : **치러야 할 대가**)

② fewer

▶ '선택의 자유가 늘어나면 우울해진다'를 '선택이 줄면 더 행복해진다'라는 반의어로 표현한 바르게 표현한 오답

③ more

▶ 선택이 증가하면 행복이 감소하지만, 더 많은 선택을 원하는 역설적 상황을 바르게 표현한 오답

④ relieved

▶ **역접 뒤에서 앞의 역설적 상황이 아닌 필자의 실제 의도가 들어가야 하는 부분임. '선택이 많으면 행복하지 않다'라는 의미가 아닌 주제와 반대가 되었으므로 정답 ('paralyzed(마비된)'로 변경)**

⑤ prompting

▶ 문장의 주어인 'This'는 앞 문장을 의미하며 '선택의 감소 ⇒ 행복 증가 ⇒ 선택(구매) 증가'라는 의미를 바르게 표현한 오답

학습날짜 ______년 ______월 ______일

학습시간 ____:____ ~ ____:____

10 일차

다. 실전 연습 문제

정답과 해설 55~56쪽

1. (A), (B), (C)의 각 네모 안에서 문맥에 맞는 낱말로 가장 적절한 것을 고르시오.

[2018 고1 6월 전국연합 29번]

People have higher expectations as their lives get better. However, the higher the expectations, the more difficult it is to be satisfied. We can increase the satisfaction we feel in our lives by (A) [controlling / raising] our expectations. Adequate expectations leave room for many experiences to be pleasant surprises. The challenge is to find a way to have proper expectations. One way to do this is by keeping wonderful experiences (B) [frequent / rare]. No matter what you can afford, save great wine for special occasions. Make an elegantly styled silk blouse a special treat. This may seem like an act of denying your desires, but I don't think it is. On the contrary, it's a way to make sure that you can continue to experience (C) [familiarity / pleasure]. What's the point of great wines and great blouses if they don't make you feel great?

(A) (B) (C)

① controlling …… frequent …… pleasure

② controlling …… rare ……… familiarity

③ controlling …… rare ……… pleasure

④ raising ……… frequent …… familiarity

⑤ raising ……… rare ……… pleasure

✐ **어휘 Box** (모르는 어휘와 표현을 아래에 정리하고 해설을 통해 복습하세요.)

✐ **비법 적용 Box** (앞에서 배운 비법을 스스로 문장에 적용하고 해설과 비교해 보세요.)

2. 다음 글의 밑줄 친 부분 중, 문맥상 낱말의 쓰임이 적절하지 않은 것을 고르시오.

[2020 고2 3월 전국연합 30번]

I was sitting outside a restaurant in Spain one summer evening, waiting for dinner. The aroma of the kitchens excited my taste buds. My future meal was coming to me in the form of molecules drifting through the air, too small for my eyes to see but ① detected by my nose. The ancient Greeks first came upon the idea of atoms this way; the smell of baking bread suggested to them that small particles of bread ② existed beyond vision. The cycle of weather ③ disproved this idea: a puddle of water on the ground gradually dries out, disappears, and then falls later as rain. They reasoned that there must be particles of water that turn into steam, form clouds, and fall to earth, so that the water is ④ conserved even though the little particles are too small to see. My paella in Spain had inspired me, four thousand years too ⑤ late, to take the credit for atomic theory.

*taste bud: 미뢰(혀의 미각 기관) **molecule: 분자 ***paella: 파에야(스페인 요리의 하나)

✐ **어휘 Box** (모르는 어휘와 표현을 아래에 정리하고 해설을 통해 복습하세요.)

✐ **비법 적용 Box** (앞에서 배운 비법을 스스로 문장에 적용하고 해설과 비교해 보세요.)

3. (A), (B), (C)의 각 네모 안에서 문맥에 맞는 낱말로 가장 적절한 것을 고르시오.

[2020 고1 6월 전국연합 30번]

The brain makes up just two percent of our body weight but uses 20 percent of our energy. In newborns, it's no less than 65 percent. That's partly why babies sleep all the time — their growing brains(A) [warn / exhaust] them — and have a lot of body fat, to use as an energy reserve when needed. Our muscles use even more of our energy, about a quarter of the total, but we have a lot of muscle. Actually, per unit of matter, the brain uses by far (B) [more / less] energy than our other organs. That means that the brain is the most expensive of our organs. But it is also marvelously (C) [creative / efficient]. Our brains require only about four hundred calories of energy a day — about the same as we get from a blueberry muffin. Try running your laptop for twenty–four hours on a muffin and see how far you get.

	(A)	(B)	(C)
①	warn	less	efficient
②	warn	more	efficient
③	exhaust	more	efficient
④	exhaust	more	creative
⑤	exhaust	less	creative

✐ **어휘 Box** (모르는 어휘와 표현을 아래에 정리하고 해설을 통해 복습하세요.)

✐ **비법 적용 Box** (앞에서 배운 비법을 스스로 문장에 적용하고 해설과 비교해 보세요.)

정답과 해설 59~61쪽

4. 다음 글의 밑줄 친 부분 중, 문맥상 낱말의 쓰임이 적절하지 <u>않은</u> 것을 고르시오.

[2020 고2 9월 전국연합 30번]

Spine-tingling ghost stories are fun to tell if they are really scary, and even more so if you claim that they are true. People get a ① <u>thrill</u> from passing on those stories. The same applies to miracle stories. If a rumor of a miracle gets written down in a book, the rumor becomes hard to ② <u>believe</u>, especially if the book is ancient. If a rumor is ③ <u>old</u> enough, it starts to be called a "tradition" instead, and then people believe it all the more. This is rather odd because you might think they would realize that older rumors have had more time to get ④ <u>distorted</u> than younger rumors that are close in time to the alleged events themselves. Elvis Presley and Michael Jackson lived too ⑤ <u>recently</u> for traditions to have grown up, so not many people believe stories like "Elvis seen on Mars."

✐ **어휘 Box** (모르는 어휘와 표현을 아래에 정리하고 해설을 통해 복습하세요.)

✐ **비법 적용 Box** (앞에서 배운 비법을 스스로 문장에 적용하고 해설과 비교해 보세요.)

라. 고난도 실전 문제

정답과 해설 61~63쪽

1. 다음 글의 밑줄 친 부분 중, 문맥상 낱말의 쓰임이 적절하지 <u>않은</u> 것을 고르시오.

[2021학년도 고3 수능 30번]

Suppose we know that Paula suffers from a severe phobia. If we reason that Paula is afraid either of snakes or spiders, and then ① <u>establish</u> that she is not afraid of snakes, we will conclude that Paula is afraid of spiders. However, our conclusion is reasonable only if Paula's fear really does concern either snakes or spiders. If we know only that Paula has a phobia, then the fact that she's not afraid of snakes is entirely ② <u>consistent</u> with her being afraid of heights, water, dogs or the number thirteen. More generally, when we are presented with a list of alternative explanations for some phenomenon, and are then persuaded that all but one of those explanations are ③ <u>unsatisfactory</u>, we should pause to reflect. Before ④ <u>denying</u> that the remaining explanation is the correct one, consider whether other plausible options are being ignored or overlooked. The fallacy of false choice misleads when we're insufficiently attentive to an important hidden assumption, that the choices which have been made explicit exhaust the ⑤ <u>sensible</u> alternatives.

*plausible: 그럴듯한 **fallacy: 오류

✐ **어휘 Box** (모르는 어휘와 표현을 아래에 정리하고 해설을 통해 복습하세요.)

✐ **비법 적용 Box** (앞에서 배운 비법을 스스로 문장에 적용하고 해설과 비교해 보세요.)

2. 다음 글의 밑줄 친 부분 중, 문맥상 낱말의 쓰임이 적절하지 않은 것을 고르시오.

[2020 고3 9월 모의 평가 30번]

If I say to you, ‘Don’t think of a white bear’, you will find it difficult not to think of a white bear. In this way, ‘thought suppression can actually increase the thoughts one wishes to suppress instead of calming them’. One common example of this is that people on a diet who try not to think about food often begin to think much ① more about food. This process is therefore also known as the rebound effect. The ② ironic effect seems to be caused by the interplay of two related cognitive processes. This dual-process system involves, first, an intentional operating process, which consciously attempts to locate thoughts ③ unrelated to the suppressed ones. Second, and simultaneously, an unconscious monitoring process tests whether the operating system is functioning effectively. If the monitoring system encounters thoughts inconsistent with the intended ones, it prompts the intentional operating process to ensure that these are replaced by ④ inappropriate thoughts. However, it is argued, the intentional operating system can fail due to increased cognitive load caused by fatigue, stress and emotional factors, and so the monitoring process filters the inappropriate thoughts into consciousness, making them highly ⑤ accessible.

어휘 Box (모르는 어휘와 표현을 아래에 정리하고 해설을 통해 복습하세요.)

비법 적용 Box (앞에서 배운 비법을 스스로 문장에 적용하고 해설과 비교해 보세요.)

2 『어법』

유형 풀이 비법

문장의 구조를 파악해라. 문장의 주어와 동사부터 구별하자.

어법 출제 영역 BEST 7

1) 수일치 : 단수동사 VS 복수동사, 단수대명사 VS 복수대명사 유형의 문제, 부분명사의 문제

밑줄 친 부분	▶ ▶ ▶ ▶ ▶ 비법 적용 단계 ▶ ▶ ▶ ▶ ▶				정답
	〈1단계〉	〈2단계〉	〈3단계〉		
is/are	주어를 수식하는 수식어구를 괄호로 묶어 제외	괄호 묶는 수식어구: 전치사구/ 분사구(-ing,-ed) /관계사절/to부정사	괄호 제외한 주어가 단수	▶	단수 정답
단수 동사 /복수 동사			괄호 제외한 주어가 복수		복수 정답
대명사	대명사가 대신하는 명사가 무엇인지 파악	앞 문장에서 지칭되는 명사의 단/복수에 따라	지칭되는 명사가 단수		단수 정답
			지칭되는 명사가 복수		복수 정답
부분 명사	A of B의 구조파악	A에 해당하는 표현: some, most, part, half, portion, all, 분수	of 뒤의 B(명사)가 단수		단수 정답
			of 뒤의 B(명사)가 단수		복수 정답

가. 비법 연습 문제 .... 정답과 해설66쪽

1. 다음 중 어법상 옳은 것을 고르시오.

1) This high concentration of cats [was / were] probably due to the laws protecting the cat.

2) While manned space missions are more costly than unmanned [it /one / ones], they are more successful.

3) Some of the good things that companion animals do for us [is / are] so easy to see on the daily life.

2) 관계사 : 관계대명사 VS 관계부사, 관계대명사 VS 접속사 유형의 문제

밑줄 친 부분	▶ ▶ ▶ ▶ ▶ 비법 적용 단계 ▶ ▶ ▶ ▶ ▶				
	〈1단계〉	〈2단계〉	〈3단계〉		정답
관계 대명사 /관계부사	뒤이은 구조의 불완전함	주어, 목적어, 보어, 전치사의 목적어 존재 여부	한 개라도 없다	▶	관계대명사 정답
	뒤이은 구조의 완전함		모두 있다		관계부사 정답
관계대명사 /접속사	뒤이은 구조의 불완전함	주어, 목적어, 보어, 전치사의 목적어 존재 여부	한 개라도 없다		관계대명사 정답
	뒤이은 구조의 완전함		모두 있다		접속사 정답

가. 비법 연습 문제 .... 정답과 해설66쪽

2. 다음 중 어법상 옳은 것을 고르시오.

1) I want to live in an apartment [which / where] they are building as soon as possible.

2) I admitted [that / what] I made a big mistake.

3) 분사 : 현재분사 VS 과거분사 유형의 문제

밑줄 친 부분	▶ ▶ ▶ ▶ ▶ 비법 적용 단계 ▶ ▶ ▶ ▶ ▶				
	〈1단계〉		〈2단계〉		정답
Ving / Ved	분사(Ved/Ving)가 수식하는 명사 먼저 파악	해석상	명사가 V(동사) 하는	▶	Ving 정답
	분사(Ved/Ving)가 수식하는 명사 먼저 파악		명사가 V(동사) 당하는		Ved 정답

가. 비법 연습 문제 .... 정답과 해설66쪽

3. 다음 중 어법상 옳은 것을 고르시오.

1) Keep the windows [closing / closed] and use air conditioners for 20 minutes.

2) Emily Tomson had printed an [insulted / insulting] editorial in the local newspaper a few hours earlier.

4) 형용사 VS 부사 유형의 문제

밑줄 친 부분	▶ ▶ ▶ ▶ ▶ 비법 적용 단계 ▶ ▶ ▶ ▶ ▶			
	〈1단계〉	〈2단계〉		정답
형용사/ 부사	수식하는 말이 명사인지 판단	보어의 위치 or 명사를 수식	▶	형용사 정답
	수식하는 말이 명사 이외의 것인지 판단	형용사/부사/ 동사/문장 수식		부사 정답

가. 비법 연습 문제 ······ 정답과 해설66쪽

4. 다음 중 어법상 옳은 것을 고르시오.

1) You need to prove how [smartly/smart] you are through deep self-observation.

2) Our immune systems are functioning as [effective/effectively] when we are well rested

5) 준동사 VS 동사 유형의 문제

밑줄 친 부분	▶ ▶ ▶ ▶ ▶ 비법 적용 단계 ▶ ▶ ▶ ▶ ▶			
	〈1단계〉	〈2단계〉		정답
준동사/ 동사	동사의 종류: be동사, 조동사, 일반동사	밑줄 친 부분이 준동사인데 문장에 동사가 없을 경우	▶	동사가 정답
	준동사의 종류: to V, Ving, Ved	밑줄 친 부분이 동사인데 문장에 동사가 있을 경우		준동사가 정답

가. 비법 연습 문제 ······ 정답과 해설66쪽

5. 다음 중 어법상 옳은 것을 고르시오.

1) Your body uses this energy [make / to make] new cells, move your bodies.

2) This experience will make it possible for your child [remember / to remember] the things he should know when he is left alone.

6) 병렬구조 찾기 유형의 문제

밑줄 친 부분	▶ ▶ ▶ ▶ ▶ 비법 적용 단계 ▶ ▶ ▶ ▶ ▶			
	〈1단계〉	〈2단계〉		정답
A and/but/ or B	밑줄 바로 앞, 병렬구조 접속사가 있는지 확인	and/but/or 뒤의 B가 준동사이면	▶	A도 같은 형태의 준동사가 정답
		and/but/or 뒤의 B가 동사이면		A도 같은 형태의 동사가 정답(수일치)

가. 비법 연습 문제 ························ 정답과 해설66쪽

6. 다음 중 어법상 옳은 것을 고르시오.

1) In the Mtro, you have to open the doors yourself by pushing a button, depressing a lever or [slide / sliding] them.

2) After feeding my brother and me breakfast, she would scrub, mop, and [dust / to dust] everything.

7) 그 밖의 기타 유형들

<table>
<tr><th rowspan="2">밑줄 친 부분</th><th colspan="4">▶ ▶ ▶ ▶ ▶ 비법 적용 단계 ▶ ▶ ▶ ▶ ▶</th></tr>
<tr><th>〈1단계〉</th><th>〈2단계〉</th><th></th><th>정답</th></tr>
<tr><td rowspan="2">do(does, did)/be</td><td rowspan="2">밑줄 친 부분에 do/be동사 외에 다른 동사가 없음</td><td>앞에 나온 동사인 be 동사를 대신하면</td><td rowspan="9">▶</td><td>be가 정답</td></tr>
<tr><td>앞에 나온 동사인 일반 동사를 대신하면</td><td>do(does, did)가 정답</td></tr>
<tr><td>do/does/did (강조동사)</td><td>밑줄 친 부분 뒤에 부정형 없이 do/does/did+동사원형 확인</td><td>수일치 및 시제에 맞는지 확인</td><td>수일치 및 시제 고려하여 do/does/did 정답 택일</td></tr>
<tr><td rowspan="2">to 부정사 / 동사원형</td><td rowspan="2">문장의 본동사가 존재하고 목적 보어 자리인지 확인</td><td>본동사가 지각, 사역동사</td><td>동사원형이 정답</td></tr>
<tr><td>to 부정사를 목적 보어로 취하는 동사 (expect, allow, want, tell, ask, order, enable 등)</td><td>to 부정사가 정답</td></tr>
<tr><td rowspan="2">대명사/ 관계 대명사</td><td rowspan="2">밑줄 친 부분을 기준으로, 앞 · 뒤 문장을 연결할 때 접속사 여부 확인</td><td>접속사가 있으면</td><td>대명사가 정답</td></tr>
<tr><td>접속사가 없으면</td><td>관계대명사가 정답</td></tr>
</table>

가. 비법 연습 문제

정답과 해설66쪽

7. 다음 중 어법상 옳은 것을 고르시오.

1) If you were a monkey, you would see things in colors, just as people [are / do].

2) They [do / does] have a wonderful time at the birthday party.

3) ESP is a sense that allows one person [reading / to read] the mind of another person.

4) Amy thought [it / which] was a normal family outing to go to a car to the picnic.

11일차

가. 비법 연습 문제

정답과 해설 66쪽

8. 다음 주어진 문장의 밑줄 친 부분이 어법상 맞는 것은 O 표시하고, 틀린 것은 바르게 고치시오.

1) In warm environments, clothes that have a wicking capacity <u>is</u> helpful in dissipating heat from the body. (   )

2) Competitive activities can be more than just performance showcases <u>which</u> the best is recognized and the rest are overlooked. (   )

3) Artificial light, which typically contains only a few wavelengths of light, <u>does</u> not seem to have the same effect on mood that sunlight has. (   )

4) With this form of agency comes the belief that individual successes <u>depending</u> primarily on one's own abilities and actions, and thus, whether by influencing the environment or trying to accept one's circumstances. (   )

나. 기출 연습 문제

정답과 해설 66~67쪽

다음 글의 밑줄 친 부분 중, 어법상 <u>틀린</u> 것을 고르시오.

[2020년 고2 3월 전국연합 29번]

Commercial airplanes generally travel airways similar to roads, although they are not physical structures. Airways have fixed widths and defined altitudes, ① <u>which</u> separate traffic moving in opposite directions. Vertical separation of aircraft allows some flights ② <u>to pass</u> over airports while other processes occur below. Air travel usually covers long distances, with short periods of intense pilot activity at takeoff and landing and long periods of lower pilot activity while in the air, the portion of the flight ③ <u>known</u> as the "long haul." During the long-haul portion of a flight, pilots spend more time assessing aircraft status than ④ <u>searching</u> out nearby planes. This is because collisions between aircraft usually occur in the surrounding area of airports, while crashes due to aircraft malfunction ⑤ <u>tends</u> to occur during long-haul flight.

*altitude: 고도 ** long haul: 장거리 비행

학습날짜 ______년 ______월 ______일
학습시간 ______ : ______ ~ ______ : ______

비법 적용

This is because collisions between aircraft usually occur in the surrounding area of airports, while crashes due to aircraft malfunction ⑤ <u>tends</u> to occur during long-haul flight.

☞ 수일치) 문장의 주어인 'crashes'가 복수 명사이므로 '<u>tend</u>'로 고쳐야 한다.

오답의 모든 것

① which
▶ 관계사) 관계대명사 which 이하에 주어가 없이 separate라는 동사가 나오므로 주격 관계대명사 which는 적절히 쓰인 오답 (which의 선행사는 'fixed widths and defined altitudes')

② to pass
▶ to 부정사) 동사 allow는 to 부정사를 목적보어로 취하는 동사이므로 적절히 쓰인 오답

③ known
▶ 분사) 장거리 비행이라고 '알려진'이라는 수동의 의미이므로 known은 적절히 쓰인 오답

④ searching
▶ 병렬 구조) spend 시간 ~ing구문에서 assessing과 병렬구조를 이루는 searching은 적절히 쓰인 오답

12 일차

다. 실전 연습 문제

정답과 해설 67~68쪽

1. 다음 글의 밑줄 친 부분 중, 어법상 틀린 것을 고르시오.

[2020년 고2 3월 전국연합 29번]

My dad worked very late hours as a musician — until about three in the morning — so he slept late on weekends. As a result, we didn't have much of a relationship when I was young other than him constantly nagging me to take care of chores like mowing the lawn and cutting the hedges, ① which I hated. He was a responsible man ② dealing with an irresponsible kid. Memories of how we interacted ③ seems funny to me today. For example, one time he told me to cut the grass and I decided ④ to do just the front yard and postpone doing the back, but then it rained for a couple days and the backyard grass became so high I had to cut it with a sickle. That took so long ⑤ that by the time I was finished, the front yard was too high to mow, and so on.

*sickle: 낫

✐ **어휘 Box** (모르는 어휘와 표현을 아래에 정리하고 해설을 통해 복습하세요.)

✐ **비법 적용 Box** (앞에서 배운 비법을 스스로 문장에 적용하고 해설과 비교해 보세요.)

정답과 해설 68~69쪽

2. 다음 글의 밑줄 친 부분 중, 어법상 틀린 것을 고르시오.

[2019년 고1 11월 전국연합 29번]

Non-verbal communication is not a substitute for verbal communication. Rather, it should function as a supplement, ① serving to enhance the richness of the content of the message that is being passed across. Non-verbal communication can be useful in situations ② where speaking may be impossible or inappropriate. Imagine you are in an uncomfortable position while talking to an individual. Non-verbal communication will help you ③ get the message across to him or her to give you some time off the conversation to be comfortable again. Another advantage of non-verbal communication is ④ what it offers you the opportunity to express emotions and attitudes properly. Without the aid of non-verbal communication, there are several aspects of your nature and personality that will not be adequately expressed. So, again, it does not substitute verbal communication but rather ⑤ complements it.

*supplement: 보충

어휘 Box (모르는 어휘와 표현을 아래에 정리하고 해설을 통해 복습하세요.)

비법 적용 Box (앞에서 배운 비법을 스스로 문장에 적용하고 해설과 비교해 보세요.)

3. 다음 글의 밑줄 친 부분 중, 어법상 틀린 것을 고르시오.

[2019년 고2 6월 전국연합 29번]

Trying to produce everything yourself would mean you are using your time and resources to produce many things ① for which you are a highcost provider. This would translate into lower production and income. For example, even though most doctors might be good at record keeping and arranging appointments, ② it is generally in their interest to hire someone to perform these services. The time doctors use to keep records is time they could have spent seeing patients. Because the time ③ spent with their patients is worth a lot, the opportunity cost of record keeping for doctors will be high. Thus, doctors will almost always find it ④ advantageous to hire someone else to keep and manage their records. Moreover, when the doctor specializes in the provision of physician services and ⑤ hiring someone who has a comparative advantage in record keeping, costs will be lower and joint output larger than would otherwise be achievable.

어휘 Box (모르는 어휘와 표현을 아래에 정리하고 해설을 통해 복습하세요.)

비법 적용 Box (앞에서 배운 비법을 스스로 문장에 적용하고 해설과 비교해 보세요.)

4. 다음 글의 밑줄 친 부분 중, 어법상 틀린 것을 고르시오.

[2020년 고2 11월 전국연합 29번]

One of the keys to insects' successful survival in the open air ① lies in their outer covering — a hard waxy layer that helps prevent their tiny bodies from dehydrating. To take oxygen from the air, they use narrow breathing holes in the body-segments, which take in air ② passively and can be opened and closed as needed. Instead of blood ③ containing in vessels, they have free-flowing hemolymph, which helps keep their bodies rigid, aids movement, and assists the transportation of nutrients and waste materials to the appropriate parts of the body. The nervous system is modular — in a sense, each of the body segments has ④ its own individual and autonomous brain — and some other body systems show a similar modularization. These are just a few of the many ways ⑤ in which insect bodies are structured and function completely differently from our own.

*hemolymph: 혈림프 **modular: 모듈식의(여러 개의 개별 단위로 되어 있는)

어휘 Box (모르는 어휘와 표현을 아래에 정리하고 해설을 통해 복습하세요.)

비법 적용 Box (앞에서 배운 비법을 스스로 문장에 적용하고 해설과 비교해 보세요.)

라. 고난도 실전 문제

정답과 해설 72~73쪽

1. 다음 글의 밑줄 친 부분 중, 어법상 <u>틀린</u> 것을 고르시오.

[2019년 고3 3월 전국연합 28번]

Baylor University researchers investigated ① <u>whether</u> different types of writing could ease people into sleep. To find out, they had 57 young adults spend five minutes before bed ② <u>writing</u> either a todo list for the days ahead or a list of tasks they'd finished over the past few days. The results confirm that not all presleep writing is created equally. Those who made todo lists before bed ③ <u>were</u> able to fall asleep nine minutes faster than those who wrote about past events. The quality of the lists mattered, too; the more tasks and the more ④ <u>specific</u> the todo lists were, the faster the writers fell asleep. The study authors figure that writing down future tasks ⑤ <u>unloading</u> the thoughts so you can stop turning them over in your mind. You're telling your brain that the task will get done — just not right now.

어휘 Box (모르는 어휘와 표현을 아래에 정리하고 해설을 통해 복습하세요.)

비법 적용 Box (앞에서 배운 비법을 스스로 문장에 적용하고 해설과 비교해 보세요.)

2. 다음 글의 밑줄 친 부분 중, 어법상 틀린 것을 고르시오.

[2021학년도 고3 수능 29번]

Regulations covering scientific experiments on human subjects are strict. Subjects must give their informed, written consent, and experimenters must submit their proposed experiments to thorough examination by overseeing bodies. Scientists who experiment on themselves can, functionally if not legally, avoid the restrictions ① associated with experimenting on other people. They can also sidestep most of the ethical issues involved: nobody, presumably, is more aware of an experiment's potential hazards than the scientist who devised ② it. Nonetheless, experimenting on oneself remains ③ deeply problematic. One obvious drawback is the danger involved; knowing that it exists ④ does nothing to reduce it. A less obvious drawback is the limited range of data that the experiment can generate. Human anatomy and physiology vary, in small but significant ways, according to gender, age, lifestyle, and other factors. Experimental results derived from a single subject are, therefore, of limited value; there is no way to know ⑤ what the subject's responses are typical or atypical of the response of humans as a group.

*consent: 동의 **anatomy: (해부학적) 구조 ***physiology: 생리적 현상

어휘 Box (모르는 어휘와 표현을 아래에 정리하고 해설을 통해 복습하세요.)

비법 적용 Box (앞에서 배운 비법을 스스로 문장에 적용하고 해설과 비교해 보세요.)

파이널 모의고사 1회

영어
오답의
모든것

파이널 모의고사 1회

[1~2] 주어진 글 다음에 이어질 글의 순서로 가장 적절한 것을 고르시오.

정답과 해설 76~78쪽

1.

[2020 고3 3월 전국연합 37번]

Distinct from the timing of interaction is the way in which time is compressed on television. Specifically, the pauses and delays that characterize everyday life are removed through editing, and new accents are added — namely, a laugh track.

(A) It is the statement that is in bold print or the boxed insert in newspaper and magazine articles. As such, compression techniques accentuate another important temporal dimension of television — rhythm and tempo.

(B) More important, television performers, or people who depend on television, such as politicians, are evaluated by viewers (voters) on their ability to meet time compression requirements, such as the one sentence graphic statement or metaphor to capture the moment.

(C) The familiar result is a compressed event in which action flows with rapid ease, compacting hours or even days into minutes, and minutes into seconds. Audiences are spared the waiting common to everyday life. Although this use of time may appear unnatural in the abstract, the television audience has come to expect it, and critics demand it.

*accentuate: 강조하다

① (A) - (C) - (B)　② (B) - (A) - (C)　③ (B) - (C) - (A)
④ (C) - (A) - (B)　⑤ (C) - (B) - (A)

어휘 Box (모르는 어휘와 표현을 아래에 정리하고 해설을 통해 복습하세요.)

비법 적용 Box (앞에서 배운 비법을 스스로 문장에 적용하고 해설과 비교해 보세요.)

정답과 해설 78~79쪽
[2020 고3 7월 전국연합 36번]

2.

The reason why any sugar molecule — whether in cocoa bean or pan or anywhere else — turns brown when heated is to do with the presence of carbon.

(A) Further roasting will turn some of the sugar into pure carbon (double bonds all round), which creates a burnt flavor and a darkbrown color. Complete roasting results in charcoal: all of the sugar has become carbon, which is black.

(B) On the whole, it is the carbonrich molecules that are larger, so these get left behind, and within these there is a structure called a carboncarbon double bond. This chemical structure absorbs light. In small amounts it gives the caramelizing sugar a yellowbrown color.

(C) Sugars are carbohydrates, which is to say that they are made of carbon ("carbo"), hydrogen ("hydr"), and oxygen ("ate") atoms. When heated, these long molecules disintegrate into smaller units, some of which are so small that they evaporate (which accounts for the lovely smell).

① (A) - (C) - (B)
② (B) - (A) - (C)
③ (B) - (C) - (A)
④ (C) - (A) - (B)
⑤ (C) - (B) - (A)

✐ **어휘 Box** (모르는 어휘와 표현을 아래에 정리하고 해설을 통해 복습하세요.)

✐ **비법 적용 Box** (앞에서 배운 비법을 스스로 문장에 적용하고 해설과 비교해 보세요.)

[3~4] 글의 흐름으로 보아 주어진 문장이 들어가기에 가장 적절한 곳을 고르시오.

정답과 해설 79~82쪽

3.

[2020 고3 3월 전국연합 38번]

Historians and sociologists of science have recently corrected this claim by showing how senses other than seeing, including listening, have been significant in the development of knowledge, notable in the laboratory.

If there is any field that is associated with seeing rather than with hearing, it is science. Scholars who emphasize the visual bias in Western culture even point to science as their favorite example. (①) Because doing research seems impossible without using images, graphs, and diagrams, science is — in their view — a visual endeavor par excellence. (②) They stress that scientific work involves more than visual observation. (③) The introduction of measurement devices that merely seem to require the reading of results and thus seeing has not ruled out the deployment of the scientists' other senses. (④) On the contrary, scientific work in experimental settings often calls for bodily skills, one of which is listening. (⑤) The world of science itself, however, still considers listening a less objective entrance into knowledge production than seeing.

*deployment: 사용

✐ **어휘 Box** (모르는 어휘와 표현을 아래에 정리하고 해설을 통해 복습하세요.)

✐ **비법 적용 Box** (앞에서 배운 비법을 스스로 문장에 적용하고 해설과 비교해 보세요.)

4.

정답과 해설 82~84쪽
[2020 고3 9월 모의평가 39번]

Rather, it evolved naturally as certain devices were found in practice to be both workable and useful.

Film has no grammar. (①) There are, however, some vaguely defined rules of usage in cinematic language, and the syntax of film — its systematic arrangement — orders these rules and indicates relationships among them. (②) As with written and spoken languages, it is important to remember that the syntax of film is a result of its usage, not a determinant of it. (③) There is nothing preordained about film syntax. (④) Like the syntax of written and spoken language, the syntax of film is an organic development, descriptive rather than prescriptive, and it has changed considerably over the years. (⑤) "Hollywood Grammar" may sound laughable now, but during the thirties, forties, and early fifties it was an accurate model of the way Hollywood films were constructed.

*preordained: 미리 정해진

✐ **어휘 Box** (모르는 어휘와 표현을 아래에 정리하고 해설을 통해 복습하세요.)

✐ **비법 적용 Box** (앞에서 배운 비법을 스스로 문장에 적용하고 해설과 비교해 보세요.)

[5~6] 다음 빈칸에 들어갈 말로 가장 적절한 것을 고르시오.

정답과 해설 84~86쪽

5.

[2020 고3 3월 전국연합 32번]

Scaling up from the small to the large is often accompanied by an evolution from simplicity to complexity while ____________________. This is familiar in engineering, economics, companies, cities, organisms, and, perhaps most dramatically, evolutionary process. For example, a skyscraper in a large city is a significantly more complex object than a modest family dwelling in a small town, but the underlying principles of construction and design, including questions of mechanics, energy and information distribution, the size of electrical outlets, water faucets, telephones, laptops, doors, etc., all remain approximately the same independent of the size of the building. Similarly, organisms have evolved to have an enormous range of sizes and an extraordinary diversity of morphologies and interactions, which often reflect increasing complexity, yet fundamental building blocks like cells, mitochondria, capillaries, and even leaves do not appreciably change with body size or increasing complexity of the class of systems in which they are embedded.

*morphology: 형태 **capillary: 모세관

① maintaining basic elements unchanged or conserved
② optimizing energy use for the structural growth
③ assigning new functions to existing components
④ incorporating foreign items from surroundings
⑤ accelerating the elimination of useless parts

✐ **어휘 Box** (모르는 어휘와 표현을 아래에 정리하고 해설을 통해 복습하세요.)

✐ **비법 적용 Box** (앞에서 배운 비법을 스스로 문장에 적용하고 해설과 비교해 보세요.)

6.

정답과 해설 86~88쪽
[2020 고3 3월 전국연합 33번]

Knowing who an author is and what his or her likely intentions are in creating text or artwork is tremendously important to most of us. Not knowing who wrote, or created, some artwork is often very frustrating. Our culture places great worth on the identity of speakers, writers, and artists. Perhaps the single most important aspect of "authorship" is the vaguely apprehended presence of human creativity, personality, and authority that nominal authorship seems to provide. It is almost unthinkable for a visitor to an art museum to admire a roomful of paintings without knowing the names of the individual painters, or for a reader not to know who the writer is of the novel she is reading. Publishers proudly display authors' names on the jackets, spines and title pages of their books. Book advertisements in The New York Review of Books and The New York Times Book Review regularly include pictures of authors and quote authors as they talk about their work, both of which show that ______________________.

① book advertising strategies are being diversified
② our interest is as much in authors as in their books
③ authors are influenced by popular works of their time
④ book cover designs show who their target readers are
⑤ book writing is increasingly dictated by book marketing

어휘 Box (모르는 어휘와 표현을 아래에 정리하고 해설을 통해 복습하세요.)

비법 적용 Box (앞에서 배운 비법을 스스로 문장에 적용하고 해설과 비교해 보세요.)

[7~8] 다음 글에서 전체 흐름과 관계 없는 문장을 고르시오.

정답과 해설 88~90쪽

[2020 고3 3월 전국연합 35번]

7.

The genre film simplifies film watching as well as filmmaking. In a western, because of the conventions of appearance, dress, and manners, we recognize the hero, sidekick, villain, etc., on sight and assume they will not violate our expectations of their conventional roles. ① Our familiarity with the genre makes watching not only easier but in some ways more enjoyable. ② Because we know and are familiar with all the conventions, we gain pleasure from recognizing each character, each image, each familiar situation. ③ The fact that the conventions are established and repeated intensifies another kind of pleasure. ④ Genre mixing is not an innovation of the past few decades; it was already an integral part of the film business in the era of classical cinema. ⑤ Settled into a comfortable genre, with our basic expectations satisfied, we become more keenly aware of and responsive to the creative variations, refinements, and complexities that make the film seem fresh and original, and by exceeding our expectations, each innovation becomes an exciting surprise.

✐ 어휘 Box (모르는 어휘와 표현을 아래에 정리하고 해설을 통해 복습하세요.)

✐ 비법 적용 Box (앞에서 배운 비법을 스스로 문장에 적용하고 해설과 비교해 보세요.)

8.

정답과 해설 90~92쪽
[2020 고3 6월 모의평가 35번]

One of the most widespread, and sadly mistaken, environmental myths is that living "close to nature" out in the country or in a leafy suburb is the best "green" lifestyle. Cities, on the other hand, are often blamed as a major cause of ecological destruction — artificial, crowded places that suck up precious resources. Yet, when you look at the facts, nothing could be farther from the truth. ① The pattern of life in the country and most suburbs involves long hours in the automobile each week, burning fuel and pumping out exhaust to get to work, buy groceries, and take kids to school and activities. ② City dwellers, on the other hand, have the option of walking or taking transit to work, shops, and school. ③ The larger yards and houses found outside cities also create an environmental cost in terms of energy use, water use, and land use. ④ This illustrates the tendency that most city dwellers get tired of urban lives and decide to settle in the countryside. ⑤ It's clear that the future of the Earth depends on more people gathering together in compact communities.

*compact: 밀집한

✐ **어휘 Box** (모르는 어휘와 표현을 아래에 정리하고 해설을 통해 복습하세요.)

✐ **비법 적용 Box** (앞에서 배운 비법을 스스로 문장에 적용하고 해설과 비교해 보세요.)

[9~10] 다음 글의 밑줄 친 부분 중, 문맥상 낱말의 쓰임이 적절하지 않은 것은?

9.

정답과 해설 92~94쪽
[2019 고3 6월 모의평가 30번]

Sometimes the awareness that one is distrusted can provide the necessary incentive for self-reflection. An employee who ① realizes she isn't being trusted by her co-workers with shared responsibilities at work might, upon reflection, identify areas where she has consistently let others down or failed to follow through on previous commitments. Others' distrust of her might then ② forbid her to perform her share of the duties in a way that makes her more worthy of their trust. But distrust of one who is ③ sincere in her efforts to be a trustworthy and dependable person can be disorienting and might cause her to doubt her own perceptions and to distrust herself. Consider, for instance, a teenager whose parents are ④ suspicious and distrustful when she goes out at night; even if she has been forthright about her plans and is not ⑤ breaking any agreed-upon rules, her identity as a respectable moral subject is undermined by a pervasive parental attitude that expects deceit and betrayal.

*forthright: 솔직한, 거리낌 없는 **pervasive: 널리 스며 있는

✐ **어휘 Box** (모르는 어휘와 표현을 아래에 정리하고 해설을 통해 복습하세요.)

✐ **비법 적용 Box** (앞에서 배운 비법을 스스로 문장에 적용하고 해설과 비교해 보세요.)

10.

정답과 해설 94~96쪽
[2021학년도 고3 수능 30번]

How the bandwagon effect occurs is demonstrated by the history of measurements of the speed of light. Because this speed is the basis of the theory of relativity, it's one of the most frequently and carefully measured ① quantities in science. As far as we know, the speed hasn't changed over time. However, from 1870 to 1900, all the experiments found speeds that were too high. Then, from 1900 to 1950, the ② opposite happened — all the experiments found speeds that were too low! This kind of error, where results are always on one side of the real value, is called "bias." It probably happened because over time, experimenters subconsciously adjusted their results to ③ match what they expected to find. If a result fit what they expected, they kept it. If a result didn't fit, they threw it out. They weren't being intentionally dishonest, just ④ influenced by the conventional wisdom. The pattern only changed when someone ⑤ lacked the courage to report what was actually measured instead of what was expected.

*bandwagon effect: 편승 효과

✐ **어휘 Box** (모르는 어휘와 표현을 아래에 정리하고 해설을 통해 복습하세요.)

✐ **비법 적용 Box** (앞에서 배운 비법을 스스로 문장에 적용하고 해설과 비교해 보세요.)

[11~12] 다음 글의 밑줄 친 부분 중, 어법상 <u>틀린</u> 것을 고르시오.

11.

정답과 해설 96~97쪽
[2020 고3 3월 전국연합 29번]

When children are young, much of the work is demonstrating to them that they ① <u>do</u> have control. One wise friend of ours who was a parent educator for twenty years ② <u>advises</u> giving calendars to preschoolage children and writing down all the important events in their life, in part because it helps children understand the passage of time better, and how their days will unfold. We can't overstate the importance of the calendar tool in helping kids feel in control of their day. Have them ③ <u>cross</u> off days of the week as you come to them. Spend time going over the schedule for the day, giving them choice in that schedule wherever ④ <u>possible</u>. This communication expresses respect — they see that they are not just a tagalong to your day and your plans, and they understand what is going to happen, when, and why. As they get older, children will then start to write in important things for themselves, ⑤ <u>it</u> further helps them develop their sense of control.

✐ **어휘 Box** (모르는 어휘와 표현을 아래에 정리하고 해설을 통해 복습하세요.)

✐ **비법 적용 Box** (앞에서 배운 비법을 스스로 문장에 적용하고 해설과 비교해 보세요.)

12.

정답과 해설 98~99쪽
[2020 고3 4월 전국연합 29번]

Mental representation is the mental imagery of things that are not actually present to the senses. In general, mental representations can help us learn. Some of the best evidence for this ① comes from the field of musical performance. Several researchers have examined ② what differentiates the best musicians from lesser ones, and one of the major differences lies in the quality of the mental representations the best ones create. When ③ practicing a new piece, advanced musicians have a very detailed mental representation of the music they use to guide their practice and, ultimately, their performance of a piece. In particular, they use their mental representations to provide their own feedback so that they know how ④ closely they are to getting the piece right and what they need to do differently to improve. The beginners and intermediate students may have crude representations of the music ⑤ that allow them to tell, for instance, when they hit a wrong note, but they must rely on feedback from their teachers to identify the more subtle mistakes and weaknesses.

어휘 Box (모르는 어휘와 표현을 아래에 정리하고 해설을 통해 복습하세요.)

비법 적용 Box (앞에서 배운 비법을 스스로 문장에 적용하고 해설과 비교해 보세요.)

파이널 모의고사 2회

영어
오답의
모든것

파이널 모의고사 2회

[1~2] 주어진 글 다음에 이어질 글의 순서로 가장 적절한 것을 고르시오.

정답과 해설 100~101쪽

1. [2020 고3 3월 전국연합 37번]

In the 1980s and '90s, some conservationists predicted that orangutans would go extinct in the wild within 20 or 30 years. Fortunately that didn't happen. Many thousands more orangutans are now known to exist than were recognized at the turn of the millennium.

(A) In fact, the overall population of orangutans has fallen by at least 80 percent in the past 75 years. It's indicative of the difficulty of orangutan research that scientist Erik Meijaard is willing to say only that between 40,000 and 100,000 live on Borneo. Conservationists on Sumatra estimate that only 14,000 survive there.

(B) This doesn't mean that all is well in the orangutans' world. The higher figures come thanks to improved survey methods and the discovery of previously unknown populations, not because the actual numbers have increased.

(C) Much of this loss has been driven by habitat destruction from logging and the rapid spread of vast plantations of oil palm, the fruit of which is sold to make oil used in cooking and in many food products.

① (A) - (C) - (B)　② (B) - (A) - (C)　③ (B) - (C) - (A)
④ (C) - (A) - (B)　⑤ (C) - (B) - (A)

✐ 어휘 Box (모르는 어휘와 표현을 아래에 정리하고 해설을 통해 복습하세요.)

✐ 비법 적용 Box (앞에서 배운 비법을 스스로 문장에 적용하고 해설과 비교해 보세요.)

2.

정답과 해설 101~103쪽
[2020 고3 9월 전국연합 36번]

In the fifth century B.C.E., the Greek philosopher Protagoras pronounced, "Man is the measure of all things." In other words, we feel entitled to ask the world, "What good are you?"

(A) Abilities said to "make us human" — empathy, communication, grief, toolmaking, and so on — all exist to varying degrees among other minds sharing the world with us. Animals with backbones (fishes, amphibians, reptiles, birds, and mammals) all share the same basic skeleton, organs, nervous systems, hormones, and behaviors.

(B) We assume that we are the world's standard, that all things should be compared to us. Such an assumption makes us overlook a lot.

(C) Just as different models of automobiles each have an engine, drive train, four wheels, doors, and seats, we differ mainly in terms of our outside contours and a few internal tweaks. But like naive car buyers, most people see only animals' varied exteriors.

*contour: 윤곽, 외형 **tweak: 조정, 개조

① (A) - (C) - (B) ② (B) - (A) - (C) ③ (B) - (C) - (A)
④ (C) - (A) - (B) ⑤ (C) - (B) - (A)

✐ **어휘 Box** (모르는 어휘와 표현을 아래에 정리하고 해설을 통해 복습하세요.)

✐ **비법 적용 Box** (앞에서 배운 비법을 스스로 문장에 적용하고 해설과 비교해 보세요.)

[3~4] 글의 흐름으로 보아 주어진 문장이 들어가기에 가장 적절한 곳을 고르시오.

정답과 해설 103~105쪽

3.

[2019 고3 3월 전국연합 38번]

However, newspapers could be posted free of charge, and this provided a loophole for thrifty Victorians.

The ancient Greek historian Aeneas the Tactician suggested conveying a secret message by pricking tiny holes under particular letters in an apparently ordinary page of text. Those letters would spell out a secret message, easily read by the intended receiver. (①) However, any other person who stared at the page would probably be unaware of pinpricks and thus the secret message. (②) Two thousand years later, British letter writers used exactly the same method, not to achieve secrecy but to avoid paying excessive postage costs. (③) Before the establishment of the postage system in the mid1800s, sending a letter cost about a shilling for every hundred miles, beyond the means of most people. (④) Instead of writing and sending letters, people began to use pinpricks to spell out a message on the front page of a newspaper. (⑤) They could then send the newspaper through the post without having to pay a penny.

*loophole: 빠져나갈 구멍 **prick: (찔러서) 구멍을 내다

✐ **어휘 Box** (모르는 어휘와 표현을 아래에 정리하고 해설을 통해 복습하세요.)

✐ **비법 적용 Box** (앞에서 배운 비법을 스스로 문장에 적용하고 해설과 비교해 보세요.)

4.

정답과 해설 106~108쪽
[2020 고3 9월 전국연합 36번]

Rather, happiness is often found in those moments we are most vulnerable, alone or in pain.

We seek out feel-good experiences, always on the lookout for the next holiday, purchase or culinary experience. This approach to happiness is relatively recent; it depends on our capacity both to pad our lives with material pleasures and to feel that we can control our suffering. (①) Painkillers, as we know them today, are a relatively recent invention and access to material comfort is now within reach of a much larger proportion of the world's population. (②) These technological and economic advances have had significant cultural implications, leading us to see our negative experiences as a problem and maximizing our positive experiences as the answer. (③) Yet, through this we have forgotten that being happy in life is not just about pleasure. (④) Comfort, contentment and satisfaction have never been the elixir of happiness. (⑤) Happiness is there, on the edges of these experiences, and when we get a glimpse of that kind of happiness it is powerful, transcendent and compelling.

*culinary: 요리의 **elixir: 특효약 ***transcendent: 뛰어난

✐ **어휘 Box** (모르는 어휘와 표현을 아래에 정리하고 해설을 통해 복습하세요.)

✐ **비법 적용 Box** (앞에서 배운 비법을 스스로 문장에 적용하고 해설과 비교해 보세요.)

[5~6] 다음 빈칸에 들어갈 말로 가장 적절한 것을 고르시오.

정답과 해설 108~110쪽
[2020 고3 7월 전국연합 31번]

5.

Both the acquisition and subsequent rejection of agriculture are becoming increasingly recognized as adaptive strategies to local conditions that may have occurred repeatedly over the past ten millennia. For example, in a recent study of the Mlabri, a modern huntergatherer group from northern Thailand, it was found that these people had previously been farmers, but had abandoned agriculture about 500 years ago. This raises the interesting question as to how many of the diminishing band of contemporary huntergatherer cultures are in fact the descendents of farmers who have only secondarily readopted huntergathering as a more useful lifestyle, perhaps after suffering from crop failures, dietary deficiencies, or climatic changes. Therefore, the process of what may be termed the 'agriculturalization' of human societies was ________________, at least on a local level. Huntergatherer cultures across the world, from midwestern Amerindians to !Kung in the African Kalahari, have adopted and subsequently discarded agriculture, possibly on several occasions over their history, in response to factors such as game abundance, climatic change, and so on.

*!Kung: !Kung족(族)

① not necessarily irreversible
② met with little resistance
③ essential for adaptation
④ started by pure coincidence
⑤ rarely subject to reconsideration

✐ **어휘 Box** (모르는 어휘와 표현을 아래에 정리하고 해설을 통해 복습하세요.)

✐ **비법 적용 Box** (앞에서 배운 비법을 스스로 문장에 적용하고 해설과 비교해 보세요.)

6.

정답과 해설 110~112쪽
[2020 고3 7월 전국연합 32번]

Sometimes it seems that contemporary art isn't doing its job unless it provokes the question, 'But is it art?' I'm not sure the question is worth asking. It seems to me that the line between art and notart is never going to be a sharp one. Worse, as the various art forms — poetry, drama, sculpture, painting, fiction, dance, etc. — are so different, I'm not sure why we should expect to be able to come up with ______________________. Art seems to be a paradigmatic example of a Wittgensteinian 'family resemblance' concept. Try to specify the necessary and sufficient condition for something qualifying as art and you'll always find an exception to your criteria. If philosophy were to admit defeat in its search for some immutable essence of art, it is hardly through lack of trying. Arguably, we have very good reasons for thinking that this has been one of the biggest wild goose chases in the history of ideas.

*paradigmatic: 전형적인 **immutable: 변치 않는

① a detailed guide to tracing the origin of art
② a novel way of perceiving reality through art
③ a single definition that can capture their variety
④ a genre that blends together diverse artistic styles
⑤ a radical idea that challenges the existing art forms

✏ **어휘 Box** (모르는 어휘와 표현을 아래에 정리하고 해설을 통해 복습하세요.)

✏ **비법 적용 Box** (앞에서 배운 비법을 스스로 문장에 적용하고 해설과 비교해 보세요.)

[7~8] 다음 글에서 전체 흐름과 관계 없는 문장을 고르시오.

정답과 해설 112~114쪽
[2019 고3 3월 전국연합 35번]

7.

New technologies encounter challenges based on both how many of our existing habits they promise to alter and the strength of these habits. ① Lasting behavioral change must occur through existing habits rather than attempts to alter them. ② People are likely to adopt innovations only if they improve rather than destroy their existing habits, in the same way that electronic calculators made mathematical computations faster. ③ The success of an electronics product is linked to the innovative technological design both of its electronic processes and of its major components. ④ Thus, public policy should encourage behavioral change by targeting the least fixed habits. ⑤ For example, developing countries could encourage increased protein consumption by offering new highprotein beverages rather than new types of highprotein foods.

✐ **어휘 Box** (모르는 어휘와 표현을 아래에 정리하고 해설을 통해 복습하세요.)

✐ **비법 적용 Box** (앞에서 배운 비법을 스스로 문장에 적용하고 해설과 비교해 보세요.)

8.

정답과 해설 114~116쪽
[2019 고3 9월 모의평가 35번]

Much of what we do each day is automatic and guided by habit, requiring little conscious awareness, and that's not a bad thing. As Duhigg explains, our habits are necessary mental energy savers. ① We need to relieve our conscious minds so we can solve new problems as they come up. ② Once we've solved the puzzle of how to ballroom dance, for example, we can do it by habit, and so be mentally freed to focus on a conversation while dancing instead. ③ But try to talk when first learning to dance the tango, and it's a disaster — we need our conscious attention to focus on the steps. ④ Tango musicians bring different genres of music together to attract a more diverse audience from varying backgrounds. ⑤ Imagine how little we'd accomplish if we had to focus consciously on every behavior — e.g., on where to place our feet for each step we take.

✐ **어휘 Box** (모르는 어휘와 표현을 아래에 정리하고 해설을 통해 복습하세요.)

✐ **비법 적용 Box** (앞에서 배운 비법을 스스로 문장에 적용하고 해설과 비교해 보세요.)

[9~10] 다음 글의 밑줄 친 부분 중, 문맥상 낱말의 쓰임이 적절하지 않은 것은?

정답과 해설 116~119쪽

9.

[2020 고3 6월 모의평가 42번]

In many mountain regions, rights of access to water are associated with the possession of land — until recently in the Andes, for example, land and water rights were ① combined so water rights were transferred with the land. However, through state land reforms and the development of additional sources of supply, water rights have become separated from land, and may be sold at auction. This therefore ② favours those who can pay, rather than ensuring access to all in the community. The situation arises, therefore, where individuals may hold land with no water. In Peru, the government grants water to communities separately from land, and it is up to the community to allocate it. Likewise in Yemen, the traditional allocation was one measure (tasah) of water to one hundred 'libnah' of land. This applied only to traditional irrigation supplies — from runoff, wells, etc., where a supply was ③ guaranteed. Water derived from the capture of flash floods is not subject to Islamic law as this constitutes an uncertain source, and is therefore free for those able to collect and use it. However, this traditional allocation per unit of land has been bypassed, partly by the development of new supplies, but also by the ④ decrease in cultivation of a crop of substantial economic importance. This crop is harvested throughout the year and thus requires more than its fair share of water. The economic status of the crop ⑤ ensures that water rights can be bought or bribed away from subsistence crops.

*irrigation: 관개(灌漑) **bribe: 매수하다 ***subsistence crop: 생계용 작물

✐ **어휘 Box** (모르는 어휘와 표현을 아래에 정리하고 해설을 통해 복습하세요.)

✐ **비법 적용 Box** (앞에서 배운 비법을 스스로 문장에 적용하고 해설과 비교해 보세요.)

10.

정답과 해설 119~121쪽
[2019 고3 6월 모의평가 42번]

Aristotle did not think that all human beings should be allowed to engage in political activity: in his system, women, slaves, and foreigners were explicitly ① <u>excluded</u> from the right to rule themselves and others. Nevertheless, his basic idea that politics is a unique collective activity that is directed at certain ② <u>common</u> goals and ends still resonates today. But which ends? Many thinkers and political figures since the ancient world have developed different ideas about the goals that politics can or should achieve. This approach is known as political moralism.

For moralists, political life is a branch of ethics — or moral philosophy — so it is ③ <u>unsurprising</u> that there are many philosophers in the group of moralistic political thinkers. Political moralists argue that politics should be directed toward achieving substantial goals, or that political arrangements should be organized to ④ <u>protect</u> certain things. Among these things are political values such as justice, equality, liberty, happiness, fraternity, or national self-determination. At its most radical, moralism produces descriptions of ideal political societies known as Utopias, named after English statesman and philosopher Thomas More's book Utopia, published in 1516, which imagined an ideal nation. Utopian political thinking dates back to the ancient Greek philosopher Plato's book the Republic, but it is still used by modern thinkers such as Robert Nozick to explore ideas. Some theorists consider Utopian political thinking to be a ⑤ <u>promising</u> undertaking, since it has led in the past to justifications of totalitarian violence. However, at its best, Utopian thinking is part of a process of striving toward a better society, and many thinkers use it to suggest values to be pursued or protected.

어휘 Box (모르는 어휘와 표현을 아래에 정리하고 해설을 통해 복습하세요.)

비법 적용 Box (앞에서 배운 비법을 스스로 문장에 적용하고 해설과 비교해 보세요.)

[11~12] 다음 글의 밑줄 친 부분 중, 어법상 틀린 것을 고르시오.

정답과 해설 122~123쪽
[2020 고3 10월 전국연합 29번]

11.

Mathematical practices and discourses should be situated within cultural contexts, student interests, and reallife situations ① where all students develop positive identities as mathematics learners. Instruction in mathematics skills in isolation and devoid of student understandings and identities renders them ② helpless to benefit from explicit instruction. Thus, we agree that explicit instruction benefits students but propose that incorporating culturally relevant pedagogy and consideration of nonacademic factors that ③ promoting learning and mastery must enhance explicit instruction in mathematics instruction. Furthermore, teachers play a critical role in developing environments ④ that encourage student identities, agency, and independence through discourses and practices in the classroom. Students who are actively engaged in a contextualized learning process are in control of the learning process and are able to make connections with past learning experiences ⑤ to foster deeper and more meaningful learning.

*render: (어떤 상태가 되게) 만들다 **pedagogy: 교수법

✐ **어휘 Box** (모르는 어휘와 표현을 아래에 정리하고 해설을 통해 복습하세요.)

✐ **비법 적용 Box** (앞에서 배운 비법을 스스로 문장에 적용하고 해설과 비교해 보세요.)

12.

정답과 해설 123~124쪽
[2019학년도 고3 수능 29번]

"Monumental" is a word that comes very close to ① expressing the basic characteristic of Egyptian art. Never before and never since has the quality of monumentality been achieved as fully as it ② did in Egypt. The reason for this is not the external size and massiveness of their works, although the Egyptians admittedly achieved some amazing things in this respect. Many modern structures exceed ③ those of Egypt in terms of purely physical size. But massiveness has nothing to do with monumentality. An Egyptian sculpture no bigger than a person's hand is more monumental than that gigantic pile of stones ④ that constitutes the war memorial in Leipzig, for instance. Monumentality is not a matter of external weight, but of "inner weight." This inner weight is the quality which Egyptian art possesses to such a degree that everything in it seems to be made of primeval stone, like a mountain range, even if it is only a few inches across or ⑤ carved in wood.

✐ **어휘 Box** (모르는 어휘와 표현을 아래에 정리하고 해설을 통해 복습하세요.)

✐ **비법 적용 Box** (앞에서 배운 비법을 스스로 문장에 적용하고 해설과 비교해 보세요.)

영어
오답의
모든것

고등학교 영어 오답의 모든 것

<4. 심화독해편> : 영끌극복 심화독해

초판 1쇄 발행 2021년 4월 30일

지은이 정동완 김표 손평화 정승덕 이자인
펴낸이 꿈구두
펴낸곳 꿈구두
디자인 맨디 디자인

출판등록 2019년 5월 16일, 제 2019-000010호
블로그 https://blog.naver.com/edu-atoz
이메일 edu-atoz@naver.com
밴드 네이버밴드 <오늘과 내일의 학교>

ISBN 979-11-91607-01-7

책값은 표지 뒤쪽에 있습니다.
파본은 구입하신 서점에서 교환해드립니다.

영어 오답의 모든것 4

정답과 해설

영끌극복
심화독해

꿈구두

영어 오답의 모든것 4

정답과 해설

영끌극복
심화독해

꿈구두

연결사를 활용한 글의 흐름 파악하기

(3) 연결사 연습 문제 정답

본문 12~20쪽

연결사	정답
1. 역접(대조)	On the other hand, (A)
2. 예시	For example (B)
3. 인과	As a result, (C)
4. 비교	① Likewise, (C) ② Likewise, (A) ③ Similarly, (B)
5. 재진술(부연)	In other words, (C)
6. 나열(순서)	Later, (C)
7. 첨가	Moreover, (C)

I 글의 논리 흐름 관련 독해 유형

1. 글의 순서

가. 비법 연습 문제

본문 25쪽

정답

1. 1) ① 2) ①

2. (A) ⇒ (C) ⇒ (B)

해석

1.

1) 미군의 연구자들은 오토바이 사고에 대한 연구를 진행했다.
   ① 그들은 오토바이 탑승자들이 가지고 있는 문신의 숫자가 가장 좋은 예측자라는 것을 찾아냈다.
   ② 그녀는 오토바이에 대한 새로운 연구를 진행하도록 뽑혔다.

2) 선을 따라 두 개의 정사각형을 잘라내세요.
   ① 그 후에, 그들을 뒤로 마주보도록 하세요.
   ② 새로운 가위를 살 때는 조심하세요.

2.

(A) 많은 사람들이 온라인 추천에 의존한다.
(B) 그러나 어떤 개인들은 종종 광범위한 소셜 네트워크를 가지고 있지 않다.
(C) 그리고 젊은이들은 그들(온라인 추천)에게 많이 의지하고 인터넷의 영향을 받을 가능성이 매우 높다.

주요 어휘 및 표현

conduct	(연구를) 진행하다	predictor	예측자
face	마주보다	recommendation	추천
individual	개인	be likely to	~할 가능성이 높다

나. 기출 연습 문제

본문 25쪽

정답 [③]

해석

여러분이 어느 날 프로젝트를 하느라 바빠서 점심 식사를 살 시간이 없다고 가정해 보자. 갑자기 가장 친한 친구가 여러분이 가장 좋아하는 샌드위치를 들고 나타난다. (B) 그는 여러분이 바쁘다는 것을 알고 있으며, 샌드위치를 사 주는 것으로 돕고 싶다고 말한다. 이런 경우에, 여러분은 친구의 도움에 고마워할 가능성이 높다. (C) 그러나 만약 낯선 사람이 같은 샌드위치를 들고 나타나 그것을 여러분에게 준다면, 여러분은 그것을 고마워하지 않을 것이다. 대신에, 혼란스러울 것이다. 여러분은 "당신은 누군데, 제가 어떤 종류의 샌드위치를 먹고 싶은지 어떻게 아세요?"라고 생각하기가 쉽다. (A) 이 두 경우의 주요 차이점은 신뢰 수준이다. 여러분은 가장 친한 친구를 아주 많이 믿어서 그 친구가 여러분을 너무 잘 알고 있다는 것에 대해 걱정하지 않겠지만, 낯선 사람에게는 분명히 같은 수준의 신뢰를 주지 않을 것이다.

주요 어휘 및 표현

all of a sudden	갑자기	show up	나타나다
key	주요한	trust	신뢰
stranger	낯선 사람	appreciate	고마워하다
offer	주다, 제공하다	confused	혼란스러운

다. 실전 연습 문제

본문 27~30쪽

1. 정답 [⑤]

해석

1824년, 페루는 스페인으로부터 독립했다. 독립 직후, 해방군을 이끌었던 장군인 Simón Bolívar는 새 나라를 위한 헌법의 초안을 작성하기 위해 회의를 소집하였다. (C) 회의가 끝난 후, 사람들은 Bolívar가 그들을 위해 해 준 모든 것에 대한 감사의 표시로 그에게 특별한 것을 해 주고 싶어 했다. 그래서 그들은 그 당시 매우 많은 돈인 백만 페소를 그에게 선물로 주었다. (B) Bolívar는 선물을 받고 나서 물었다. "페루에 노예가 몇 명입니까?" 그는 대략 3천 명이 있다고 들었다. "그리고 노예 한 명은 얼마에 팔립니까?" 그는 알고 싶어 했다. "한 사람당 약 350페소입니다."라는 대답이 있었다. (A) Bolívar가 말했다. "그렇다면, 나는 당신들이 나에게 준 이 백만 페소에 필요한 것은 무엇이든 다 더해 페루에 있는 모든 노예를 사서 그들을 해방시켜 주겠습니다. 모든 시민 또한 자유를 누리지 못한다면, 한 국가를 해방시킨다는 것은 의미가 없습니다."

비법 적용

In 1824, Peru won its freedom from Spain. Soon after, Simón Bolívar, the general who had led the liberating forces, called <u>a meeting</u> to write the first version of the constitution for the new country.

☞ 스페인과의 전쟁에서 승리를 이끈 Simón Bolívar 장군이 새로운 헌법을 제정하기 위해 '회의(a meeting)'를 소집했다는 내용이다.

(A) "Then," said Bolívar, "I'll add whatever is necessary to this million pesos you have given me and I will buy all the slaves in Peru and set them free. It makes no sense to free a nation, unless all its citizens enjoy freedom as well."

☞ (this+명사) (A)에서 장군의 대사와 함께, '이 백만 페소(this million pesos)', '모든 노예(all the slaves)'라는 말이 나왔으므로 (A)의 앞에 이에 해당하는 말들이 먼저 나와야 한다.

(B) Bolívar accepted the gift and then asked, "How many slaves are there in Peru?" He was told there were about three thousand. "And how much does a slave sell for?" he wanted to know. "About 350 pesos for a man," was the answer.

☞ (the+명사) (B)에서 'the gift'라 하였으므로 이에 해당하는 말이 (B)의 앞에 먼저 나와야 한다.

☞ (B)의 뒷부분에서 장군은 사람들에게 '노예 한 명(a slave)'의 가격이 얼마인지 묻고 있다.

(C) After the meeting, the people wanted to do something special for Bolívar to show their appreciation for all he had done for them, so they offered him a gift of one million pesos, a very large amount of money in those days.

☞ (the+명사) (C)의 앞부분에서 '그 회의(the meeting)'라고 하였으므로, 이에 해당하는 말이 (C) 앞에 먼저 나와야 한다.

☞ (C)의 뒷부분에서 장군에게 감사를 표시하기 위해 사람들이 '백만 페소의 선물(a gift of one million pesos)'을 주었다고 하였다.

오답의 모든 것

(1) 첫 번째 문단 찾기

▶ **주어진 글의 'a meeting'은 (C)의 'the meeting'으로 연결되므로 주어진 글 뒤에 (C)는 정답**

▶ (A)의 "Then," 'this million pesos', 'all the slaves' 등은 주어진 글에서 언급되지 않았으므로 주어진 글 뒤에 (A)는 오답

▶ (B)의 'the gift'는 주어진 문장에 언급되지 않은 말이므로 주어진 글 뒤에 (B)는 오답

(2) 두 번째 문단 찾기

▶ **(B)의 'the gift'는 (C)의 'a gift of one million pesos'을 의미하므로 (C)뒤에 (B)는 정답**

▶ (A)의 "Then," 'all the slaves' 등은 (C)에서 언급되지 않았으므로 (C) 뒤에 (A)는 오답

(3) 세 번째 문단 찾기

▶ **(B)의 마지막 부분에서 노예 한명의 값을 답하는 묻고 난 뒤에 (A)에서 이에 대한 대화를 이어나가는 것이 자연스럽고, 'this million pesos', 'all the slaves'가 (B)에서 언급된 내용이므로 (B) 뒤에 (A)는 정답**

주요 어휘 및 표현

general	장군	constitution	헌법
liberate	해방시키다	appreciation	감사

2. 정답 [④]

해석

AI 로봇과 보통 로봇의 기본적 차이는 센서로부터 얻는 데이터에 기반하여 결정을 내리고, 학습하여 환경에 적응하는 로봇과 그것의 소프트웨어의 능력이다. (C) 좀 더 구체적으로 말해서 보통 로봇은 결정론적인(이미 정해진) 행동을 보인다. 다시 말해, 일련의 입력에 대해 그 로봇은 항상 똑같은 결과를 만들 것이다. (A) 예를 들어, 장애물을 우연히 마주치는 것과 같이 동일한 상황에 직면한다면 그 로봇은 그 장애물을 왼쪽으로 돌아서 가는 것과 같이 항상 똑같은 행동을 할 것이다. 하지만 AI 로봇은 보통 로봇이 할 수 없는 두 가지, 즉, 결정을 내리고 경험으로부터 학습하는 것을 할 수 있다. (B) 그것은 환경에 적응할 것이고, 어떤 상황에 직면할 때마다 다른 행동을 할 수 있다. AI 로봇은 경로에서 장애물을 밀어내거나 새로운 경로를 만들거나 목표를 바꾸려고 할 수도 있다.

비법 적용

The basic difference between an AI robot and a normal robot is the ability of the robot and its software to make decisions, and learn and adapt to its environment based on data from its sensors.

☞ AI 로봇과 보통 로봇은 데이터를 기반으로 의사를 결정하고 학습하여 환경에 적응하는 능력의 차이가 있다는 글이다. 그러한 능력 면에서 어떤 차이가 있는지에 대한 구체적인 설명이 이어질 것이라 예상할 수 있다.

(A) For instance, if faced with the same situation, such as running into an obstacle, then the robot will always do the same thing, such as go around the obstacle to the left. An AI robot, however, can do two things the normal robot cannot: make decisions and learn from experience.

☞ (For instance) 예시에 해당하는 일반적인 문장이 먼저 오고 그 뒤에 (A)가 들어가야 한다.

☞ (the robot) '그 로봇(the robot)'은 (A)앞에 이것에 해당하는 로봇이 먼저 언급되었음을 의미한다. (A)에서 '그 로봇(the robot)'은 같은 상황에서 같은 것을 하는 로봇이라 하였으므로, 문맥상 '보통 로봇(the normal robot)'이라 볼 수 있다. (A)의 두 번째 문장에서 역접 연결사와 함께 'AI 로봇(An AI Robot)'에 대해 설명이 이어지는 것을 보아 '그 로봇(the robot)'은 '보통 로봇'을 의미한다.

(B) It will adapt to circumstances, and may do something different each time a situation is faced. The AI robot may try to push the obstacle out of the way, or make up a new route, or change goals.

☞ (대명사 It) 주어 대명사 'It'에 해당하는 것은 환경에 적응하고 매 상황마다 다르게 행동한다고 말하고 있다. 따라서 문맥상 대명사 'It'은 'AI 로봇'을 의미한다고 볼 수 있다.

(C) To be a bit more specific, the normal robot shows deterministic behaviors. That is, for a set of inputs, the robot will always produce the same output.

☞ (to be specific) '보통 로봇(the normal robot)'의 행동에 대한 구체적 설명이 이어지고 있다.

☞ (that is) 재진술 연결사 앞과 뒤는 서로 동일한 의미의 문장이 나온다. 따라서 (C)에 언급된 '결정론적 행동(deterministic behaviors)'이란 항상 '같은 결과(the same output)'를 만드는 보통 로봇의 특징이다.

오답의 모든 것

(1) 첫 번째 문단 찾기

▶ **주어진 글에서 보통 로봇과 AI 로봇의 차이점을 말하였으므로, 두 가지 로봇 중 '보통 로봇'에 관해 구체적인 설명이 이어지는 (C)는 정답**

▶ 대명사 'It'으로 시작하려면 무엇을 지칭하는지 분명해야 하는데, 주어진 글에서는 두 가지 로봇이 모두 언급되었으므로 어떤 것을 말하는지 알 수 없으므로 (B)는 오답

▶ 예시의 내용으로 보아 같은 상황에서 항상 같은 것을 하는 '그 로봇(the robot)'은 주어진 글의 두 가지 로봇 중 어떤 로봇의 예시인지 알 수 없으므로 (A)는 오답

(2) 두 번째 문단 찾기

▶ **첫 번째 문단인 (C)에서 보통 로봇이 항상 '같은 결과(the same output)'을 만든다고 하였는데, 이에 대한 구체적 사례가 나오는 (A)는 정답**

▶ 첫 번째 문단인 (C)에서 보통 로봇이 항상 '같은 결과(the same output)'을 만든다고 하였으나, 환경에 적응하는 (B)의 로봇은 상황마다 다른 행동을 한다는 의미이므로 (B)는 오답

(3) 세 번째 문단 찾기

▶ **(A)의 두 번째 문장에서 'AI 로봇'에 관한 설명이 나오고, 이를 대명사 'It'으로 받아주는 (B)는 정답**

주요 어휘 및 표현

obstacle	장애물	circumstance	상황
run into	...와 우연히 만나다	deterministic	결정론적인

3. 정답 [②]

해석

내가 South Milwaukee의 각 교실에서 한 첫 번째 일 중 하나는 학생들을 알아보기 위한 보조물로 그들의 이름을 적은, 학생들의 좌석표를 그리는 것이었다. (B) 내가 들어간 첫째 날 1학년 교실에서 점심시간에 한 무리의 학생들이 다가와 좌석표를 보고는 내가 그린 그림에서 자신의 이름을 찾기 시작했다. (A) 한 학생이 "선생님 이름은 어디 있어요?"라고 말하더니, 내 이름을 적은, 책장 옆 내가 앉아 있던 의자 그림을 내가 포함하고 나서야 비로소 흡족해했다. 나는 내가 포함될 필요가 있다는 생각을 하지 못했었다. 어쨌든 나는 내가 어디 앉아 있는지 알고 있었고, 내 이름을 알고 있었다. (C) 하지만 그녀에게는 교실에서의 나의 존재가 그날 일어난 가장 새롭고 가장 주목할 만한 일이었으며, 나를 포함시키는 것이 타당했다. 그녀의 관점은 내 관점과 달랐고, 그 결과 교실의 좌석표가 달라졌다.

비법 적용

One of the first things I did in each classroom in South Milwaukee was to draw a diagram of the students' desks, labelled with their names, as an aid to recognizing them.
☞ South Milwaukee에서 필자가 처음으로 한 일 중에 하나는 학생들의 이름을 붙인 다이어그램(a diagram)을 그린 것이라 하며 이야기를 시작하고 있다.

(A) One said, "Where's your name?" and was not satisfied until I included a sketch of the chair by the bookcase where I was sitting, labelled with my name. It had not occurred to me that I needed to be included: after all, I knew where I was sitting, and knew my name.
☞ (대명사 one) 문장을 해석해 보았을 때 대명사 'One'은 앞에 언급된 여러 사람들 중 하나임을 알 수 있다.

(B) At lunch in the first grade classroom the first day I was present, a group of students came over, saw the diagram, and began finding their names on my picture.
☞ (the diagram) '그 다이어그램(the diagram)'은 앞에서 다이어그램이 이미 언급되었음을 의미한다.
☞ '한 무리의 학생들(a group of students)'이 새롭게 등장하였다.

(C) But to her, my presence in the classroom was the newest, most noteworthy thing that had occurred that day, and it was logical to include me. Her point of view was different from mine, and resulted in a different diagram of the classroom.
☞ (대명사 her) 앞내용에서 'her'이라고 지칭할 여자가 등장해야 함을 알 수 있다

오답의 모든 것

(1) 첫 번째 문단 찾기
▶ **주어진 글의 'a diagram' 뒤에서 이를 가리키는 'the diagram'이 나오는 것이 흐름상 자연스러우므로 (B)가 정답**
▶ (A)의 앞부분에서 'One'이 가리킬 만한 대상이 주어진 글에 없었기 때문에 (A)는 오답
▶ 대명사 'her'가 가리킬만한 대상이 주어진 글에 없었기 때문에 (C)는 오답

(2) 두 번째 문단 찾기
▶ **(B)에서 '한 무리의 학생들(a group of students)'이 자신의 이름을 다이어그램에서 찾기 시작했고, 그 한 무리의 학생들 중 '하나(One)'가 선생님의 이름이 어디있는지 묻는 것이 흐름상 자연스러우므로 (A)가 정답**
▶ 대명사 'her'가 가리킬만한 대상을 (B)에서 찾을 수 없으므로 (C)는 오답

(3) 세 번째 문단 찾기
▶ **(A)에서 질문한 '하나(One)'의 학생을 대명사 'her'로 받아 설명을 이어나가고 있으므로 (A) 뒤에 (C)는 정답**

주요 어휘 및 표현

label	이름 붙이다	occur	일어나다
noteworthy	주목할 만한	point of view	관점, 입장

4. 정답 [⑤]

해석

돈이 없다면, 사람들은 물물 교환만 할 수 있을 것이다. 우리 대다수는 우리가 호의에 보답할 때, 작은 규모에서 물물 교환을 한다. (C) 예를 들어, 한 사람은 몇 시간 동안 아기를 돌봐준 것에 대한 보답으로 이웃의 고장난 문을 수리해줄 것을 제안할지도 모른다. 그러나 이러한 개인적인 교환들이 더 큰 규모로 작동하는 것을 상상하기 어렵다. (B) 만약 당신이 빵 한 덩어리를 원하고 교환하기 위해 가지고 있는 전부가 새 자동차뿐이라면 어떤 일이 일어날까? 물물 교환은 원하는 바의 이중의 우연의 일치에 달려있는데, 다른 사람이 내가 원하는 것을 우연히 가지고 있을 뿐만 아니라 또한 나도 그가 원하는 것을 가지고 있는 경우이다. 돈은 이러한 모든 문제를 해결한다. (A) 당신이 교환하기 위해 가지고 있는 것을 원하는 누군가를 찾을 필요가 없다. 당신은 단순히 돈으로 물건 값을 지불하면 된다. 그러면 판매자는 돈을 받고 다른 누군가로부터 구매할 수 있다. 돈은 이동 가능하고 (지불을) 연기할 수 있다 – 판매자는 그것을 쥐고 있다가 시기가 적절한 때에 구매할 수 있다.

비법 적용

Without money, people could only barter. Many of us barter to a small extent, when we return favors.

☞ 돈이 없을 경우에 이루어지는 물물 교환(barter)에 관한 내용이다. 호의에 보답할 때는 '작은 규모(a small extent)'로 물물교환(barter)을 한다는 내용으로 문장을 마무리하였으므로, 이에 관련한 내용이 뒤에 나올 것이라 예상할 수 있다.

(A) There is no need to find someone who wants what you have to trade; you simply pay for your goods with money. The seller can then take the money and buy from someone else. Money is transferable and deferrable – the seller can hold on to it and buy when the time is right.

☞ 눈에 보이는 단서가 없으므로 내용 파악에 좀 더 집중해야 한다. 거래할 사람을 찾을 필요 없이 '돈으로(with money)' 지불하면 된다고 말하고 있다. 돈의 두 가지 속성으로 '이동가능성(transferable)'과 '지불 연기(deferrable)'에 대해 언급하였다.

(B) What would happen if you wanted a loaf of bread and all you had to trade was your new car? Barter depends on the double coincidence of wants, where not only does the other person happen to have what I want, but I also have what he wants. Money solves all these problems.

☞ '빵 한 조각(a loaf of bread)', 새 자동차'(new car)'와 같은 단어로 거래 규모의 차이를 구체적으로 보여주고 있다.

☞ '큰 규모(a larger scale)'의 물물 교환에 대한 서술이 선행되어야 함을 추론할 수 있다.

☞ 이러한 거래 규모의 차이가 있을 때, 서로 원하는 것이 일치하지 않을 때 '돈(Money)'이 해결책이 될 수 있다. 이에 관련한 내용이 (B) 뒤에 나올 것이라 예상할 수 있다.

(C) A man might offer to mend his neighbor's broken door in return for a few hours of babysitting, for instance. Yet it is hard to imagine these personal exchanges working on a larger scale.

☞ (for instance) 아이를 돌봐주는 대가로 이웃의 고장난 문을 수리하는 상황을 사례로 들고 있다.

☞ (yet, these personal exchanges) 역접 연결사 'Yet' 뒤에서 '이러한 개인적인 거래(these personal exchanges)'가 '더 큰 규모(on a larger scale)'로 작동하기는 어렵다고 하였으므로, (C)의 예시는 주어진 글에서 말한 '작은 규모(a small extent)'임을 알 수 있다.

오답의 모든 것

(1) 첫 번째 문단 찾기

▶ **주어진 글에서 호의에 보답할 때 작은 규모로 물물 교환을 한다고 하였으므로 이에 대한 구체적 사례인 (C)가 정답**

▶ 주어진 글에서는 돈이 없을 경우에 물물 교환을 한다고 하였는데 돈으로 지불하면 된다는 (A)는 오답

▶ 빵 한 덩어리와 새 차의 거래는 주어진 글에서 말하는 작은 규모의 거래가 아니므로 (B)는 오답

(2) 두 번째 문단 찾기

▶ **(C)에서 '큰 규모의 물물 교환은 상상하기 어렵다'라고 이야기한 뒤에, 그에 대한 사례인 빵 한 덩어리와 차를 바꾸는 '큰 규모의 물물 교환'은 흐름상 자연스러우므로 (B)는 정답**

▶ 주어진 글에서 물물 교환은 돈이 없을 경우에 한다고 하였는데, '큰 규모의 물물 교환' 뒤에서 돈으로 지불하면 된다고 하는 (A)는 오답

(3) 세 번째 문단 찾기

▶ **물물 교환의 어려움에 대한 해결책으로 돈을 제시하는 (B) 뒤에서, 물물 교환할 상대를 찾을 필요 없이 돈으로 지불하면 된다고 하는 (A)가 흐름상 자연스럽게 이어지므로 정답**

주요 어휘 및 표현

barter	물물 교환	goods	상품
transferable	이동가능한	deferrable	연기할 수 있는
in return for	~의 대가로	coincidence	우연의 일치, 동시 발생

1. 정답 [③]

해석

(사람들이) 새에게 사로잡힐 만한 것이 도대체 '무엇'이 있는지 많은 사람들은 이해하지 못한다. 조류관찰자들은 숲, 늪, 그리고 들판에 나가 실제로 무엇을 하고 있을까? (B) 조류관찰에 대한 열정을 이해하는 비결은 조류관찰이 실은 사냥이라는 점을 깨닫는 것이다. 하지만 사냥과 달리, 여러분이 모은 전리품들은 여러분의 마음속에 있다. (C) 물론 여러분이 어디를 가든지 전리품들을 갖고 다니게 되기 때문에 여러분의 마음은 그것들로 가득 채우기에 훌륭한 장소이다. 여러분은 그것들을 먼지가 쌓이도록 벽이나 다락 위에 두지 않는다. 여러분의 조류관찰 경험은 여러분 삶의 일부, 여러분 자신의 일부가 된다. (A) 그리고 조류관찰자들은 인간이기 때문에 이러한 조류관찰의 기억들은, 인간의 기억 대부분이 그러하듯이, 시간이 지남에 따라 향상된다. 돌이켜 생각해 보면, 깃털의 색은 더 풍부해지고, 새소리는 더 달콤해지며, (기억에) 흐릿했던 눈에 띄는 외견상의 그 특징들은 더욱더 선명해지고 뚜렷해진다.

비법 적용

Many people cannot understand what there is about birds to become obsessed about. What are bird-watchers actually doing out there in the woods, swamps, and fields?
☞ 조류의 매력과 조류관찰자들이 하는 일에 대한 질문으로 시작하고 있다.

(A) And because birders are human, these birding memories—like most human memories—improve over time. The colors of the plumages become richer, the songs sweeter, and those elusive field marks more vivid and distinct in retrospect.
☞ (these birding memories) 'these 명사'의 형태이므로 앞에서 '조류관찰 기억(birding memories)'에 대한 서술이 선행되었어야 한다.

(B) The key to comprehending the passion of birding is to realize that bird-watching is really a hunt. But unlike hunting, the trophies you accumulate are in your mind.
☞ (the passion of birding) 'the 명사'의 형태이므로 앞에서 '조류관찰에 대한 열정(the passion of birding)'이 언급되었어야 한다. 주어진 글에 있었던 '조류관찰'에 대한 설명이 (B)에서 이어지고 있다.

(C) Of course, your mind is a great place to populate with them because you carry them around with you wherever you go. You don't leave them to gather dust on a wall or up in the attic. Your birding experiences become part of your life, part of who you are.
☞ (대명사 them) 앞에서 복수 대명사 'them'이 나타내는 것이 무엇인지 파악해야 한다. 'your mind'로 문장을 시작하는 것으로 보아 앞에서 'your mind'에 관련된 내용이 언급된 뒤에 (C)가 나올 수 있다.

오답의 모든 것

(1) 첫 번째 문단 찾기

▶ **주어진 글에 나온 '조류관찰에 사로잡힌(obssessd)다'는 내용을 (B)의 '조류관찰에 대한 열정(the passion of birding)'으로 설명하여 관련 내용이 자연스럽게 이어지고 있으므로 (B)가 정답**

▶ '이러한 조류관찰의 기억(these birding memories)'이 주어진 글에서 언급되지 않았으므로 (A)는 오답

▶ 주어진 글에서 조류관찰자들의 이야기로 끝이 났는데, '여러분의 마음(your mind)'이 그것들을(them) 채우기에 충분한 곳이라는 내용은 어색하며, 대명사 'them'이 가리킬만한 구체적인 명사를 주어진 글에서 찾을 수 없으므로 (C)는 오답

(2) 두 번째 문단 찾기

▶ **첫 번째 순서인 (B)에서 '여러분이 모은 전리품들은 여러분의 마음속에 있다(the trophies you accumulate are in your mind)'는 표현과 '여러분의 마음은 그것들로 가득 채우기에 훌륭한 장소이다(your mind is a great place to populate with them)'라는 표현은 서로 동일한 의미이며, 대명사 'them'이 'the trophies'를 받아주고 있기 때문에 (C)가 정답 (마음속에 전리품을 채운다는 것은 마음속에 조류관찰의 경험을 채운다는 것과 동일한 의미)**

▶ '이러한 조류관찰의 기억(these birding memories)'이 (B)에서 언급되지 않았으므로 (B) 뒤에 (A)는 오답

(3) 세 번째 문단 찾기

▶ **두 번째 순서인 (C)의 마지막 부분에 언급된 '조류관찰 경험(Your birding experiences)'은 (A)의 이러한 조류관찰의 기억these birding memories)'을 의미하므로 (C) 뒤에 (A)는 정답**

주요 어휘 및 표현

obsess about	~에 사로잡히다	swamp	늪
elusive	흐릿한, 기억하기 힘든	vivid	생생한
distinct	두드러진	in retrospect	되돌아보면
accumulate	축적하다	attic	다락

2. 정답 [③]

해석

인간은 현재 지구에서 가장 많은 포유동물이기 때문에 우리가 언젠가 멸종되는 것을 상상하기란 다소 어렵다. (B) 하지만, 바로 그것은 사실 여러 번 일어날 뻔했던 일이다. 화석 기록과 DNA 분석으로부터 우리는 우리의 조상이 거의 멸종될 뻔했으며 셀 수 없이 여러 번 그들의 인구가 매우 작은 수로 줄었다는 것을 알 수 있다. (C) 게다가 정말로 멸종한 진화 인류 모체가 된 사람이나 동물의 혈통들이 많이 있다. 우리 조상과 침팬지 조상 사이의 분리 이래로 우리의 혈통은 점진적으로 변화한 단일한 계통이 아니었다. 진화는 결코 그런 방식으로 작용하지 않는다. (A) 대신에 많은 가지들이 서로로부터 갈라졌고 그들만의 가지들로 발전했다. 지난 오백만 년 대부분 동안 동시에 살고 있는 다른 진화 인류 모체가

된 사람이나 동물의 종들이 최소 서넛 있었다. 이 모든 가지들 중에서 오직 하나, 즉 우리(의 가지)만이 오늘날까지 살아남았다.

비법 적용

Because humans are now the most abundant mammal on the planet, it is somewhat hard to imagine us ever going extinct.
☞ 인간은 지구상에서 가장 수가 많은 포유동물이기 때문에 멸종하는 것은 상상하기 어렵다고 말하고 있다.

(A) Many branches broke off from each other and developed branches of their own, instead. There were at least three or four different species of hominids living simultaneously for most of the past five million years. Of all these branches, only one survived until today: ours.
☞ (instead) 앞내용에 대한 대안으로, 많은 가지들이 서로로부터 갈라졌고 그들만의 가지들로 발전했다고 언급하고 있다. 'instead'는 아래와 같은 형식으로 쓰이는 것이 일반적이므로, 앞에서 '~가 아니다'라는 내용이 언급되었음을 예상할 수 있다.

'A는 ~한 것이 아니다' + ' instead , A는 ~한 것이다.'

(B) However, that is exactly what almost happened—many times, in fact. From the fossil record and from DNA analysis, we can tell that our ancestors nearly went extinct, and their population shrunk to very small numbers countless times.
☞ (However) 역접을 통해 앞부분에 상반된 내용을 예상할 수 있다. 즉 (B)에서는 우리가 '거의 멸종할 뻔(nearly went extinct)' 했고 수가 줄었다고 하였으므로 앞에서는 그렇지 않다(멸종하지 않았다)는 내용이 언급되었을 것이다. 또한, 'that'이 가리키는 것이 무엇이지 생각하며 읽도록 한다.

(C) In addition, there are many lineages of hominids that did go extinct. Since the split between our ancestors and those of the chimps, our lineage has not been a single line of gradual change. Evolution never works that way.
☞ (in addition) 'in addition'은 앞에서 언급된 소재에 대한 추가적 설명을 나열할 때 사용하는 연결사이다. '멸종한 진화 인류 모체가 된 사람이나 동물의 혈통(many lineages of hominids that did go extinct)'에 대한 언급으로 보아 앞내용에도 멸종한 다른 존재에 대한 언급이 있었음을 예상할 수 있다. (C)의 마지막 문장에서 '진화는 그런 식으로 일어나지 않았다(Evolution never works that way)'는 문장에 주목하자.

오답의 모든 것

(1) 첫 번째 문단 찾기

▶ 주어진 글에서 인간의 멸종을 상상하기 어려우나, (B)의 역접의 연결사 'however'와 함께, 사실 거의 멸종될 뻔했다는 내용이 흐름상 자연스러우므로 주어진 글 뒤에 (B)는 정답 (따라서 (B)의 'that'이 가리키는 것은 '인간의 멸종')

▶ 주어진 글의 인간의 멸종에 대한 이야기와 (A)의 'instead'가 서로 어색하므로 (A)는 오답
▶ 주어진 글에서 인간의 멸종을 상상하기 어렵다는 내용과 멸종한 종이 있었다는 내용을 'in addition'으로 연결하는 것은 어색하므로 (C)는 오답

(2) 두 번째 문단 찾기
▶ 첫 번째 순서인 (B) 뒤에서 추가적으로 멸종한 다른 존재에 대한 언급을 'in addition'을 이용해 연결하는 것이 자연스러우므로 (B) 뒤에 (C)가 정답
▶ 멸종할 뻔한 인간에 대해 언급한 (B)의 뒤에서 (A)의 'instead'가 서로 어색하므로 (B) 뒤에 (A)는 오답

(3) 세 번째 문단 찾기
▶ (C)의 뒷부분에서 '진화는 그런 식으로 일어나지 않았다(Evolution never works that way)'는 내용은 '대신에(instead)' 앞에 오기에 적절하며, 단일계통이 아니라 대신에 많은 가지들이 서로로부터 갈라져서 그들만의 가지들로 발전했다고 말하는 전개가 흐름상 자연스러우므로 (A)가 정답

주요 어휘 및 표현

abundant	풍부한	go extinct	멸종하다
simultaneously	동시에	ancestor	조상
shrink	줄어들다	countless	셀 수 없이 많은

2. 문장 삽입

가. 비법 연습 문제

본문 34쪽

정답 1) ② (B) 2) ① (A) 3) ② (C)

주요 어휘 및 표현

compose	작곡하다, 구성하다	diagnose	진단하다
be supposed to V	to V ~하기로 되어있다	owe	빚지다

나. 기출 연습 문제

본문 34쪽

정답 [⑤]

해석

나는 국제사회가 연간 투자를 오늘날 GDP의 24%에서 2052년에 36%로 늘릴 것으로 예상한다. 이 투자의 많은 부분은 저렴한 에너지 시대를 위해 고안된 구식의 물건보다는 더 비싼 에너지 효율이 높은 제품에 이루어질 것이다. (이 투자의) 다른 몫은 석탄에서 재래식 가스와 같은 더 비싼 연료로의 이동에 투자될 것이다. (투자의) 일부는 신재생 에너지 공급이 경쟁력이 있게 되기 여러 해 전이라도 그것의 구축으로 들어갈 것이다. 그리고 (투자의) 많은 부분은 기후 변화로 인한 피해를 복구하거나, 예를 들어 해수면 상승을 막기 위해 해안을 따라 새로운 보호벽에 투자하는 것처럼 미래 기후 변화로 인한 피해에 적응하는 일로 들어갈 것이다. 이러한 엄청난 투자의 증가는 투자가 시장에 맡겨진다면 일어나지 않을 것이다. <u>오히려, 그것(투자의 엄청난 증가)은 의회의 결정에 근거한 국가의 개입을 통해서만 일어날 것이다.</u> 그것은 정부가 가장 필요하다고 여기는 어떤 생산 능력에라도 세금을 투자한다는 점에서 직접적이고, 아니면 정부가 바람직한 활동을 더 수익성이 있게 만드는 법률을 통과시킨다는 점에서 간접적일 것이다.

주요 어휘 및 표현

intervention	개입	adaptation	적응
parliamentary	의회의	come about	일어나다, 발생하다
annual	연간의, 매년의	tax dollar	세금
investment	투자	capacity	생산 능력, 수용력
old-fashioned	구식의	legislation	법률
conventional	재래식의	desired	바라던, 희망했던
competitive	경쟁력이 있는	profitable	수익성이 있는

1. 정답 [⑤]

해석

우리가 의사소통하는 방식은 강하고 건강한 공동체를 만드는 우리의 능력에 영향을 미친다. 공동체를 만드는 전통적인 방식은 토론과 논쟁을 강조해왔다. 예를 들어, 미국은 공동체 내의 중요한 쟁점들을 숙고하기 위해 타운홀 미팅을 활용하는 확고한 전통을 갖고 있다. 이러한 환경에서 쟁점의 각 입장에 있는 옹호자들이 자신의 입장에 대한 논거들을 제시하고, 공공의 쟁점들이 그러한 공개적인 토론회에서 논의되었다. 그러나 토론과 논쟁이 효력을 잘 발휘하기 위해서는 사람들이 비슷한 가정과 가치를 가지고 그러한 토론회에 올 필요가 있다. 공유된 가정과 가치가 논의를 위한 기반의 역할을 한다. 하지만 사회가 더욱 다양해짐에 따라, 사람들이 가정과 가치를 공유할 가능성은 줄어든다. 결과적으로 논쟁과 토론 같은 의사소통의 형태는 양극화되고, 이것은 공동체를 결합하는 것이 아니라 멀어지도록 몰아갈 수 있다.

비법 적용

However, as society becomes more diverse, the likelihood that people share assumptions and values diminishes.

☞ (역접) 역접의 연결사로 앞・뒤 내용을 예상한다.

☞ 주어진 문장에서 '그러나 사회가 다양화되면서 가정과 가치를 공유할 가능성이 줄어든다'고 하였다. 따라서 주어진 문장 앞부분에는 '가정과 가치(assumptions and values)를 공유해야 한다'와 같은 긍정적인 내용이, 뒷부분에는 공유의 가능성이 감소함에 따른 부정적 내용이 언급될 것으로 예상할 수 있다.

The way we communicate influences our ability to build strong and healthy communities. Traditional ways of building communities have emphasized debate and argument.

☞ 건강한 공동체를 만드는 의사소통의 방법으로 토론과 논쟁을 언급하고 있다.

① For example, the United States has a strong tradition of using town hall meetings to deliberate important issues within communities.

☞ (예시) 앞에서 토론과 논쟁을 중시하는 공동체에 관한 설명의 예시로 '타운홀 미팅(town hall meetings)'을 언급하였다.

② In these settings, advocates for each side of the issue present arguments for their positions, and public issues have been discussed in such public forums.

☞ (these/such+명사) 'these'와 'such'는 앞내용을 예상 및 확인할 수 있는 단서이다. 두 단어 모두 'town hall meetings'과 같은 논쟁의 공간과 상황을 의미한다.

③ Yet for debate and argument to work well, people need to come to such forums with similar assumptions and values.

☞ (역접과 such+명사) 역접의 연결사 'Yet'을 사용해 토론과 논쟁이 원활히 진행되기 위해 앞에서 언급한 포럼장(such forums)에 모일 필요성을 강조하고 있다. 역접의 연결사는 강조의 기능도 있다.

④ The shared assumptions serve as a foundation for the discussion.
☞ (the+명사) 앞에서 사람들이 포럼장에 모일 필요가 있다고 하였고, 그렇게 모였을 때의 '공유되는 가정(The shared assumptions)'의 역할에 대해 언급하고 있다. 'the+명사'는 앞내용을 예상하고 확인할 수 있는 단서이다.

⑤ As a result, forms of communication such as argument and debate become polarized, which may drive communities apart as opposed to bringing them together.
☞ (인과) 논쟁과 토론의 형태가 양극화된다는 내용은 앞내용과 논리적으로 맞지 않는 부분이다. 역접의 연결사로 글의 흐름을 바꿔줄 필요가 있다. 인과의 연결사는 순접의 기능을 하므로 앞내용이 부정적이면 뒷내용도 부정적이고, 앞내용이 긍정적이면 뒷내용도 긍정적이어야 한다.

오답의 모든 것

① For example, the United States has a strong tradition of using town hall meetings to deliberate important issues within communities.
▶ 주어진 문장에 있는 '가정과 가치 공유'가 '미국의 타운홀 미팅에서 가정과 가치를 공유'한다는 것으로 혼동할 수 있는 오답

② In these settings, advocates for each side of the issue present arguments for their positions, and public issues have been discussed in such public forums.
▶ '이러한 환경(in these settings)'을 주어진 문장의 '사회의 다양화' 상황으로 혼동할 수 있는 오답

③ Yet for debate and argument to work well, people need to come to such forums with similar assumptions and values.
▶ 주어진 문장에서 부정적 내용이 언급된 뒤, 역접으로 긍정적 내용이 나올 것이라고 혼동할 수 있는 오답

④ The shared assumptions serve as a foundation for the discussion.
▶ 주어진 문장은 공유의 가능성이 줄어든다고 하였으나, ④번은 공유된 가정이 토론의 기반이 된다고 하였으므로 상반된 내용임. 이러한 문맥을 고려하지 않고 'share'라는 단어와 ④번의 'The shared assumptions'을 동일시하여 혼동할 수 있는 오답

⑤ As a result, forms of communication such as argument and debate become polarized, which may drive communities apart as opposed to bringing them together.
▶ **주어진 문장의 부정적 상황(원인)에 대하여 소통의 양극화라는 결과가 문맥상 자연스럽게 이어지고 있는 정답**

주요 어휘 및 표현

likelihood	가능성	advocate	지지자, 옹호자
assumption	가정, 가설	position	위치, 입장
diminish	감소하다	polarize	양극화하다
deliberate	숙고하다, 신중한, 의도적인	community	공동체

2. 정답 [④]

해석

현재, 우리는 인간을 다른 행성으로 보낼 수 없다. 한 가지 장애물은 그러한 여행이 수년이 걸릴 것이라는 점이다. 우주선은 긴 여행에서 생존에 필요한 충분한 공기, 물, 그리고 다른 물자를 운반할 필요가 있을 것이다. 또 다른 장애물은 극심한 열과 추위 같은, 다른 행성들의 혹독한 기상 조건이다. 어떤 행성들은 착륙할 표면조차 가지고 있지 않다. 이러한 장애물들 때문에, 우주에서의 대부분의 연구 임무는 승무원이 탑승하지 않은 우주선을 사용해서 이루어진다. 이런 탐험들은 인간의 생명에 아무런 위험도 주지 않으며 우주 비행사들을 포함하는 탐험보다 비용이 덜 든다. 이 우주선은 행성의 구성 성분과 특성을 실험하는 기구들을 운반한다.

비법 적용

Because of these obstacles, most research missions in space are accomplished through the use of spacecraft without crews aboard.

☞ (인과) 인과의 표현인 'Because of'를 통해 앞 • 뒤에 나올 내용을 예상한다.

☞ (these+명사) 앞내용에 장애물이 등장하였음을 알 수 있다. 'accomplish'라는 단어로 보아 주어진 문장 뒤에서 장애물들을 해결하는 상황을 예상해 볼 수 있다.

Currently, we cannot send humans to other planets. One obstacle is that such a trip would take years.

☞ (such+명사) 인간을 다른 행성으로 보낼 수 없다는 첫 문장의 내용을 'such a trip'으로 표현하였다. 이에 대한 첫 번째 장애물로 시간이 오래 걸린다는 점을 언급하였다.

① A spacecraft would need to carry enough air, water, and other supplies needed for survival on the long journey.

☞ (the+명사) 'the 명사'의 형태는 앞에서 언급된 것을 가리킬 때 쓰는 말이다. 'the long journey'는 앞에서 언급된 '시간이 많이 걸리는 여행(장애물)'을 의미한다.

② Another obstacle is the harsh conditions on other planets, such as extreme heat and cold.

☞ (another+명사) 'another'은 '또 다른 하나'라는 의미이므로 앞내용을 예상하고 확인할 수 있는 단서이다. 즉 앞에서 장애물이 있었음을 의미하며, 시간에 관한 첫 번째 장애물에 이어 두 번째 장애물을 언급하고 있다.

③ Some planets do not even have surfaces to land on.

☞ (some+명사) ②번에 나온 '혹독한 조건(harsh conditions)'의 행성의 예시로 착륙할 표면조차 없는 '일부 행성(Some planets)'을 언급하였다.

④ These explorations pose no risk to human life and are less expensive than ones involving astronauts.

☞ (these+명사) '이러한 탐험들(these explorations)'이라는 것은 앞에서 탐험들이 언급되었음을 의미하는데, 여기서 인간의 생명에 어떠한 위험도 없다는 것은 앞에서 제시된 장애물들과는

흐름이 맞지 않다. 무엇보다 '우주 비행사들이 타고 있는 탐험(ones involving astronauts)'과 비교할만한 것이 제시되어 있지 않다.

⑤ The spacecraft carry instruments that test the compositions and characteristics of planets.
☞ (the+명사) 'The spacecraft'이라고 언급할 만한 것이 앞 부분에 위치할 필요가 있다.

오답의 모든 것

① A spacecraft would need to carry enough air, water, and other supplies needed for survival on the long journey.
▶ 주어진 문장에서는 장애물들이라고 하였으나 'obstacle'이라는 단어만 보고 단수, 복수조차 확인하지 않을 경우에 선택할 수 있는 오답

② Another obstacle is the harsh conditions on other planets, such as extreme heat and cold.
▶ ①번의 생존을 위한 공기, 물을 운반할 필요가 없다는 내용을 주어진 문장이 말하는 장애물이라 생각하여 선택할 수 있는 오답

③ Some planets do not even have surfaces to land on.
▶ 앞에서 두 가지 장애물이 언급된 것만 보고 ②번과 ③번이 같은 내용을 말하고 있다는 점을 확인하지 않으면 선택할 수 있는 오답

④ These explorations pose no risk to human life and are less expensive than ones involving astronauts.
▶ **앞 내용에서 말하는 장애물이라는 부정적인 내용 뒤에 인간에게 해가 없다는 긍정적인 내용이 뒤이어 나오는 것이 논리적으로 어색함. 주어진 문장의 무인 탐사 내용을 'These explorations'로 연결하였고, 이와 비교의 대상인 우주 비행사들이 탑승한 것과도 잘 어울리는 정답** ('한정사+명사'의 표현은 앞에서 등장한 단어를 그대로 사용하지 않을 수도 있음. 예를 들어 '상황(situation)', '과정(process)'과 같은 추상 명사는 글 전체의 맥락이나 상황을 통해 유추해야 함.)

⑤ The spacecraft carry instruments that test the compositions and characteristics of planets.
▶ 앞에서 이미 이러한 탐험이 인간에게 해가 없다고 하였으므로, 위험성에 대해 언급하고 있는 주어진 문장은 오답

주요 어휘 및 표현

obstacle	장애물	harsh	극심한
aboard	탑승하여	pose	위험을 제기하다
planet	행성	involve	수반하다, 관련시키다

3. 정답 [③]

해석

20세기 후반 연구자들은 얼마나 빨리 그리고 얼마나 멀리 뉴스, 소문, 혁신이 이동하는지를 측정하고자 했다. 더 최근의 연구는 생각 즉 감정 상태와 상황까지도 사회 관계망을 통해 전파될 수 있다는 것을 보여주어 왔다. 이러한 종류의 전염의 증거는 분명하며, 즉 '학구적인 룸메이트와 함께 하는 학생들은 더욱 학구적이 되며 폭식하는 사람 옆에 앉아 식사하는 사람은 더 많은 음식을 먹는다.' 그러나 Christakis와 Fowler에 따르면 우리는 우리의 친구의 친구의 친구를 훨씬 넘어서서, 다시 말해 고작 세 단계의 떨어짐을 건너서는 생각과 행동을 전파할 수 없다. 이것은 생각이나 행동의 전파와 수용이 편지나 어떤 고용 기회가 있다는 정보를 전달하는 것보다 더 강한 연결을 요구하기 때문이다. 단지 사람을 아는 것은 그들이 더 공부하거나 과식하도록 영향을 미칠 수 있는 것과는 같지 않다. 모방은 그것이 무의식적일 때조차도 실로 가장 순수한 형태의 아첨이다.

비법 적용

However, according to Christakis and Fowler, we cannot transmit ideas and behaviours much beyond our friends' friends' friends (in other words, across just three degrees of separation).

☞ (역접) 역접의 연결사를 통해 앞 • 뒤에 올 내용을 예상해 본다.

☞ 세 단계가 떨어지면 생각과 행동을 전파할 수 없다는 점을 통해 앞내용은 전파 가능한 상황을 예상해 본다.

In the late twentieth century, researchers sought to measure how fast and how far news, rumours or innovations moved.

☞ 뉴스, 소문, 혁신이 얼마나 빨리 그리고 얼마나 멀리 이동하는지를 측정하는 연구에 대해 소개하고 있다.

① More recent research has shown that ideas—even emotional states and conditions—can be transmitted through a social network.

☞ 주어진 문장에서 예상한 대로 전파 가능한 상황이 제시되어 있다.

② The evidence of this kind of contagion is clear: 'Students with studious roommates become more studious. Diners sitting next to heavy eaters eat more food.'

☞ (this+명사) 앞 내용에서 '이러한 종류의 전염(this kind of contagion)'이 나왔음을 의미한다. '생각이 전파될 수 있다(ideas can be transmitted)'는 말을 '전염(contagion)'이라는 단어를 이용하여 문장을 연결하고 있다.

③ This is because the transmission and reception of an idea or behaviour requires a stronger connection than the relaying of a letter or the communication that a certain employment opportunity exists.

☞ (인과) 이 문장에서 말하는 '생각이나 행동의 전파와 수용이 더 강력한 연결을 필요로 한다'는 것은

생각이나 행동의 전파가 쉬운 일이 아님을 의미한다. 그러나 인과의 표현 앞·뒤는 유사한 문맥으로 이어져야 하므로, 전파가 확실히 일어난다는 말 뒤에 오기에 어색한 문장이 된다. 또한 'this is because SV' 뒤에 이어지는 '더 강한 연결을 필요로 한다(requires a stronger connection)'는 표현에서 강한 연결을 필요로 하는 상황이 먼저 제시되어야 함을 알 수 있다. 즉, 세 단계 건너의 친구에게는 좀 더 강한 연결을 필요로 한다는 내용이 흐름상 적절하다.

> **예시** I don't feel well all day. (결과) + <u>This is because</u> I got up too early this morning. (원인)
> I studied hard last night. (원인) + <u>This is why</u> I could pass the test. (결과)

④ Merely knowing people is not the same as being able to influence them to study more or overeat.
☞ '단순히 사람을 안다(Merely knowing people)'는 것은 주어진 문장의 '친구의 친구의 친구를 안다'는 것과 같은 의미이며, 강력하지 않은 관계를 뜻한다. 또한 '생각이나 행동의 전파' 강력한 관계에서 일어난다고 하였으므로 '공부나 과식'과 같은 '생각이나 행동의 전파'는 이러한 '단순히 아는 사람'에게는 전파될 수 없을 것이다. ③번과 같은 의미의 문장이면서 ②번까지의 내용과 상충되기 때문에 중간에 흐름을 바꿔줄 내용이 필요하다는 사실을 다시 한 번 확인할 수 있다.

⑤ Imitation is indeed the sincerest form of flattery, even when it is unconscious.
☞ 여기서 '모방(Imitation)'은 앞내용의' 공부와 과식'과 같은 생각과 행동의 전파를 의미한다. 무의식적으로라도 누군가를 모방한다는 것은 단순히 누군가를 안다는 것을 넘어선 '순수한 형태의 아첨'임을 강조하고 있다.

오답의 모든 것

① More recent research has shown that ideas—even emotional states and conditions—can be transmitted through a social network.
▶ 첫 문장의 연구자들과 주어진 문장의 연구자들이 역접을 통해 서로 반대 의견을 제시한다고 잘못 생각하여 선택할 수 있는 오답

② The evidence of this kind of contagion is clear: 'Students with studious roommates become more studious. Diners sitting next to heavy eaters eat more food.'
▶ 뒤의 내용을 고려하지 않은 채 ①번의 'can be transmittted'와 주어진 문장의 'cannot be transmitted'를 역접 관계로 생각하여 잘못 선택할 수 있는 오답

③ This is because the transmission and reception of an idea or behaviour requires a stronger connection than the relaying of a letter or the communication that a certain employment opportunity exists.
▶ 주어진 문장의 역접과 'this is because ~' 뒤에서 '더 강력한 연결(a stronger connection)'이 필요하다는 표현을 통해 앞내용과의 어색함을 파악하였다면 고를 수 있는 정답

④ Merely knowing people is not the same as being able to influence them to study more or overeat.
▶ 이미 ③번에서 논리적인 어색함이 발생하였으나, 이를 보지 못하였다면 선택할 수 있는 오답

⑤ Imitation is indeed the sincerest form of flattery, even when it is unconscious.
▶ 주어진 문장의 세 단계를 건너면 전파할 수 없다는 내용을 보고, 그만큼 모방이라는 것이 은밀한 것이라는 나름의 결론을 내려 잘못 선택할 수 있는 오답

주요 어휘 및 표현

transmit	전달하다, 전송하다	separation	분리, 떨어짐
contagion	전염	heavy eater	많이 먹는 사람
studious	학구적인	imitation	모방
diner	식사하는 사람	flattery	아첨

4. 정답 [③]

해석

예술 표상 이론은 예술가가 하는 일을 과학자가 하는 일과 유사한 것으로 취급한다. 말하자면, 둘 다 외부 세계를 묘사하는 것과 관련이 있다. 하지만 19세기 무렵에, 과학자와 예술가 사이의 비교는 어떤 것이든 세상에 관한 발견을 하거나 자연을 있는 그대로 묘사하는 것에 있어 예술가를 천덕꾸러기(과학자보다 열등한 것)처럼 보이게 만들 가능성이 컸다. 여기서, 과학은 분명히 우위를 가졌다. 그래서 예술이 그것(예술)을 과학과 구별하는 동시에 수준에 있어 그것을 과학과 동일하게 만드는 어떤 소명을 제시해야 한다는 사회적 압력이 있었다. 예술이 감정의 표현을 전문으로 한다는 개념은 이런 관점에서 특히 매력적이었다. 그것은 과학 그것 자체의 것, 즉 객관적 세계의 탐구를 주었고, 동시에 예술이 해야 하는 (과학과) 비슷하게 중요한 것, 즉 감정이라는 내적 세계를 탐구하는 것을 남겨두었다. 만약 과학이 자연을 있는 그대로 묘사했다면, 예술은 거울의 방향을 자아와 그것의 경험으로 돌렸다.

비법 적용

So, there was a social pressure for art to come up with some vocation that both distinguished it from science and, at the same time, made it equal in stature to science.

☞ (인과) 인과 연결사 'So'를 통해 앞 • 뒤에 나올 내용을 예상한다

☞ 주어진 문장에서 예술을 향한 사회적 압박이 있다(결과)는 내용으로 보아 앞내용에 예술 세계에 대한 부정적인 상황(원인)을 예상해 볼 수 있다.

☞ 'So'와 같은 인과 관계에서 주어진 문장과 같이 무언가를 해결할 필요성이 언급된 경우에는 'So'의 앞내용은 문제의 상황이 제시되어 있고 뒤에는 해결한 이후의 긍정적 상황이 제시되어 있을 수 있어 이를 잘 파악하는 것이 핵심이다.

Representational theories of art treat the work of the artist as similar to that of the scientist. Both, so to speak, are involved in describing the external world.

☞ 예술가와 과학자에 관한 내용으로 예술가와 과학자는 외부 세상을 묘사한다는 점에서 유사하다고 말하고 있다.

① But by the nineteenth century, any comparison between the scientist and the artist was bound to make the artist look like a poor relation in terms of making discoveries about the world or holding a mirror up to nature.

☞ (역접) 과학자와 예술가를 유사하게 보았다는 내용 뒤에 역접을 통해 예술가에 대한 '부정적 인식(a poor relation)'이 언급되어 있다.

② Here, science clearly had the edge.
☞ 과학이 우위를 차지했다는 말을 바꿔 말하면, 예술가의 입장이 열등하다는 의미이다. 따라서 'Here'은 앞 문장의 'the artist look like a poor relation'의 상황을 가리킨다.

③ The notion that art specialized in the expression of the emotions was particularly attractive in this light.
☞ (this+명사) '이러한 점(this light)'에서 예술이 매력적이라고 하였으므로 앞에서 예술의 매력적인 '점(light)'이 언급되었는지 확인해야 한다. 그러나 어떤 점이 예술의 매력인지 언급되지 않았으며, 예술가를 천덕꾸러기로 보는 앞내용과 예술이 매력적이라는 점은 모순 된다.

④ It rendered unto science its own – the exploration of the objective world – while saving something comparably important for art to do – to explore the inner world of feeling.
☞ (대명사 it) '그것(It)'이 과학에게는 그 자체의 것(객관적 세계의 탐구)을 주었고 예술에게는 내적 세계를 탐구하게 해주었다고 하였다. 따라서 '그것(it)'은 앞 문장의 'the notion'을 의미하며, 과학과 예술이 동등한 입장에서 각각의 것을 탐구하는 역할을 하고 있음을 알 수 있다.

⑤ If science held the mirror up to nature, art turned a mirror at the self and its experiences.
☞ 앞내용에 이어 과학과 예술의 각각의 역할을 동등하게 서술하고 있다.

오답의 모든 것

① But by the nineteenth century, any comparison between the scientist and the artist was bound to make the artist look like a poor relation in terms of making discoveries about the world or holding a mirror up to nature.
▶ 인과의 연결사 'so'는 앞·뒤가 동일한 맥락으로 연결되어야 한다는 점을 모르면 선택할 수 있음. 예술과 과학이 외부 세상을 묘사한다는 점이 유사하다는 말 뒤에 예술과 과학을 구별하라는 사회적 압박이 있었다는 내용은 논리적으로 어색하므로 오답

② Here, science clearly had the edge.
▶ 예술에 대한 부정적 평가가 곧 과학에 대한 긍정적인 평가임을 추론하지 못하거나, 'edge'의 뜻(이점, 장점)을 제대로 알지 못하면 선택할 수 있는 오답

③ The notion that art specialized in the expression of the emotions was particularly attractive in this light.
▶ **앞내용에 언급된 예술에 대한 부정적 내용과 이 문장에 언급된 '예술의 긍정적 측면'이 논리적으로 어색하므로 정답**

④ It rendered unto science its own – the exploration of the objective world – while saving something comparably important for art to do – to explore the inner world of feeling.
▶ 대명사 'It'을 주어진 문장의 'a social pressure'로 오해하였거나, 주어진 문장의 'equal'을 'comparably'와 잘못 연결지어 선택할 수 있는 오답

⑤ If science held the mirror up to nature, art turned a mirror at the self and its experiences.
▶ 앞내용에서 주어진 단서들을 제대로 찾지 못하고 주어진 문장의 'a social pressure'에 대한 해결책으로 이 문장이 제시되었다고 잘못 선택할 수 있는 오답

주요 어휘 및 표현

come up with	(생각 등을) 떠올리다, 생각해내다	a poor relation	천덕꾸러기
comparison	비교	edge	이점, 장점

라. 고난도 실전 문제

본문 40~41쪽

1. 정답 [⑤]

해석

반딧불이는 짝의 주의를 끌기 위해서 꽁무니에 불을 밝히는 것만이 아니라, 박쥐에게 자기들을 먹지 말라고 말하기 위해 빛을 내기도 한다. 반딧불이의 이름을 지어주는 특성에 대한 이야기의 이 반전은 Jesse Barber와 그의 동료들에 의해 발견되었다. 빛이 하는 경고 역할은 반딧불이와 박쥐 모두에게 유익한데, 왜냐하면 이 곤충이 그 포유동물(박쥐)에게는 역겨운 맛이 나기 때문이다. 반딧불이를 삼키면, 반딧불이가 배출하는 화학 물질 때문에 박쥐가 그것을 다시 토해내게 낸다. 연구팀은 여덟 마리의 박쥐를 서너 마리의 반딧불이와, 그보다 세 배가 많은 딱정벌레와 나방을 포함한 맛이 좋은 곤충들과 함께 어두운 방에 나흘 동안 두었다. 첫날 밤 동안에, 모든 박쥐는 적어도 한 마리의 반딧불이를 잡았다. 그러나 네 번째 밤에 이르러서는, 대부분의 박쥐는 반딧불이를 피하고 대신 다른 모든 먹이를 잡는 법을 배웠다. 그 팀이 반딧불이에서 빛이 나는 기관을 어둡게 칠했을 때, 새로운 한 무리의 박쥐는 그것들을 피하는 법을 배우는 데 두 배의 시간이 걸렸다. 오랫동안 반딧불이의 생물 발광(發光)은 주로 짝짓기 신호의 역할을 한다고 생각되었지만, 새로운 연구 결과는 짝짓기를 하기에 미숙함에도 불구하고 반딧불이 애벌레 역시 빛을 내는 이유를 설명해 준다.

비법 적용

When the team painted fireflies' light organs dark, a new set of bats took twice as long to learn to avoid them.

☞ (the+명사, 대명사) 앞내용에 '그 팀(the team)'에 대한 언급이 있어야 함을 예상할 수 있다. 본문 속에서 'them'이 가리키는 것이 무엇인지 생각하며 읽는다.

☞ '반딧불이의 빛이 나는 기관(fireflies' light organs)'을 어둡게 칠했다는 점을 통해 앞내용에 반딧불이의 빛이나는 기관을 칠하지 않았다는 내용이 먼저 언급되어야 함을 예상할 수 있다.

☞ '새로운 종류의 박쥐(a new set of bats)'가 어둡게 칠한 반딧불이를 피하는 법을 배우는 데 시간이 오래 걸렸다'는 말을 통해 이미 다른 박쥐들이 반딧불이를 피하는 법을 배웠다는 내용이 먼저 언급되어 이 두 가지를 비교하고 있음을 예상해 볼 수 있다.

Fireflies don't just light up their behinds to attract mates, they also glow to tell bats not to eat them. This twist in the tale of the trait that gives fireflies their name was discovered by Jesse Barber and his colleagues. The glow's warning role benefits both fireflies and bats, because these insects taste disgusting to the mammals.

☞ 반딧불이의 불빛이 짝의 관심을 끌기 위해서 뿐만 아니라, 자신을 먹지 말라는 경고이기도 하다는 반딧불이의 특성에 대해 언급하고 있다.

① When swallowed, chemicals released by fireflies cause bats to throw them back up.
☞ 반딧불이가 배출하는 화학 물질 때문에 맛이 역겹다는 내용으로 앞에서 반딧불이의 불빛이 자신들을 먹지 말라는 경고의 역할을 한다는 점과 자연스럽게 연결되고 있다.

② The team placed eight bats in a dark room with three or four fireflies plus three times as many tasty insects, including beetles and moths, for four days.
☞ (the+명사) 주어진 문장에 언급된 '그 팀(the team)'이라는 단어가 본문에서 처음 등장하였음을 주목한다. 문맥상 'Jesse Barber와 그의 동료들(Jesse Barber and his colleagues)'임을 파악한다.
☞ 실험을 위해 8마리의 박쥐와 서너 마리의 반딧불 등이 등장하였다.

③ During the first night, all the bats captured at least one firefly.
☞ 시간의 흐름을 통해 실험과정을 알 수 있다, 적어도 한 마리의 반딧불이를 먹었다고 하였으므로 박쥐들은 경험을 통해 반딧불이의 맛이 역겹다는 것을 알았을 것이다.

④ But by the fourth night, most bats had learned to avoid fireflies and catch all the other prey instead.
☞ (역접) 첫날에는 반딧불이를 잡아 먹었으나, 이후 4일째에 박쥐들이 (반딧불이의 불빛을 보고) 피하는 법을 학습했다는 내용이다. 주어진 문장에 언급된 표현 및 내용과 유사한 것들이 등장하고 있음을 주목한다.

⑤ It had long been thought that firefly bioluminescence mainly acted as a mating signal, but the new finding explains why firefly larvae also glow despite being immature for mating.
☞ (the+명사) 새로운 연구 결과에 대한 내용을 언급하며 글을 마무리하고 있으나, '새로운 연구 결과(the new finding)'라고 할 만한 내용이 존재하지 않았다.

오답의 모든 것

① When swallowed, chemicals released by fireflies cause bats to throw them back up.
▶ 앞내용에 제시된 '불빛(glow)'을 주어진 문장의 'dark'와 조합하거나, 'Jesse Barber and his colleagues' 바로 뒤에 이들을 'the team'으로 연결지어 잘못 선택할 수 있는 오답

② The team placed eight bats in a dark room with three or four fireflies plus three times as many tasty insects, including beetles and moths, for four days.
▶ 전체적 문맥에 대한 이해없이 'the team'이라는 단어만 성급히 연결 짓거나 'dark'라는 단어가 공통으로 나오는 것을 보고 잘못 선택할 수 있는 오답

③ During the first night, all the bats captured at least one firefly.
▶ 실험의 전후관계를 제대로 파악하지 않고, 주어진 문장의 박쥐가 언급된 것만 보고 잘못 선택할 수 있는 오답

④ But by the fourth night, most bats had learned to avoid fireflies and catch all the other prey instead.
▶ 'them'이 나타낼 만한 대상이 없는데도 확인하지 않거나, 단순히 'to learn to avoid'만 보고 선택할 수 있는 매력적인 오답

⑤ It had long been thought that firefly bioluminescence mainly acted as a mating signal, but the new finding explains why firefly larvae also glow despite being immature for mating.

▶ **네 번째 밤에 반딧불이를 피하는 법을 배운 기존의 박쥐들에 비해, 빛을 내는 기관이 어둡게 칠해지자 새로운 박쥐들은 배우는 데 두 배나 더 걸렸다는 사실이 역접 연결사로 잘 연결되어 있는 정답** (비교급에는 비교 대상이 있어야 하므로, 다른 박쥐들이 피하는 법을 배우는 데 걸린 시간보다 두 배 더 걸렸다는 내용이 먼저 나와야 한다는 사실을 주어진 문장을 통해 예측하였다면 쉽게 접근할 수 있음. 답을 고른 뒤에도 주어진 문장의 대명사 'them'이 가리키는 것이 앞의 'fireflies'라는 것을 확인하는 과정이 필요함.

주요 어휘 및 표현

firefly	반딧불이	throw up	~을 토하다
twist	반전	beetle	딱정벌레
trait	특성, 특징	moth	나방
disgusting	역겨운	prey	먹이
swallow	삼키다	finding	연구 결과
chemical	화학 물질	immature	미숙한

2. 정답 [④]

해석

디자이너는 새로운 프로젝트에 접근할 때 자신의 디자인 경험을 이용한다. 이것에는 효과가 있다고 그들이 알고 있는 이전의 디자인, 즉 그들이 직접 만들었던 디자인과 다른 사람들이 만들었던 디자인을 둘 다 활용하는 것이 포함된다. 다른 사람들의 창작물은 흔히 새로운 아이디어와 혁신으로도 이어지는 영감을 불러일으킨다. 이는 잘 알려져 있고 이해되는 일이다. 그러나 한 아이디어의 표현은 저작권에 의해 보호되며, 그 저작권을 침해하는 사람들은 법정에 끌려가고 기소될 수 있다. 저작권은 아이디어의 표현을 다루지, 아이디어 그 자체를 다루지는 않는다는 점에 유의하라. 이것은 예를 들어, 모두 유사한 기능을 가진 많은 스마트폰이 있지만, 그 아이디어가 서로 다른 방식으로 표현되었고 저작권 보호를 받은 것은 그 표현이기 때문에 이것이 저작권 침해를 나타내지 않는다는 것을 의미한다. 저작권은 무료이며 저작자, 예를 들어 어떤 책의 저자나 프로그램을 개발하는 프로그래머가 저작권을 다른 누군가에게 양도하지 않는 한 그 저작자에게 자동으로 부여된다.

비법 적용

Note that copyright covers the expression of an idea and not the idea itself.

☞ (the+명사) 주어진 문장 앞에 'the + 명사'에 해당하는 말과 저작권(copyright)에 대한 설명이 먼저 언급되어야 함을 예상할 수 있다.

Designers draw on their experience of design when approaching a new project. This includes the

use of previous designs that they know work – both designs that they have created themselves and those that others have created.
☞ 디자이너는 자신의 경험, 즉 이전의 효과가 있던 디자인을 활용하여 새로운 프로젝트를 진행한다는 내용이다.

① Others' creations often spark inspiration that also leads to new ideas and innovation.
☞ 다른 사람들이 만든 디자인이 새로운 아이디어와 혁신으로 이어진다는 앞내용에 대한 부연 설명이 이어지고 있다.

② This is well known and understood.
☞ (this) 문맥상 'this'는 앞내용을 나타낸다. 다른 사람이 만든 것을 보고 새로운 아이디어를 얻는 것은 너무도 당연한(well known and understood) 사실이다.

③ However, the expression of an idea is protected by copyright, and people who infringe on that copyright can be taken to court and prosecuted.
☞ (역접) 앞에서 다른 사람의 창작물을 통해 영감을 받아 새로운 아이디어를 얻는 일은 종종 있는 일이라고 한 뒤에, 역접의 연결사(however)를 이용해 그러한 아이디어의 표현은 저작권으로 보호되며 저작권을 침해하는 경우에는 법적인 문제가 생길 수 있음을 언급하고 있다.
☞ 주어진 문장에 있던 'the expression of an idea'라는 표현과 '저작권(copyright)'라는 단어가 처음 등장하였으므로 ④ 또는 ⑤번에 주어진 문장이 들어가야 한다.

④ This means, for example, that while there are numerous smartphones all with similar functionality, this does not represent an infringement of copyright as the idea has been expressed in different ways and it is the expression that has been copyrighted.
☞ (this와 예시) 문맥상 'this'는 앞내용을 의미하며, 예시는 앞내용에 대한 구체적 사례여야 한다. 그러나 비슷한 기능의 스마트폰이 모두 저작권 침해는 아니라고 하는 이 문장은 저작권을 위반하면 법적인 문제가 생길 수 있다는 앞 문장의 예시가 되기에는 논리적으로 어색하다.

⑤ Copyright is free and is automatically invested in the author, for instance, the writer of a book or a programmer who develops a program, unless they sign the copyright over to someone else.
☞ 저작권에 대한 추가 설명이 이어지고 있다.

오답의 모든 것

① Others' creations often spark inspiration that also leads to new ideas and innovation.
▶ 'new ideas'보다 주어진 문장에 있는 'an idea'가 먼저 나와야 한다고 잘못 생각하여 선택할 수 있는 오답

② This is well known and understood.
▶ 'This'가 주어진 문장을 의미한다고 잘못 생각하여 선택할 수 있는 오답

③ However, the expression of an idea is protected by copyright, and people who infringe on that copyright can be taken to court and prosecuted.
▶ 주어진 문장과 이 문장이 유사한 맥락의 말임을 이해하지 못하여 역접 연결사로 이어져야

한다고 생각하거나, 'the expression of an idea'가 주어진 문장에 공통으로 등장하는 것을 보고 선택할 수 있는 매력적인 오답

④ This means, for example, that while there are numerous smartphones all with similar functionality, this does not represent an infringement of copyright as **the idea has been expressed** in different ways and it is the expression that has been copyrighted.

▶ 주어진 예시의 내용이 저작권을 어겼을 때 법정에 끌려갈 수 있다는 앞 문장의 내용과 달라 앞뒤의 문맥이 어색함을 발견하였거나, 저작권이 아이디어 자체가 아닌 아이디어의 표현에 있다는 주어진 문장의 내용과 같은 의미를 담고 있음을 파악하였다면 선택할 수 있는 정답

⑤ Copyright is free and is automatically invested in the author, for instance, the writer of a book or a programmer who develops a program, unless they sign the copyright over to someone else.

▶ 저작권이 무료이며 저작자에게 자동으로 부여된다는 내용은 주어진 문장과는 조금 거리가 먼 저작권에 대한 추가적 사실이므로 오답

주요 어휘 및 표현

copyright	저작권; 저작권을 보호하다	functionality	(컴퓨터·전자 장치의) 기능
cover	다루다	represent	나타내다
draw on	~을 이용하다, ~에 의지하다	automatically	자동으로
spark	불러일으키다	invest	부여하다, 투자하다
inspiration	영감	sign ~ over to …	…에게 ~을 양도하다

II 논리 추론 및 논리 판단 관련 독해 유형

1. 빈칸 추론

가. 비법 연습 문제

본문 45쪽

정답

1. ①

2. 1) ③ 2) ④

해석

1. 우리 대부분은 신속하게 하는 인식을 의심한다. 우리는 결정의 질은 결정을 내리는 데 들어간 시간과 노력과 직접적인 관계가 있다고 생각한다. 그게 우리가 자녀들에게 말하는 것인데, "서두르면 일을 망친다." "돌다리도 두드려 보고 건너라." "멈춰서 생각하라." "겉만 보고 판단하지 마라."이다. 우리는 최대한 많은 정보를 모아서 최대한 많은 시간을 주의 깊게 숙고하는 데 시간을 보내면 우리가 늘 더 나을 것이라고 생각한다. 하지만 특히 시간에 쫓기는 중대한 상황 속에서는 서두르는데도 일을 망치지 않는, 즉 우리의 순식간에 내리는 판단과 첫인상이 세상을 파악하는 더 나은 수단을 제공할 수 있는 순간이 있다. 생존자들은 어쨌든 이 교훈을 배웠고, 신속하게 인식하는 능력을 발전시켜서 연마했다.

2. 1) 사람들은 일란성 쌍둥이가 모든 면에서 정확히 같다고 생각한다. 하지만 일란성 쌍둥이는 독특한 개인들이다. 예를 들어 나의 자녀들은 항상 몸무게에서 약 25%의 차이를 보였다. 또한, 그들은 똑같이 행동하지 않습니다.

① 활동적인 ② 짝 지워진 ③ 독특한 ④ 재능있는 ⑤ 사려깊은

2) 연구원들의 목표는 성취도가 높은 사람들의 공통점을 파악하는 것이었다. 그들 모두 한 가지 공통점이 있었다: 오랜 시간, 힘든 시간을 기꺼이 일하려는 마음이다. 그들 모두는 성공이 그들에게 갑자기 일어난 일이 아니라는 것에 동의했다. 그것은 그들이 지속적인 노력을 통해 그것을 실현시켰기 때문에 일어난 일이었다.

① 위험을 감수하는
② 미리 계획하는
③ 나쁜 습관을 버리는
④ 오랜 시간, 힘든 시간을 일하는
⑤ 다른 사람의 의견을 존중하는

주요 어휘 및 표현 (비법 연습 문제 1)

identical	동일한	high-achieving	성취도가 높은
willingness	의지	continuous	지속적인

주요 어휘 및 표현 (비법 연습 문제 2)

cognition	인지	be related to	~와 관련된
haste	서두름	leap	뛰다
judge	판단하다	snap	빠른

나. 기출 연습 문제 A

본문 46쪽

정답 [⑤]

해석

어떤 식당이 대체로 붐빈다는 것을 알게 되면 우리가 그 식당에서 식사할 가능성이 더 크다. 아무도 우리에게 어떤 식당이 좋다고 말하지 않을 때조차도, 우리의 무리 행동은 우리의 의사를 결정한다. 당신이 두 개의 텅 빈 식당 쪽으로 걸어가고 있다고 가정하자. 당신은 어느 곳에 들어가야 할지 모른다. 하지만, 갑자기 당신은 여섯 명의 무리가 둘 중 하나의 식당으로 들어가는 것을 보게 된다. 당신은 텅 빈 식당 혹은 나머지 식당, 둘 중 어느 식당에 들어갈 가능성이 더 높겠는가? 대부분의 사람들은 사람들이 있는 식당에 들어갈 것이다. 당신과 친구가 그 식당에 들어간다고 가정하자. 이제, 그 식당 안에는 여덟 명이 있다. 다른 사람들은 한 식당은 텅 비어 있고 다른 식당은 여덟 명이 있는 것을 보게 된다. 그래서, 그들도 다른 여덟 명과 같은 행동을 하기로 결정한다.

① 두 식당이 모두 더 바빠진다.
② 당신과 당신의 친구는 망설이기 시작한다.
③ 당신의 결정은 다른 사람들에게 영향력이 없다.
④ 그들은 다른 많은 사람들이 하는 것을 거절한다.
⑤ 그들도 다른 여덟 명과 같은 행동을 하기로 결정한다.

주요 어휘 및 표현

behavior	행동	decisionmaking	의사 결정

나. 기출 연습 문제 B

본문 48쪽

정답 [③]

해석

우리는 우리의 '모든' 주의력을 활용하려는 매우 강렬한 욕구가 우리 안에 항상 존재한다는 것을 인정해야 한다. 그리고 이것은 우리의 주의력 전체가 사용되지 않고 있을 때마다 우리가 느끼는 엄청난 양의 불쾌감에서 꽤 명백해진다. 이런 경우가 되면, 우리는 사용되지 않은 주의력의 배출구를 찾으려 할 것이다. 만약 우리가 더 약한 상대와 체스 게임을 하고 있다면, 우리는 이 활동을 또 다른 것, 즉 TV 시청이나 음악 감상, 또는 동시에 다른 체스 게임 하기와 같은 것으로 보충하려고 할 것이다. 이것은 자기 손안의 무언가를 가지고 놀거나 방을 돌아다니는 것과 같은 무의식적인 움직임들로 매우 자주 나타나며, 만약 그런 행동이 기쁨을 증가시키거나 불쾌감을 덜어주는 데에도 또한 도움이 된다면 더할 나위 없이 좋을 것이다.
① 우리가 잘하는 것으로 다른 사람을 기쁘게 해주려
② 주어진 일에 더욱더 집중하려
③ 사용되지 않은 주의력의 배출구를 찾으려
④ 더 강력한 상대와 게임을 하려
⑤ 우리 뇌에 짧은 휴식을 주려

주요 어휘 및 표현

utilize	활용하다	evident	명확한
displeasure	불쾌감	entirety	전체
supplement	보충하다	unconscious	무의식적인
pace	걷다	relieve	완화시키다

다. 실전 연습 문제

본문 50~53쪽

1. 정답 [⑤]

해석

한 문화가 다른 문화보다 나은지를 결정하는 방법을 알기는 어렵다. 록, 재즈, 고전 음악의 문화적인 순위는 어떻게 될까? 문화적 변화가 더 나아지는 것인지 더 나빠지는 것인지에 관한 여론 조사에 관한 한, 앞을 내다보는 것과 뒤돌아보는 것은 아주 다른 대답으로 이어진다. 우리 아이들은 조부모의 문화로 되돌아가야 한다는 말을 들으면 겁이 날 것이다. 우리 부모님은 손주의 문화에 참여해야 한다고 들으면 겁이 날 것이다. 인간은 자신이 자라고 익숙해진 것을 좋아하는 경향이 있다. 특정한 나이 이후에는 갑작스러운 문화적 변화가 다가오고 있을 때 불안감이 생긴다. 우리 문화는 우리의 정체성과 우리의 입지의 일부이고, 우리는 우리의 정체성과 우리의 입지가 오래가지 못한다고 생각하고 싶어 하지 않는다.

비법 적용

〈빈칸에서 묻는 말 파악하기〉
Humans tend to ________________________ .
☞ 인간의 특성(성향)에 대해 묻고 있다. 지문을 읽으면서 인간에 대한 설명에 주목하도록 한다.

It is difficult to know how to determine whether one culture is better than another. What is the cultural rank order of rock, jazz, and classical music? When it comes to public opinion polls about whether cultural changes are for the better or the worse, looking forward would lead to one answer and looking backward would lead to a very different answer.
☞ 어떤 문화가 더 좋은지, 즉 문화의 우열을 가리기가 어렵고 문화적 변화에 대한 여론 조사의 답 역시 다르다고 말하고 있다.

Our children would be horrified if they were told they had to go back to the culture of their grandparents. Our parents would be horrified if they were told they had to participate in the culture of their grandchildren.

☞ 아이들에게 조부모의 세대로 돌아가라고 하거나, 부모님에게 손주의 문화에 참여하라는 말에 사람들은 겁을 먹는다고 하였다. '우리 아이들(Our children)', '우리 부모님(Our parents)' 등은 빈칸에서 묻는 'humans'를 의미한다.

Humans tend to ______________________.

☞ 앞에서 언급된 사람들 즉, 아이들과 부모님의 공통점을 찾아 빈칸을 채우라는 의미이다.

After a certain age, anxieties arise when sudden cultural changes are coming. Our culture is part of who we are and where we stand, and we don't like to think that who we are and where we stand are short-lived.

☞ 특정 나이가 지나, 문화 변화가 생겨날 때 인간은 불안감을 느낀다고 하였다. 즉 우리의 문화는 우리의 입지의 일부이자 정체성이며, 우리의 인간들은 우리의 입지나 정체성이 짧아지는 것을 원치 않는다 말하고 있다. 여기서 'we'는 빈칸의 'humans'를 의미한다. 요컨대 인간은 변화를 싫어하고 문화를 자신의 일부로 여기기 때문에 그러한 문화가 변하는 것에 대해 불안해 한다는 내용으로 빈칸을 채워야 한다.

오답의 모든 것

① 세대 간의 협력을 필요로 한다

▶ 자녀, 조부모, 손주 등의 단어를 세대 간의 협력으로 잘못 생각할 수 있는 오답

② 그들이 경험한 것을 잊어버린다

▶ 그들의 경험을 잊어버리기보다는 오히려 변하지 않고 유지되기를 바란다는 의미이기 때문에 오답

③ 새로운 환경에 빠르게 적응한다

▶ 새로운 환경은 변화를 의미하며, 변화에 불안감을 느낀다고 하였기 때문에 오답

④ 조상들이 한 일을 기억하려고 노력한다

▶ 조상의 일을 기억하기보다는 자신의 문화에 더 익숙하기 때문에 오답

⑤ 자신이 자라고 익숙해진 것을 좋아한다

▶ 자라고 익숙해진 것은 인간이 처한 문화를 의미하며, 변화를 원치 않는다는 말이 내포되었기 때문에 정답

주요 어휘 및 표현

when it comes to	~에 대해 말하자면	public opinion polls	여론조사
be horrified	겁먹다, 두려워하다	cooperation	협력

2. 정답 [②]

해석

실리콘 밸리의 가장 혁신적인 회사들 중 한 회사의 최고 경영자는 지루하고 창의력을 해치는 판에 박힌 일처럼 보이는 것을 한다. 그는 일주일에 하루 오전 9시에 시작하는 세 시간짜리 회의를 연다. 그 회의에 빠지거나 다른 시간으로 일정이 변경되는 일은 결코 없다. 그것은 의무적인데 너무 그러하여 심지어 이 다국적 기업의 모든 경영자들은 그 회의와 시간이 겹치는 어떠한 이동 일정도 절대로 잡지 않아야 한다는 것을 알고 있다. 언뜻 보아, 이것에 대한 특별히 독특한 점은 없다. 그러나 정말로 독특한 것은 이 정기적인 회의들로부터 나오는 아이디어의 질이다. 최고경영자는 회의를 계획하거나 누가 회의에 참여하고 참여하지 않을지에 대해 생각하는 것과 관련된 정신적 비용을 없앴기 때문에, 사람들은 창의적인 문제 해결에 초점을 맞출 수 있다.

비법 적용

〈빈칸에서 묻는 말 파악하기〉

But what is unique is the quality of ideas that come out of ____________________.

☞ 역접의 연결사가 있으므로 단서는 주로 빈칸 문장의 뒤에 있음을 알 수 있다.

☞ 역접 뒤에서 독특한 점에 대해 언급하고 있는 것으로 보아 앞부분은 독특하지 않은 점에 대한 설명이 있었음을 예상할 수 있다.

☞ 빈칸 문장은 '아이디어(ideas)'를 수식하는 관계대명사절의 구조이다. 그러므로, '아이디어(ideas)가 어디에서 나오는지(come out of)'를 찾는 것이 이 문제의 핵심이다.

One CEO in one of Silicon Valley's most innovative companies has what would seem like a boring, creativitykilling routine.

☞ 실리콘 밸리의 가장 혁신적인 회사들 중 한 경영자가 사실 굉장히 따분한 판에 박힌 일처럼 보이는 일을 한다는 이야기로 시작하고 있다.

He holds a threehour meeting that starts at 9:00 A.M. one day a week. It is never missed or rescheduled at a different time. It is mandatory—so much so that even in this global firm all the executives know never to schedule any travel that will conflict with the meeting. At first glance there is nothing particularly unique about this.

☞ 앞에서 언급된 경영자의 판에 박힌 일처럼 보이는 것이 무엇인지 구체적으로 말해주고 있다. 정기적인 회의에 의무적으로 모든 경영자들이 참석하는 상황이 언급되어 있다.

But what is unique is the quality of ideas that come out of ____________________.

☞ 앞에서 경영자들이 매일 똑같은 일상을 반복하는 것이 얼핏 보기에는 특별하지 않다고 한 뒤에 빈칸 문장에서 역접의 연결사 'But'으로 연결하여 독특한 점이 무엇인지 묻고 있다.

Because the CEO has eliminated the mental cost involved in planning the meeting or thinking about who will or won't be there, people can focus on creative problem solving.

☞ '그 경영자(the CEO)'는 회의에 관련된 정신적 비용을 없애고 창의적 문제 해결에 집중할 수 있게 되었다고 말하고 있다. '창의적 문제 해결(creative problem solving)'은 빈칸 문장의 질 좋은 아이디어를 의미한다. 즉 질 좋은 아이디어는 정신적 비용을 없앴기 때문이고 정신적 비용이 없었던 이유는 정기적이고 의무적인 회의를 개최했기 때문이다.

오답의 모든 것

① 소비자 불만
▶ 소비자 불만에 대해 언급하지 않았으므로 오답

② 정기적 회의들
▶ 경영자들이 정해진 시간에 의무적인 회의를 통해 정신적 비용을 없앴다고 하였으므로 정답

③ 여행 경험
▶ 지문에 나온 'travel'은 실제 여행보다는 회의에 관련된 이동의 의미에 가까우므로 오답

④ 유연한 근무시간
▶ 유연한 근무시간이라기보다는 오히려 일요일에 의무적인 회의를 가졌다고 하였으므로 오답

⑤ 재정적 인센티브
▶ 재정적인 인센티브에 대해 언급하지 않았으므로 오답

주요 어휘 및 표현

mandatory	의무적인	firm	회사
executive	경영진	at first glance	첫 눈에

3. 정답 [①]

해석

현대의 불교 스승인 Dainin Katagiri는 죽음을 앞두고, '침묵으로의 회귀'라는 주목할 만한 책을 집필했다. 그는 삶이란 "위험한 상황이다."라고 썼다. 삶을 소중하게 만드는 것은 바로 삶의 취약함이며, 그의 글은 자신의 삶이 끝나가고 있다는 바로 그 사실로 채워져 있다. "자기 그릇은 언젠가 깨질 것이기 때문에 아름답다…. 그 그릇의 생명은 늘 위험한 상황에 놓여 있다." 그런 것이 우리의 고행이다. 이 불안정한 아름다움. 이 피할 수 없는 상처. 우리는 사랑과 상실이 친밀한 동반자라는 것을, 우리가 진짜 꽃을 플라스틱 꽃보다 훨씬 더 사랑하고 산 중턱을 가로지르는 한 순간만 지속하는 황혼의 색조를 사랑한다는 것을 잊어버린다(그것도 너무나 쉽게). 우리의 마음을 여는 것은 바로 이 연약함이다.

비법 적용

〈빈칸에서 묻는 말 파악하기〉
It is this very ______________ that opens our hearts.
☞ 우리의 마음을 여는 것이 무엇인지를 'it ~ that' 강조 구문을 통해 묻고 있다.

When he was dying, the contemporary Buddhist teacher Dainin Katagiri wrote a remarkable book called Returning to Silence. Life, he wrote, "is a dangerous situation." It is the weakness of life that makes it precious; his words are filled with the very fact of his own life passing away.

☞ 죽음을 앞둔 Dainin Katagiri라는 승려의 책에 쓰인 말을 소개하고 있다.
☞ '위험한 상황(a dangerous situation)', '취약함(the weakness of life)' 등의 표현을 통해 인간이 죽는다는 사실이 바로 삶의 취약함이며, 그것이 우리의 삶을 소중하게 만들어준다는 점을 알 수 있다.

"The china bowl is beautiful because sooner or later it will break.... The life of the bowl is always existing in a dangerous situation."
☞ 인생이 위험하다는 첫 문장과 자기 그릇의 생명이 늘 위험하다는 점을 통해, '자기 그릇(The china bowl)'은 문맥상 '인생(life)'을 빗대는 말이며, 이것이 깨진다는 것은 인간의 죽음을 비유하는 말임을 알 수 있다.

Such is our struggle: this unstable beauty. This inevitable wound. We forget—how easily we forget—that love and loss are intimate companions, that we love the real flower so much more than the plastic one and love the cast of twilight across a mountainside lasting only a moment.
☞ 우리의 삶을 '불안정한 아름다움(unstable beauty)', '피할 수 없는 상처(inevitable wound)'등에 비유하고 있다. '진짜 꽃(the real flower)', '한순간만 지속하는 황혼의 색조(the cast of twilight lasting only a moment)'등은 '자기 그릇'과 우리의 인생처럼 오래 지속되지 않는다는 공통점이 있다.

It is this very ________________ that opens our hearts.
☞ 우리의 맘을 연다는 것은 우리가 좋아한다는 것을 의미한다. 또한 앞에서 플라스틱 꽃보다 진짜 꽃과 한순간만 지속하는 황혼의 색조를 좋아한다고 하였는데, 이들의 공통점은 모두 '사라지는 것, 불안정한 것', '취약함'이라고이라고 볼 수 있다.

오답의 모든 것

① 연약함
▶ **글에서 반복적으로 등장한 'dangerous situation', 'weakness', 'passing away', 'break', 'unstable', 'lasting only a moment'과 같은 키워드와 유사한 의미이므로 정답**

② 안정감
▶ 불안정하고 일시적인 것에서 아름다움을 느낀다고 했으므로 반대의 의미이기 때문에 오답

③ 조화
▶조화에 대해 언급되지 않았으므로 오답

④ 만족
▶ 만족에 대해 언급되지 않았으므로 오답

⑤ 다양성
▶ 다양성에 대해 언급되지 않았으므로 오답

주요 어휘 및 표현

contemporary	현대의	remarkable	놀랄만한
pass away	죽다	sooner or later	머지않아
inevitable	피할 수 없는	intimate	친밀한

4. 정답 [④]

해석

사회학자들은 사람들이 그들 자신의 관점이나 가치를 그들이 직면하는 문화로 가져온다는 것을 입증해 왔다. 책, TV 프로그램, 영화, 그리고 음악은 모두에게 영향을 줄지도 모르지만, 그것들은 다양한 사람들에게 다른 방식으로 영향을 준다. 한 연구에서, Neil Vidmar와 Milton Rokeach는 인종에 관한 다양한 관점을 가진 시청자들에게 시트콤 All in the Family의 에피소드들을 보여주었다. 이 쇼는 자주 그의 더 진보적인 가족 구성원들과 싸움에 휘말리는 편협한 고집쟁이 Archie Bunker라는 인물에 초점을 맞춘다. Vidmar와 Rokeach는 Archie Bunker의 관점을 공유하지 않는 시청자들이 Archie의 어처구니없는 인종 차별주의를 비웃는 방식에 있어 그 쇼가 아주 재미있다고 생각했다는 것을 발견했다–사실, 이것이 제작자의 의도였다. 그러나 반면에, 스스로가 고집쟁이인 시청자들은 Archie Bunker가 그 쇼의 영웅이라고 생각했고, 제작자가 Bunker의 어리석은 가족들을 비웃으려고 한다고 생각했다! 이것이 특정 문화적 산물이 모든 사람에게 똑같은 영향을 줄 것이라고 가정하는 것이 잘못인 이유를 보여준다.

비법 적용

〈빈칸에서 묻는 말 파악하기〉

This demonstrates why it's a mistake to assume that a certain cultural product ____________.

☞ '특정한 문화적 산물(a certain cultural product)'에 대해 묻고 있다. 단, 빈칸 문장과 같이 생각하는 것이 실수라고 하였으므로 실제 필자의 주장과 반대되는 내용이 빈칸에 들어가야 한다.

Sociologists have proven that people bring their own views and values to the culture they encounter; books, TV programs, movies, and music may affect everyone, but they affect different people in different ways.

☞ 사람들이 그들 자신의 관점이나 가치를 그들이 마주하는 '문화(the culture)'로 가져온다는 글이다. 문화는 다양한 사람들에게 다양한 영향을 미친다고 하였다. 이 문장의 뒤에서 구체적인 연구 사례가 나오고 있으므로, 이 문장은 주제문에 해당한다고 볼 수 있다.

In a study, Neil Vidmar and Milton Rokeach showed episodes of the sitcom All in the Family to viewers with a range of different views on race. The show centers on a character named Archie Bunker, an intolerant bigot who often gets into fights with his more progressive family members. Vidmar and Rokeach found that viewers who didn't share Archie Bunker's views thought the show was very funny in the way it made fun of Archie's absurd racism–in fact, this was the producers' intention. On the other hand, though, viewers who were themselves bigots thought Archie Bunker was the hero of the show and that the producers meant to make fun of his foolish family!

☞ '연구(a study)'는 주제를 뒷받침하는 하나의 사례이다. 따라서 사람들이 자신이 마주한 문화에 자신만의 관점과 가치를 부여하며, 같은 문화라도 사람마다 다양한 영향을 받을 수 있다는 내용이라 볼 수 있다. 역접의 연결사를 통해 서로 다른 영향을 받은 사람들을 예를 구체적으로 보여주고 있다.

This demonstrates why it's a mistake to assume that a certain cultural product ____________.

☞ 빈칸에 들어갈 말은 '문화적 산물'에 대한 설명으로 글 도입부에서 찾은 주제인 '문화는 다양한 사람들에게 다양한 영향을 준다'는 말이 들어가야 한다. 단, '실수(a mistake)'라는 표현이 있으므로, 주제의 반대인 '사람들에게 동일한 영향을 준다'는 내용의 선택지를 고르면 된다.

오답의 모든 것

① 많은 가치 있는 견해를 제공할 수 있다고
▶ 첫 문장의 'views'를 이용한 매력적인 오답

② 사회학자의 아이디어를 반영한다고
▶ 사회학자들이 입증했다는 첫 문장의 표현을 활용한 오답

③ 특정한 캐릭터들에게 선입견을 형성한다고
▶ 예시에 있던 인종 문제를 이용한 매력적인 오답

④ 모두에게 똑같은 영향을 줄 것이라고
▶ 주제의 반대 의미이지만, 'a mistkae'와 함께 결합하여 바르게 쓰인 정답

⑤ 사람들 사이의 사회적 갈등을 해결할 것이라
▶ 예시에 있던 다른 반응의 사람들을 이용한 오답

주요 어휘 및 표현

sociologist	사회학자	encounter	마주치다
absurd	터무니없는	intention	의도
demonstrate	보여주다, 설명하다	assume	가정하다, 추정하다

라. 고난도 실전 문제

본문 54~55쪽

1. 정답 [①]

해석

인간 본성의 두드러지는 정서적 특징은 동료 인간들을 주의 깊게 지켜보고 그들의 이야기를 알게 되어, 그것으로 그들의 인격과 신뢰 가능성을 판단하는 것이다. 그리고 홍적세 이후 계속 그래 왔다. 인간 속[인류]으로 분류할 수 있는 첫 번째 무리와 그들의 후손은 수렵 채집인이었다. 오늘날의 칼라하리 사막의 Ju/'hoansi 부족과 같이, 그들은 그저 하루하루 생존하기 위해 잘 발달된 협력 행위에 의존했던 것이 거의 확실하다. 그 결과 그것은 무리 속 동료 각자의 개인사와 개인적 성과에 대한 정확한 지식을 필요로 했고 마찬가지로 그들은 다른 사람들의 감정과 성향에 대한 공감 감각을 가질 필요가 있었다. 동료가 말하는 이야기가 불러일으키는 감정을 알게 될 뿐만 아니라 공유하게 되는 것은 깊은 만족감을 주는데, 원한다면 이를 인간의 본능이라고 부를 수 있다. 이러한 행위 전체는 생존과 번식에 이익이 된다. 남 이야기와 스토리텔링은 다윈적인(진화적으로 의미 있는) 현상이다.

비법 적용

〈빈칸에서 묻는 말 파악하기〉

__________________ are Darwinian phenomena.

☞ 글에서 말하는 다윈적인(진화적 의미가 있는) 현상이 무엇인지 묻는 문제이다.

☞ 다윈이라는 단어를 통해 인간의 진화에 관련된 내용들을 예상해 볼 수 있다.

A distinct emotional trait of human nature is to watch fellow humans closely, to learn their stories, and thereby to judge their character and dependability.

☞ '인간 본성의 두드러지는 정서적 특징(A distinct emotional trait of human nature)'에 관해 언급하고 있다. 인간은 관찰과 이야기를 통해 서로의 인격과 신뢰도를 판단한다는 것이 그 특징이다.

And so it has ever been since the Pleistocene. The first bands classifiable to the genus Homo and their descendants were huntergatherers. Like the Kalahari Ju/'hoansi of today, they almost certainly depended on sophisticated cooperative behavior just to survive from one day to the next. That, in turn, required exact knowledge of the personal history and accomplishments of each of their groupmates, and equally they needed an empathetic sense of the feelings and propensities of others.

☞ 인류 최초의 무리들이 생존을 위해 협력에 의존했고 그 결과(in turn) 서로에 대해 잘 알고 공감능력이 필요했다고 말하고 있다. 직접적인 언급은 없지만 인류의 기원을 말하고 있으므로 빈칸에서 언급한 다윈의 진화론과 관련이 있는 부분이다.

It gives deep satisfaction—call it, if you will, a human instinct—not just to learn but also to share emotions stirred by the stories told by our companions. The whole of these performances pays off in survival and reproduction.

☞ '인간의 본능(a human instinct)'은 타고나는 것이며, '생존과 번식에 유리(pays off in survival and reproduction)하도록 진화'하는 것이 일반적인 다윈의 진화론이다. 여기서 인간의 본능은 이야기를 통해 서로의 감정에 대해 잘 알고 이를 공유하는데서 오는 만족을 의미한다.

__________________ are Darwinian phenomena.

☞ 진화에 관련한 현상은 앞에서 말한 인간의 본능, 첫 문장에 언급된 이야기를 공유하면서 공감하는 것들을 의미한다.

오답의 모든 것

① 남 이야기와 스토리텔링

▶ **인간의 본능(본질)은 이야기를 공유하고 공감하는 것이며, 이것이 생존과 번식에 도움이 되었다고 하였으므로 정답**

② 계획과 실행

▶ 계획하고 연습하는 것에 대해 언급된 적이 없으므로 오답

③ 실행과 수정

▶ 실행하고 수정하는 것에 대해 언급된 적이 없으므로 오답

④ 보여주기와 질투

▶ 보여주기와 질투에 대해 언급된 적이 없으므로 오답

⑤ 경쟁과 보상

▶ 경쟁과 보상에 대해 언급된 적이 없으므로 오답

주요 어휘 및 표현

distinct	두드러진	fellow	동료
dependability	신뢰도	classifiable	분류 가능한
genus	(생물 분류상의) 속	descendant	후손
hunter-gatherer	수렵채집가	sophisticated	정교한
empathetic	감정 이입의	propensities	경향성
reproduction	번식	pay off	도움(이익)이 되다

2. 정답 [④]

해석

프로토피아는 목적지라기보다는 생성의 상태이다. 그것은 과정이다. 프로토피아적인 방식에서는 어제보다 오늘, 비록 그저 약간 더 나아졌을 뿐이라도, 상황이 더 낫다. 그것은 점진적인 개선이나 가벼운 진보이다. 프로토피아적이라는 말에서 '프로'는 과정과 진보라는 개념에서 비롯된다. 이 미묘한 진보는 극적이지도 않고 자극적이지도 않다. 프로토피아는 거의 새로운 이점만큼 많은 새로운 문제를 발생시키기 때문에 그것을 놓치기 쉽다. 오늘의 문제는 어제의 기술적 성공이 가져온 것이고, 오늘의 문제에 대한 기술적 해결책은 내일의 문제를 유발할 것이다. 문제와 해결책의 이런 순환적 팽창은 시간이 지남에 따라 작은 순이익의 꾸준한 축적을 보이지 않게 한다. 계몽주의와 과학의 발명 이래로 줄곧, 우리는 매년 파괴해 온 것보다 조금 더 많은 것을 만들어냈다. 그러나 그 작은 몇 퍼센트의 긍정적인 차이는 수십 년에 걸쳐 우리가 문명이라고 부를 수 있는 것으로 조합된다. 그것의 장점은 영화에서 주연을 맡아 돋보이는 법이 없다.

비법 적용

〈빈칸에서 묻는 말 파악하기〉

This circular expansion of both problems and solutions ________________.

☞ 문제와 해결책의 순환적 팽창에 대한 설명을 묻는 문제이다.

☞ 'This'라는 지시사를 통해 '문제와 해결책의 순환적 팽창(circular expansion of both problems and solutions)'은 앞에서 나온 개념이며, 이에 대한 답의 근거는 주로 뒤에 있음을 예상할 수 있다.

Protopia is a state of becoming, rather than a destination. It is a process. In the protopian mode, things are better today than they were yesterday, although only a little better. It is incremental improvement or mild progress. The "pro" in protopian stems from the notions of process and progress.

☞ '프로토피아(Protopia)'의 정의를 '생성(becoming)', '과정(a process)', '점진적인 개선이나 가벼운 진보(incremental improvement or mild progress)'라고 소개하고 있다.

This subtle progress is not dramatic, not exciting. It is easy to miss because a protopia generates almost as many new problems as new benefits.

☞ 앞에서 말한 프로토피아의 점진적인 발전에 대해 '미묘한(subtle)', '극적이지 않은(not dramatic)', '놓치기 쉬운(easy to miss)' 등으로 반복해서 표현하고 있다.

The problems of today were caused by yesterday's technological successes, and the technological solutions to today's problems will cause the problems of tomorrow.
☞ 빈칸에서 묻는 '문제와 해결책의 순환적 팽창(circular expansion of both problems and solutions)'의 개념이 언급되었다.

This circular expansion of both problems and solutions ________________.
☞ '문제와 해결책의 순환적 팽창(circular expansion of both problems and solutions)'의 개념이 앞에서 소개되었고 이것에 대한 설명은 빈칸 뒤에서 찾아야 한다.

Ever since the Enlightenment and the invention of science, we've managed to create a tiny bit more than we've destroyed each year. But that few percent positive difference is compounded over decades into what we might call civilization. Its benefits never star in movies.
☞ 계속해서 우리의 발전은 '크지 않다, 작은 차이가 쌓여 조합된 것이다, 돋보이지 않는다, 놓치기 쉽다' 등으로 표현하고 있다. 따라서 빈칸에 들어갈 내용은 '문제와 해결책의 순환적 팽창(circular expansion of both problems and solutions)'으로 인해 우리의 발전이 '크게 돋보이지 않는다, 영화 주연처럼 두드러지지 않는다' 등의 말이 나와야 한다,

오답의 모든 것

① 현재의 혁신의 한계를 감춘다
▶ 어제의 성공이 오늘의 문제를 가져오고, 오늘의 문제에 대한 기술적 해결책은 내일의 문제를 유발한다는 표현을 이용한 오답

② 자신감을 가지고 미래를 예견하기 어렵게 한다
▶ 문제와 해결책이 반복된다는 점을 이용한 오답

③ 프로토피아 문명을 빠르게 성취하도록 동기를 부여한다
▶ 문명을 빠르게 성취하도록 하기보다는 오히려 점진적으로 미묘한 변화라 하였으므로 오답

④ 시간이 지남에 따라 작은 순이익의 꾸준한 축적을 보이지 않게 한다
▶ **과거와 오늘, 그리고 내일의 문제와 해결이 반복되어 꾸준히 발전했음에도 불구하고 그러한 발전이 미묘하여 영화 주연처럼 돋보이지 않는다고 하였으므로 정답**

⑤ 기술적인 성공에 큰 변화를 만든다
▶ 여러 문제들로 인해 기술적인 성공이 오히려 크지 않다고 볼수 있으므로 오답

주요 어휘 및 표현

incremental	점진적인	circular	선형의
expansion	팽창	the Enlightenment	개화기
compound	혼합시키다	conceal	숨기다
net	순(純)	star in	주연을 맡다

2. 무관한 문장

가. 비법 연습 문제 ······ 본문 57쪽

정답 무관한 문장 (②) - 근거 (b)

나. 기출 연습 문제 ······ 본문 57쪽

정답 [④]

해석

2006년에, 조사에 응한 미국 쇼핑객의 81%가 구매를 계획할 때 온라인 고객 평점과 후기를 중요하게 고려한다고 말했다. 온라인 평가는 긍정적인 것이든 부정적인 것이든 사람 간의 직접적인 의견 교환만큼 강력하지는 않지만, 사업에 매우 중요할 수 있다. ① 많은 사람이 온라인 추천에 의존한다. ② 그리고 젊은 사람들은 그것에 크게 의존하고, 어떤 영화를 볼지, 혹은 어떤 앨범을 살 것인지를 결정할 때 인터넷에 의해 영향을 받을 가능성이 크다. ③ 이 사람들은 흔히 폭넓은 인간관계망을 보유하고 있으며, 수십 명의 다른 사람들과 정기적으로 소통하는데, 수천 명에 영향을 미칠 잠재력이 있다. ④ 전문가들은 젊은 사람들이 불필요한 것에 돈을 낭비하기를 그만두고 저축을 시작해야 한다고 권한다. ⑤ 6세에서 24세의 젊은 사람들이 미국 전체 지출의 약 50%에 영향을 미치는 것으로 보고되었다.

주요 어휘 및 표현

survey	조사하다	rating	평점, 등급, 평가
review	후기, 논평, 비평	purchase	구매; 구매하다
positive	긍정적인	negative	부정적인
direct	직접적인	interpersonal	사람과 사람 사이의
exchange	의견 교환, 교환	depend on	~에 의존하다
recommendation	추천	heavily	크게, 몹시
individual	사람, 개인	widereaching	폭넓은, 광범위한
regularly	정기적으로	dozens of	수십 명[개]의
potential	잠재력	reach	영향을 미치다, 도달하다
waste	낭비하다	unnecessary	불필요한

다. 실전 연습 문제

본문 59~62쪽

1. 정답 [④]

해석

연사들은 연설하는 동안 청중에게 '귀 기울이기' 때문에 대중 연설은 청중 중심이다. 그들은 청중의 피드백, 즉 청중이 연사에게 주는 언어적, 비언어적 신호를 주시한다. ① 청중의 피드백은 흔히 청중들이 연사의 생각을 이해하고, 관심을 갖고, 받아들일 준비가 되었는지를 보여 준다. ② 이 피드백은 연사를 여러모로 도와준다. ③ 그것은 연사가 언제 속도를 늦출지, 언제 무언가를 더 주의해서 설명할지, 혹은 언제 연설의 끝에 있는 질의응답 시간에 어떤 주제로 되돌아 갈 것이라고 청중에게 말할지까지도 파악하는 데 도움이 된다. ④ 무대 불안을 줄이기 위해 연사가 자신의 원고를 암기하는 것이 중요하다. ⑤ 청중의 피드백은 연사가 청중과 존중하는 관계를 만드는 것을 도와준다.

비법 적용

Public speaking is audience centered because speakers "listen" to their audiences during speeches. They monitor audience feedback, the verbal and nonverbal signals an audience gives a speaker.

☞ 글의 주제 : 대중 연설은 청중의 피드백에 의존한다.
글의 핵심 소재 : public speaking, audience feedback

① Audience feedback often indicates whether listeners understand, have interest in, and are ready to accept the speaker's ideas.

☞ 핵심 소재인 '청중의 피드백'에 대한 구체적인 설명이 이어지고 있다.

② This feedback assists the speaker in many ways.

☞ '청중의 피드백'이라는 핵심 소재가 일관성을 유지하고 있다. 'in many ways'는 나열을 암시하며, 연설자에게 청중의 피드백이 어떤 방식으로 도움이 될지에 대한 설명이 뒤에 이어질 것이라 예상할 수 있다.

③ It helps the speaker know when to slow down, explain something more carefully, or even tell the audience that she or he will return to an issue in a questionandanswer session at the close of the speech.

☞ 대명사 'It'이 가리키는 것은 핵심 소재인 'audience feedback'를 가리키며, 앞에서 말한 'many ways'를 나열하고 있다.

④ It is important for the speaker to memorize his or her script to reduce on-stage anxiety.

☞ 비법 1, 2 오류) 'It'은 가주어로 to memorize 이하가 진주어이다. 핵심 소재가 빠져있으며 '무대 불안'이라는 흐름과 관계없는 소재가 등장하였다.

⑤ Audience feedback assists the speaker in creating a respectful connection with the audience.

☞ 핵심 소재인 '청중의 피드백'이 도움이 되는 상황을 계속해서 나열하고 있다.

오답의 모든 것

① Audience feedback often indicates whether listeners understand, have interest in, and are ready to accept the speaker's ideas.
▶ 핵심 소재가 주제에 맞게 서술되고 있는 오답

② This feedback assists the speaker in many ways.
▶ '청중의 피드백이 연설자에게 도움이 된다'는 것은 핵심 소재가 주제에 맞게 서술되고 있으므로 오답

③ It helps the speaker know when to slow down, explain something more carefully, or even tell the audience that she or he will return to an issue in a questionandanswer session at the close of the speech.
▶ 대명사 'It'으로 핵심 소재가 주제에 맞게 서술되고 있는 오답

④ It is important for the speaker to memorize his or her script to reduce onstage anxiety.
▶ 핵심 소재가 누락되어 있고 주제와도 관련 없는 무관한 문장이므로 정답

⑤ Audience feedback assists the speaker in creating a respectful connection with the audience.
▶ 청중의 피드백이 연설자에게 도움이 된다는 내용으로 핵심 소재가 주제에 맞게 서술되고 있는 오답

주요 어휘 및 표현

public speaking	대중 연설	audience	청중
monitor	주시하다	nonverbal	비언어적인
indicate	보여주다, 나타내다	accept	받아들이다
assist	돕다	question-and-answer session	질의응답 시간
memorize	암기하다	onstage anxiety	무대 불안
respectful	존중하는	connection	관계, 연결

2. 정답 [④]

해석

전자 통신에서 이모티콘이 널리 사용되고 있다는 점을 고려할 때, 중요한 문제는 인터넷 사용자들이 온라인상의 의사소통에서 감정을 이해하는데 그것들이 도움을 주는가의 여부이다. ① 이모티콘, 특히 문자에 기반한 것들은, 면대면을 통한 단서에 비해 훨씬 더 모호하며 결국 다른 사용자들에 의해 매우 다르게 해석될 수 있다. ② 그럼에도 불구하고, 연구는 그것들이 온라인상의 텍스트 기반 의사소통에서 유용한 도구라는 것을 보여준다. ③ 137명의 인스턴트 메시지(실시간 텍스트 통신) 사용자들을 대상으로 한 연구는 이모티콘이 사용자들로 하여금 감정, 태도, 주의력 표현의 정도와 방향을 정확하게 이해할 수 있게 해주고 이모티콘이 비언어적 의사소통에서 확실한 장점이라는 것을 밝혀냈다. ④ 사실, 언어적 의사소통과 비언어적 의사소통 간의 관계에 관한 연구는 거의 없었다. ⑤ 마찬가지로, 또 다른 연구는 이모티콘이 풍자의 표현에서 뿐만 아니라, 언어적 메시지의 강도를 강화하는 데 유용하다는 것을 보여주었다.

비법 적용

Given the widespread use of emoticons in electronic communication, an important question is whether they help Internet users to understand emotions in online communication.
☞ 글의 주제 : 이모티콘의 사용이 온라인 의사소통시 감정 이해에 도움이 되는가?
글의 핵심 소재 : emoticons, communition, to understand emotions

① Emoticons, particularly character-based ones, are much more ambiguous relative to face-to-face cues and may end up being interpreted very differently by different users.
☞ 핵심 소재인 'emoticons'이 다소 모호하고 사용자마다 다른 해석이 가능할 수도 있다는 설명이다.

② Nonetheless, research indicates that they are useful tools in online text-based communication.
☞ 'they'는 문맥상 이 글의 핵심 소재인 'emoticons'를 가리킨다. 앞에서 다소 애매하고 다양한 해석이 나올 수 있지만, 그럼에도 불구하고(nontheless) 온라인상의 텍스트 기반 소통에서 유용한 도구라고 말하고 있다.

③ One study of 137 instant messaging users revealed that emoticons allowed users to correctly understand the level and direction of emotion, attitude, and attention expression and that emoticons were a definite advantage in non-verbal communication.
☞ 핵심 소재인 '이모티콘'이 감정 이해에 도움이 된다는 긍정적 내용이 앞 문장에 이어 자연스럽게 연결되고 있다.

④ In fact, there have been few studies on the relationships between verbal and nonverbal communication.
☞ 비법 1, 2 오류) 핵심 소재가 누락되어 있고 '언어적, 비언어적 의사소통에 관한 연구'가 거의 없다는 주제와는 관련 없는 내용이 등장하고 있다.

⑤ Similarly, another study showed that emoticons were useful in strengthening the intensity of a verbal message, as well as in the expression of sarcasm.
☞ 핵심 소재인 이모티콘의 긍정적 측면이 ②, ③번에 이어 자연스럽게 이어지고 있으며, 연결사 'Similarly'와 함께 ③번에 소개된 연구 이외의 또 다른 연구를 언급하며 주제의 일관성을 보여주고 있다.

오답의 모든 것

① Emoticons, particularly character-based ones, are much more ambiguous relative to face-to-face cues and may end up being interpreted very differently by different users.
▶ 뒤 문장의 'Nonetheless'와 연결하지 못하고 자칫 이모티콘의 부정적 측면을 언급하고 있다고 잘못 생각하여 선택할 수 있는 오답

② Nonetheless, research indicates that they are useful tools in online text-based communication.
▶ 앞에서 이모티콘에 관한 해석이 다양할 수 있지만, 그럼에도 불구하고(Nonetheless) 유용한 도구라는 필자의 의도가 역접의 연결사로 자연스럽게 이어지고 있는 오답

③ One study of 137 instant messaging users revealed that emoticons allowed users to correctly understand the level and direction of emotion, attitude, and attention expression and that emoticons were a definite advantage in non-verbal communication.

▶ 이모티콘이 감정 이해에 도움이 되며, 비언어적 의사소통의 강점이 된다는 이 글의 주제를 구체적인 연구 사례를 통해 보여주는 오답

④ In fact, there have been few studies on the relationships between verbal and nonverbal communication.

▶ **핵심소재가 누락되어 있고 주제와 무관한 문장이므로 정답**

⑤ Similarly, another study showed that emoticons were useful in strengthening the intensity of a verbal message, as well as in the expression of sarcasm.

▶ 이모티콘이 언어적, 비언어적 메시지 전달에 유의미하다는 또 다른 연구 결과로 주제를 뒷받침하는 오답

주요 어휘 및 표현

given	~을 고려할 때	expression	표현
widespread	널리 퍼진, 광범위한	definite	확실한
character	문자, 부호	advantage	이점, 장점
ambiguous	모호한	verbal	언어적인
relative to ~	~에 비해	strengthen	강화하다
cue	단서, 신호	intensity	강도, 강렬함
end up ~ing	결국 ~이 되다	sarcasm	풍자
attitude	태도, 사고방식	expression	표현

3. 정답 [③]

해석

최초의 상업용 철도 서비스는 1830년 Liverpool과 Manchester 간 운행을 시작했다. 10년 후, 최초의 열차 운행 시간표가 발표되었다. 기차가 낡은 마차보다 훨씬 더 빨라서, 지역 시간의 고유한 차이는 심각한 골칫거리가 되었다. ① 1847년에 영국 철도 회사들은 머리를 맞대어 논의했고, 그 이후 모든 열차 운행 시간표를 Liverpool, Manchester 또는 Glasgow의 지역 시간 대신, Greenwich 천문대 시간에 맞춰 조정할 것에 동의했다. ② 점점 더 많은 기관들이 열차 회사들의 선례를 따랐다. ③ 철도 회사들은 역, 선로, 그리고 다른 시설과 관련된 문제와 같은 기간 시설 관련 문제에 직면했다. ④ 마침내, 1880년에 영국 정부는 영국의 모든 시간표가 Greenwich 시간을 따라야 한다는 것을 입법화하는 전례 없는 조치를 취했다. ⑤ 역사상 최초로, 한 국가가 국가 지정 시간을 채택하고 국민들이 지역 시간이나 일출 일몰 주기 대신에 인위적인 시간에 따라서 생활하도록 의무화했다.

비법 적용

The first commercial train service began operating between Liverpool and Manchester in 1830. Ten years later, the first train timetable was issued. The trains were much faster than the old carriages, so the peculiar differences in local hours became a severe nuisance.

☞ 글의 주제 : 철도 서비스에서의 통일된 시간의 필요성
글의 핵심 소재 : train, timetable, differences in local hours

① In 1847, British train companies put their heads together and agreed that henceforth all train timetables would be adjusted to Greenwich Observatory time, rather than the local times of Liverpool, Manchester, or Glasgow.

☞ 핵심 소재와 주제를 포함하고 있으며, 통일된 시간 문제 관한 해결책을 제시하고 있다.

② More and more institutions followed the lead of the train companies.

☞ '그 기차 회사들의 선례(the lead of the train companies)'는 앞 문장에 언급된 회사들의 내용을 의미한다

③ Railways faced infrastructure-related challenges such as those related to stations, tracks, and other facilities.

☞ 비법 1,2 오류) 'timetable'이라는 핵심 소재가 누락되어 있으며, '철도 시설 관련 문제'라는 무관한 주제가 등장하고 있다.

④ Finally, in 1880, the British government took the unprecedented step of legislating that all timetables in Britain must follow Greenwich.

☞ 영국 정부의 시간 차이를 해결하기 위한 입법화 과정을 설명하고 있다.

⑤ For the first time in history, a country adopted a national time and obliged its population to live according to an artificial clock rather than local ones or sunrisetosunset cycles.

☞ 영국의 '국가 지정 시간(a national time)'에 대해 앞 문장에 이어 자연스럽게 설명이 이어지고 있다.

오답의 모든 것

① In 1847, British train companies put their heads together and agreed that henceforth all train timetables would be adjusted to Greenwich Observatory time, rather than the local times of Liverpool, Manchester, or Glasgow.

▶ 철도 서비스에서 통일된 시간의 필요성을 해결하기 위한 과정을 시간 순서대로 설명하고 있는 오답

② More and more institutions followed the lead of the train companies.

▶ ①번에 언급된 철도 회사들 이후에 있었던 상황이 자연스럽게 이어지고 있으므로 오답

③ Railways faced infrastructurerelated challenges such as those related to stations, tracks, and other facilities.

▶ **철도 회사들의 시설 기반 문제라는 무관한 문장으로 '철도 회사들'이라는 단어를 이용한 매력적인 정답**

④ Finally, in 1880, the British government took the unprecedented step of legislating that all timetables in Britain must follow Greenwich.
▶ 통일된 시간 문제를 해결하는 과정이 시간적 순서대로 자연스럽게 이어지고 있는 오답

⑤ For the first time in history, a country adopted a national time and obliged its population to live according to an artificial clock rather than local ones or sunrisetosunset cycles.
▶ 'a country'가 ④번의 영국임을 알지 못하면 잘못 선택할 수 있는 오답

주요 어휘 및 표현

commercial	상업적인	lead	선례
operate	가동하다, 운행하다	observatory	천문대
timetable	시간표	unprecedented	전례 없는
carriage	마차	adopt	채택하다
peculiar	고유의, 독특한	legislate	입법화하다
nuisance	골칫거리	oblige	의무를 지우다
adjust	조정하다	artificial	인위적인, 인공의
henceforth	그 이후	sunrise-to-sunset cycles	일출 일몰 주기

4. 정답 [③]

해석

마케팅 경영은 수요를 찾고 증가시키는 것뿐만 아니라 그것을 바꾸고 또는 심지어 줄이는 것과도 관련이 있다. 예를 들어, Uluru (Ayers Rock)에는 그것을 등반하기를 원하는 너무 많은 관광객이 있을지도 모르고, 그리고 North Queensland의 Daintree 국립공원은 관광 시즌에 과도하게 붐비게 될 수 있다. ① 전력 회사들은 때때로 최고 사용기간 동안 수요를 충족시키는 데 어려움이 있다. ② 과도한 수요의 이러한 그리고 다른 경우들에서, 필요로 되어지는 반 마케팅이라고 불리는 마케팅 과업은 일시적으로 혹은 영구적으로 수요를 줄이는 것이다. ③ 공급의 증가에 의해 유발된 손실들을 보상하기 위해서 노력해야 한다. ④ 반 마케팅의 목적은 수요를 완전히 없애는 것이 아니라, 단지 그것을 줄이거나 또는 다른 시기 또는 심지어 다른 제품으로 이동시키는 것이다. ⑤ 따라서, 마케팅 경영은 조직이 그것의 목표들을 달성하는 것을 돕는 방식으로 수요의 수준, 시기, 그리고 특성에 영향을 주는 것을 추구한다.

비법 적용

Marketing management is concerned not only with finding and increasing demand but also with changing or even reducing it. For example, Uluru (Ayers Rock) might have too many tourists wanting to climb it, and Daintree National Park in North Queensland can become overcrowded in the tourist season.
☞ 글의 주제 : 마케팅 경영은 수요의 변화 혹은 감소와도 관련이 있다.
글의 핵심 소재 : Marketing management, demand

① Power companies sometimes have trouble meeting demand during peak usage periods.
☞ 앞에서 말한 '수요(demand)'가 많은 상황에서는 전기 회사들이 수요를 충족하기 힘들다고 말하고 있다.

② In these and other cases of excess demand, the needed marketing task, called demarketing, is to reduce demand temporarily or permanently.
☞ '과도한 수요(excess demand)'는 앞내용의 '최고 사용 기간(peak usage periods)' 중의 수요를 의미하며, 이 기간 동안 수요를 감소시키는 마케팅 경영의 예시로 '반 마케팅(demarketing)'에 대해 소개하고 있다.

③ Efforts should be made to compensate for the losses caused by the increase in supply.
☞ 비법 1, 2 오류) 핵심 소재가 없으며, '공급(supply)'이라는 주제와 무관한 내용이 이어지고 있다.

④ The aim of demarketing is not to completely destroy demand, but only to reduce or shift it to another time, or even another product.
☞ 핵심 소재인 'demand'와 ③번의 '반마케팅(demarketing)'의 목적에 대한 설명이 다시 이어지고 있다.

⑤ Thus, marketing management seeks to affect the level, timing, and nature of demand in a way that helps the organisation achieve its objectives.
☞ '마케팅 경영(marketing management)'이 '수요(demand)'의 수준, 시기 등에 영향을 준다는 내용으로 처음에 언급했던 글의 주제를 다시 한번 진술하고 있다.

오답의 모든 것

① Power companies sometimes have trouble meeting demand during peak usage periods.
▶ 앞에서 언급된 수요가 많은 사례들 뒤에서 그러한 상황에서 수요를 충족하기 힘든 곳이 있다는 내용이 자연스러우므로 오답

② In these and other cases of excess demand, the needed marketing task, called demarketing, is to reduce demand temporarily or permanently.
▶ 'these+명사'의 표현으로 '과도한 수요'에 대한 앞 내용에 이어 자연스럽게 이어지므로 오답

③ Efforts should be made to compensate for the losses caused by the increase in supply.
▶ 공급 증가로 인한 손실을 보상하기 위한 노력은 핵심 소재 및 주제와 무관하므로 정답

④ The aim of demarketing is not to completely destroy demand, but only to reduce or shift it to another time, or even another product.
▶ 수요를 감소시킨다는 'demarketing'의 목표가 주제와 전체 흐름에 맞게 자연스럽게 이어지므로 오답

⑤ Thus, marketing management seeks to affect the level, timing, and nature of demand in a way that helps the organisation achieve its objectives.
▶ 연결사 'Thus'로 글 전체의 주제를 다시 한 번 강조 및 정리하고 있으므로 오답

주요 어휘 및 표현

demand	수요	completely	완전히
overcrowded	너무 붐비는	destroy	파괴하다, 없애다
peak	절정, 최고점	affect	영향을 주다
excess	과도, 초과	achieve	이루다, 달성하다
temporarily	임시로	objective	목표
permanently	영구적으로	organisation	조직

라. 고난도 실전 문제

본문 63~64쪽

1. 정답 [④]

해석

개가 마약, 폭발물, 밀수품, 혹은 다른 품목들을 탐지하도록 훈련받을 때, 조련사는 사실 개에게 냄새 맡는 법을 가르치지 않는데, 개는 이미 한 냄새를 다른 냄새와 구별하는 법을 알고 있기 때문이다. 오히려 개는 다른 냄새와 대조하여 한 냄새에 의해 감정적으로 자극을 받도록 훈련된다. ① 단계적 훈련 과정에서, 조련사는 어느 특정한 냄새에 '정서적 감흥'을 부여하며, 그래서 개는 다른 모든 냄새에 우선하여 그 냄새에 이끌린다. ② 그런 다음, 그 개는 조련사가 개의 행동을 통제하거나 발산시킬 수 있도록 신호에 따라 바라는 품목을 찾아내도록 훈련된다. ③ 이러한 정서적 자극은 또한 개와 당기기 놀이를 하는 것이 단지 개에게 맛있는 특별한 먹이를 주는 것보다 훈련 체계에서 더욱 강력한 정서적 보상이 되는 이유이기도 한데, 왜냐하면 조련사가 당기기 게임에 더 많은 감정을 투입하기 때문이다. ④ 조련사가 정기적으로 개에게 먹이를 주는 한, 개는 자신의 '좋은' 행동이 보상을 초래한다는 것을 이해할 수 있다. ⑤ 개의 관점에서 그 당기기 장난감은 조련사가 그 장난감에 의해 '흥분하기' 때문에 흥미진진하다.

비법 적용

When a dog is trained to detect drugs, explosives, contraband, or other items, the trainer doesn't actually teach the dog how to smell; the dog already knows how to discriminate one scent from another. Rather, the dog is trained to become emotionally aroused by one smell versus another.
☞ 글의 주제 : 정서적 자극을 이용한 탐지견 훈련
글의 핵심 소재 : dog, trained, emotionally

① In the step-by-step training process, the trainer attaches an "emotional charge" to a particular scent so that the dog is drawn to it above all others.

☞ '정서적 감흥(emotional charge)을 이용한 개의 훈련 과정(training process)'이라는 핵심 소재가 앞 문장과 자연스럽게 이어지고 있다.

② And then the dog is trained to search out the desired item on cue, so that the trainer can control or release the behavior.
☞ 앞 문장에 이어 정서적 감흥을 이용한 개 훈련에 관한 설명이 계속되고 있다.

③ This emotional arousal is also why playing tug with a dog is a more powerful emotional reward in a training regime than just giving a dog a food treat, since the trainer invests more emotion into a game of tug.
☞ 정서적 감흥에 대한 추가적 설명이 이어지고 있다. 'This emotional arousal'과 'emotional reward'와 같은 감정적 자극을 통한 훈련이라는 핵심 소재에 대한 설명이다.

④ As long as the trainer gives the dog a food reward regularly, the dog can understand its "good" behavior results in rewards.
☞ 비법 2 오류) 개 훈련이라는 핵심 소재는 등장하지만, '먹이'라는 보상은 ③번에 등장하는 단어를 활용한 무관한 문장이다.

⑤ From a dog's point of view, the tug toy is compelling because the trainer is "upset" by the toy.
☞ ③번에 언급된 감정적 보상인 '당기기 장난감(the tug toy)'에 대한 설명이 다시 이어지고 있다. 'compelling', 'upset'은 감정과 관련된 표현들이다.

오답의 모든 것

① In the step-by-step training process, the trainer attaches an "emotional charge" to a particular scent so that the dog is drawn to it above all others.
▶ 핵심 소재와 주제가 앞내용과 일관되게 유지되고 있으므로 오답

② And then the dog is trained to search out the desired item on cue, so that the trainer can control or release the behavior.
▶ 감정을 이용한 훈련과정으로 'and then'을 이용하여 앞 문장에 이어지는 훈련 단계를 의미하므로 오답

③ This emotional arousal is also why playing tug with a dog is a more powerful emotional reward in a training regime than just giving a dog a food treat, since the trainer invests more emotion into a game of tug.
▶ 'playing tug with dog'은 개와의 감정적인 자극을 하는 훈련 과정인 동시에 주제와 연관된 표현이므로 오답

④ As long as the trainer gives the dog a food reward regularly, the dog can understand its "good" behavior results in rewards.
▶ 개의 먹이, 보상이라는 핵심 소재가 누락되고 주제를 벗어난 내용이므로 정답

⑤ From a dog's point of view, the tug toy is compelling because the trainer is "upset" by the toy.
▶ '당기기 장난감(tug toy)'이라는 감정적 보상에 대한 설명으로 ③번에 이어지는 자연스러운 내용이므로 오답

주요 어휘 및 표현

detect	탐지하다, 찾다	explosive	폭발물
discriminate	구별하다	scent	냄새
arouse	자극하다, 각성시키다	emotional charge	정서적 감흥
be drawn to	~에 끌리다	search out	~을 찾아내다
on cue	신호에 따라	release	발산하다, 해방시키다
arousal	자극, 흥분	regime	관리 체계
treat	특별한(아주 좋은) 것	invest	투입하다, 쏟다
point of view	관점	upset	흥분한, 화가 난

2. 정답 [③]

해석

미국처럼 고도로 상업화된 환경에서는 많은 경관이 상품으로 여겨지는 것이 놀라운 일이 아니다. 다시 말해 경관은 그것들의 시장 잠재력 때문에 가치 있게 여겨진다. 주민들은 경관이 지역 사회를 위해 어떻게 소득을 창출할 수 있는가에 부분적으로 기초하여 정체성을 발전시킨다. ① 이 과정에는 자연의 요소를 상품으로 전환하는 것 그 이상의 것이 포함된다. ② 사람들과 그들의 자아의식을 포함하여 경관 자체가 상품의 형태를 띤다. ③ 미국에서 경관 보호는 일반적으로 산악지대에 있는 황무지 지역을 보호하는 데 전통적으로 초점을 두고 있다. ④ 시간이 흐르면서 경관 정체성은 경관에 대한 이야기를 판매하기 위해 사용될 수 있는 일종의 '로고'로 발전할 수 있다. ⑤ 따라서 California의 'Wine Country(포도주의 고장)', Florida의 'Sun Coast(태양의 해변)', 혹은 South Dakota의 'Badlands(악지)'는 외지인과 거주자가 모두 장소를 인식하는 방식을 형성하며, 이런 호칭들은 그곳에 사는 사람들의 문화와 관련된 일련의 기대치를 형성한다.

비법 적용

In a highly commercialized setting such as the United States, it is not surprising that many landscapes are seen as commodities. In other words, they are valued because of their market potential. Residents develop an identity in part based on how the landscape can generate income for the community.

☞ 글의 주제 : 시장 상품으로서의 가치를 지닌 경관

글의 핵심 소재 : landscapes, commodities, market potential, income for the community

① This process involves more than the conversion of the natural elements into commodities.

☞ '이 과정(This process)'은 자연 요소를 상품화하는 그 이상의 것과 관련이 있다고 말하고 있다. 바로 앞내용인 '경관이 지역 사회를 위해 소득을 창출'하는 과정에 대한 부연 설명이다.

② The landscape itself, including the people and their sense of self, takes on the form of a commodity.
☞ 경관의 상품화라는 핵심 소재가 주제와 일관성을 유지하고 있다.

③ Landscape protection in the US traditionally focuses on protecting areas of wilderness, typically in mountainous regions.
☞ 비법 2 오류) 주제와 무관한 '경관 보호'에 관한 내용으로 흐름에서 벗어난다.

④ Over time, the landscape identity can evolve into a sort of " logo" that can be used to sell the stories of the landscape.
☞ '경관 정체성(landscape identity)'이 일종의 'logo' 즉, 상품화된다는 설명은 주제와 일치한다.

⑤ Thus, California's "Wine Country," Florida's "Sun Coast," or South Dakota's "Badlands" shape how both outsiders and residents perceive a place, and these labels build a set of expectations associated with the culture of those who live there.
☞ '외지인과 거주자가 장소를 인식하는 방식(how both outsiders and residents perceive a place)'은 앞 문장의 '경관 정체성(the landscape identity)'을 의미한다. 이에 대한 구체적 사례를 언급하면서 '경관을 상품'으로 여긴다는 일관된 주제를 확인할 수 있다.

오답의 모든 것

① This process involves more than the conversion of the natural elements into commodities.
▶ 'This process'와 앞 문장의 내용이 문맥상 자연스럽게 이어지고 있으므로 오답

② The landscape itself, including the people and their sense of self, takes on the form of a commodity.
▶ 경관 자체가 상품이라는 주제가 일관성을 보이고 있으므로 오답

③ Landscape protection in the US traditionally focuses on protecting areas of wilderness, typically in mountainous regions.
▶ **경관을 보호한다는 것은 주제와 무관한 설명이므로 정답**

④ Over time, the landscape identity can evolve into a sort of "logo" that can be used to sell the stories of the landscape.
▶ ②번의 내용을 '경관 정체성(the landscape identity)'으로 표현하여 주제와 일치하고 있으므로 오답

⑤ Thus, California's "Wine Country," Florida's "Sun Coast," or South Dakota's "Badlands" shape how both outsiders and residents perceive a place, and these labels build a set of expectations associated with the culture of those who live there.
▶ '경관 정체성'을 예시와 함께 다시 한번 주제와 밀접하게 연관시키고 있으므로 오답

주요 어휘 및 표현

commercialized	상업화된	commodity	상품, 일용품
identity	정체성	generate	창출하다, 만들어 내다
conversion	전환, 변환	wilderness	황무지
mountainous region	산악 지대	evolve	발전하다, 진화하다
perceive	인식하다	associated with ~	~와 관련된

III 글의 흐름상 적합한 표현 관련 독해 유형

1. 어휘

가. 비법 연습 문제

본문 69쪽

정답

1. ① Distance (인과)
② changing (병렬)
③ weakness (역접)

해석

① 만약 당신이 계층에 대한 선호를 가지고 있다면 거리를 두는 것이 좋은 것으로 여겨진다.

② 정적이기는 커녕 환경은 끊임없이 변하고 있으며 진화하는 개체들에게 새로운 난제를 안겨주고 있다.

③ 심지어 이상적인 상황에서도, 이런 빠른 동물을 창이나 활과 화살로 사냥하는 것은 불확실한 일이다. 그러나 순록에게는 인류가 인정사정없이 이용할 약점이 있었는데, 그것은 순록이 수영을 잘 못한다는 것이었다.

주요 어휘 및 표현

outcome	결과	hierarchical	계급의, 계급에 따른
far from	~은 커녕	preference	선호

나. 기출 연습 문제

본문 69쪽

정답 [④]

해석

오늘날 시장에서 선택 항목의 과잉은 당신에게 더 많은 선택의 자유를 준다. 그러나 행복의 관점에서 치러야 할 대가가 있을지도 모른다. 심리학자 David Myers와 Robert Lane의 연구에 따르면 모든 이러한 선택은 자주 사람들을 우울하게 만든다. 연구자들이 어떤 쇼핑객들에게는 24개의 잼을 맛보게 했고 다른 사람들에게는 오직 6개만 맛보게 했다. 더 적은 선택 항목을 가진 사람들이 맛볼 때 더 행복했다. 훨씬 더 놀랍게도, 더 넓은 범위의 선택 사항을 가진 사람들 중 오직 그 당시 3%만이 잼을 구매한 반면, 더 적은 선택 사항을 가진 사람들 중에서는 그 당시 31%가 잼을 구매했다. 아이러니한 점은 사람들이 거의 항상 더 많은 선택 항목을 원한다고 말한다는 것이다. 그러나 그들이 더 많은 선택 항목을 가질수록 그들은 더 안도한다(→마비된다). 사리에 밝은 레스토랑 사장들은 더 적은 선택 항목을 제공한다. 이것은 고객들이 더 편안함을 느끼게 하고, 그들이 쉽게 선택하여 그 선택에 더 만족하도록 촉진한다.

주요 어휘 및 표현

overabundance	과잉, 과다	prompt	촉진하다
ironic	역설적인, 모순의	paralyze	마비시키다

다. 실전 연습 문제 본문 71~74쪽

1. 정답 [③]

해석

사람들은 삶이 나아질수록 더 높은 기대감을 지닌다. 하지만 기대감이 더 높아질수록 만족감을 느끼기는 더욱 어려워진다. 우리들은 기대감을 (A)통제함으로써 삶에서 느끼는 만족감을 향상시킬 수 있다. 적절한 기대감은 많은 경험들을 즐거운 놀라움이 되도록 하는 여지를 남긴다. 문제는 적절한 기대감을 가지는 방법을 찾는 것이다. 이것을 위한 한 방법은 멋진 경험들을 (B)드문 상태로 유지하는 것이다. 당신이 무엇이든 살 여유가 있더라도, 특별한 경우를 위해 훌륭한 와인을 아껴두어라. 품위 있는 실크 블라우스를 특별한 즐거움이 되게 하라. 이것은 당신의 욕구를 억제하는 행동처럼 보일 수도 있지만, 내 생각은 그렇지 않다. 반대로, 그것은 당신이 (C)즐거움을 계속해서 경험할 수 있도록 보장해 주는 방법이다. 멋진 와인과 멋진 블라우스가 당신을 기분 좋게 만들지 못한다면 무슨 의미가 있겠는가?

비법 적용

We can increase the satisfaction we feel in our lives by (A) controlling/raising our expectations.

☞ (인과) 앞에서 'the 비교급, the 비교급'을 이용해 '기대가 높을수록 만족감이 낮아진다'고 하였다. 역접의 단서가 없으면 앞말의 말과 동일한 의미로 만들어주면 된다. 따라서 만족감을 높이려면 기대치를 '통제(controlling)'해야 한다.

One way to do this is by keeping wonderful experiences (B) frequent/rare .

☞ (병렬-예시) 적절한 기대감을 갖는 방법에 대한 내용이다. 와인과 블라우스의 예시를 통해 멋진 경험들에 대한 부연 설명을 해주고 있다. 'save(아끼다)', 'special occasions(특별한 경우)', 'a special treat(특별한 즐거운)'라는 표현으로 보아 '드문(rare)'이 적절하다.

On the contrary, it's a way to make sure that you can continue to experience (C) familiarity/pleasure .

☞ (역접) 앞에서 특별한 경우를 위해 멋진 경험을 아껴두는 것이 '욕망을 억제(an act of denying your desires)'하는 것처럼 보일 수도 있다고 하였다. 따라서, 'On the contrary' 뒤에는 '욕망의 억제'와 반대되는 '즐거움(pleasure)'이 적절하다. 바로 앞 문장의 'I don't think it is'에 있는 'not'은 'On the contrary'와 함께 'not A but B'의 의미를 갖는다.

오답의 모든 것

(A) raising

▶ 동사인 increase만 보고 비슷한 의미인 'raising'을 선택할 수 있는 오답

(B) frequent
▶ 앞·뒤 문맥을 고려하지 않고 단순히 '멋진 경험들(wonderful experiences)'을 '자주(frequent)' 유지하는 것이 좋다고 잘못 생각하여 선택할 수 있는 오답

(C) familiarity
▶ 'On the contrary'만 보고 (B)의 'rare'와 반대 의미를 지닌 '익숙함(familiarity)'이라고 혼동할 수 있는 오답

주요 어휘 및 표현

expectation	기대, 예상	raise	올리다
treat	한 턱, 즐거움	deny	부정하다, 억제하다

2. 정답 [③]

해석

나는 어느 여름날 저녁 스페인의 한 식당 밖에 앉아 저녁 식사를 기다리고 있었다. 주방의 향기가 나의 미뢰를 자극했다. 곧 먹게 될 내 음식은, 너무 작아 눈으로 볼 수는 없지만 코로는 감지되는, 공중을 떠다니는 분자의 형태로 내게 오고 있었다. 고대 그리스인들에게 이런 식으로 원자의 개념이 최초로 떠올랐는데, 빵 굽는 냄새는 그들에게 작은 빵 입자가 눈에 보이지 않게 존재한다는 생각이 들게 했다. 날씨의 순환이 이 생각이 틀렸음을 입증했다(→ 강화했다). 지면 위 물웅덩이는 점차 말라 사라지고, 그런 다음 나중에 비가 되어 떨어진다. 수증기로 변하여 구름을 형성하고 땅으로 떨어지는 물 입자가 존재하는 게 틀림없고, 그래서 그 작은 입자들이 너무 작아 눈에 보이지 않더라도 그 물은 보존된다고 그들은 추론했다. 스페인에서의 나의 파에야가 원자 이론에 대한 공로를 인정받기에는 4천 년이나 너무 늦게 내게 영감을 주었다.

비법 적용

My future meal was coming to me in the form of molecules drifting through the air, too small for my eyes to see but ① detected by my nose.
☞ (역접) 밑줄 어휘 앞의 but이 단서이다. 너무 작아서 눈으로는 볼 수 없지만, 코로는 감지할 수 있었다는 의미이므로 옳은 표현이다.

The ancient Greeks first came upon the idea of atoms this way; the smell of baking bread suggested to them that small particles of bread ② existed beyond vision.
☞ (부연 설명) 'this way'라는 표현을 통해 앞·뒤의 내용이 같은 의미임을 알 수 있다. 따라서 세미콜론(;)을 이용해 '눈에는 보이지 않으나 냄새를 통해 감지한다'는 부연 설명이 앞내용의 'aroma(향)'의 원리와 동일한지 확인한다.

The cycle of weather ③ disproved this idea: a puddle of water on the ground gradually dries out, disappears, and then falls later as rain.

☞ (부연 설명) 'this way'는 앞내용의 '눈에 보이지 않아도 존재하는 빵 입자'를 의미한다. 콜론(:)은 앞내용에 대한 부연설명을 뜻하므로, 날씨의 원리인 '물웅덩이가 점차 말라 비로 내린다'가 냄새의 원리(앞내용)와 같은지 확인한다. 또한 'disprove'는 '틀렸음을 입증하다'라는 의미의 단어로 뒤에 이어지는 사례와 앞내용이 서로 상반된 내용이어야 한다. 그러나 이 글은 냄새와 날씨의 순환이 '눈에 보이지 않아도 존재한다'는 점에서 같은 원리라고 설명하고 있으므로 'disproved'를 'reinforced'로 바꿔야 한다.

They reasoned that there must be particles of water that turn into steam, form clouds, and fall to earth, so that the water is ④ conserved even though the little particles are too small to see.

☞ (인과) '눈에 보이지 않아도 분자가 존재한다'는 앞·뒤의 내용이 서로 유사한 의미로 'so that'을 이용한 인과 관계의 문장이다.

My paella in Spain had inspired me, four thousand years too ⑤ late, to take the credit for atomic theory.

☞ (부연 설명) 글쓴이가 파에야 요리를 통해 '원자 이론'을 깨달았다는 내용이다. 그런데 깨달은 시기는 고대 그리스인들보다 4천 년 뒤의 일임을 설명하고 있다.

오답의 모든 것

① detected

▶ 'too~ toV ...(너무 ~해서 ...할 수 없다)'를 해석하지 못하거나 역접의 'but'을 제대로 적용하지 못하면 선택할 수 있는 오답 (눈에 보이지 않는다. 그러나(but) 코로는 맡을 수 있다.)

② existed

▶ 'beyond'가 부정의 의미를 갖고 있으나 이를 알지 못하여 'beyond vision'의 의미를 '시선 너머에' 등으로 잘못 해석하였거나, 'exist'를 'exit'등으로 혼동하면 선택할 수 있는 오답

③ disproved

▶ **날씨의 순환과 this idea의 의미가 서로 같은 맥락이기 때문에 '틀렸음을 입증했다'는 것은 잘못 표현된 정답**

④ conserved

▶ 'so that', 'even though', 'too ~ to V' 구문으로 문장이 복잡하여 바르게 이해하지 못했다면 선택할 수 있는 오답 (빵입자는 눈에 보이지 않음. 그러나 냄새로 존재 = 물 입자가 증발해 보이지 않음. 그러나 존재함)

⑤ late

▶ 상단의 'The ancient Greeks first came upon the idea of atoms'를 보지 못했다면 선택할 수 있는 오답

주요 어휘 및 표현

aroma	향기	puddle	물웅덩이
excite	자극하다, 흥분시키다	gradually	점차

drift	떠다니다, 떠돌다	reason	추론하다
detect	감지하다, 알아채다	steam	수증기
come upon an idea	생각이 떠오르다	conserve	보존하다
suggest	생각나게 하다, 암시하다	inspire	영감을 주다
particle	알갱이, 입자	take the credit for ~	~에 대한 공로를 인정받다
vision	시야	atomic	원자의

3. 정답 [③]

해석

뇌는 몸무게의 2 퍼센트만을 차지하지만 우리의 에너지의 20 퍼센트를 사용한다. 갓 태어난 아기의 경우, 그 비율은 65 퍼센트에 달한다. 그것은 부분적으로 아기들이 항상 잠을 자고 (뇌의 성장이 그들을 소진시키고), 체지방을 보유하는 이유인데, 필요할 때 보유한 에너지를 사용하기 위한 것이다. 근육은 약 4분의 1 정도로 훨씬 더 많은 에너지를 사용하기도 하지만, 많은 근육을 가지고 있기도 하다. 실제로, 물질 단위당, 뇌는 다른 기관보다 훨씬 많은 에너지를 사용한다. 그것은 우리 장기 중 뇌가 단연 가장 에너지 소모가 많다는 것을 의미한다. 하지만 그것은 또한 놀랍도록 효율적이다. 뇌는 하루에 약 400 칼로리의 에너지만 필요로 하는데, 블루베리 머핀에서 얻는 것과 거의 같다. 머핀으로 24시간 동안 노트북을 작동시켜서 얼마나 가는지 보라.

비법 적용

That's partly why babies sleep all the time — their growing brains (A) warn/exhaust them — and have a lot of body fat, to use as an energy reserve when needed.

☞ (대쉬(—) 뒤 부연 설명) 'babies sleep all the time' 뒤에 삽입된 부분으로 앞내용에 대한 부연 설명이다. 따라서 뇌에서 상당한 비율의 에너지를 소모하는 아기들이 하루종일 잠을 자는 이유는 뇌의 성장이 그들을 소진(exhaust) 시키기 때문이라 볼 수 있다.

Actually, per unit of matter, the brain uses by far (B) more/less energy than our other organs.

☞ (병렬) 뇌와 근육의 에너지 사용에 대한 앞내용의 설명을 잘 이해하고 있는지 묻는 부분이다. 앞에서 우리 몸무게의 2퍼센트 정도인 뇌는 20%의 에너지를 사용한다 하였다. 이를 근육의 에너지 사용량인 전체의 4분의 1 정도, 즉 약 25%와 비교하고 있다. 따라서 물질 단위당(per unit of matter) 비교했을 때 근육보다 더 작은 물질인 뇌의 에너지 사용량이 훨씬 많다(more)고 볼 수 있다.

But it is also marvelously (C) creative/efficient .

☞ (추가 설명) 뇌의 에너지 소모가 많다는 내용 뒤에서 'also'를 이용해 뇌의 또 다른 특징을

나열하고 있다. 머핀 한 개 정도의 적은 칼로리로 정상 작동하는 것은 뇌가 '효율적인(efficient)' 것이라 볼 수 있다.

오답의 모든 것

(A) warn

▶ 필자의 의도를 파악하지 못하고 단순히 하루 종일 잠자는 아이에게 경고를 준다고 잘못 고를 수 있는 오답

(B) less

▶ 'per unit of matter'를 못 보고 'Our muscles use even more of our energy'라는 문장만 읽고 잘못 고를 수 있는 오답

(C) creative

▶ 글 전체 내용과 관계없이 단순히 뇌는 '창의적'이라는 일반적인 생각으로 고를 수 있는 오답

주요 어휘 및 표현

newborn	신생아	marvelously	놀랍게도

4. 정답 [②]

해석

스릴 넘치는 유령 이야기는 정말 무섭다면 들려주기에 재밌고, 만약 당신이 그 이야기가 사실이라고 주장하면 훨씬 더 그렇다, 사람들은 그런 이야기를 전달하는 것으로부터 스릴을 느낀다. 이것은 기적 이야기에도 동일하게 적용된다. 만약 기적에 대한 소문이 어떤 책에 쓰인다면, 특히 그 책이 먼 옛날의 것이라면, 그 소문은 믿기(→의문을 제기하기) 힘들어진다. 만약 소문이 충분히 오래된 것이라면, 그것은 대신 '전통'으로 불리기 시작하고, 그러고 나서 사람들은 그것을 한결 더 믿는다. 이것은 다소 이상한데, 그 이유는 그들이 (근거 없이) 주장된 사건 그 자체에 시간상 가까운 최근의 소문보다 오래된 소문이 왜곡될 시간이 더 있다는 점을 깨달을 것이라고 당신이 생각할 수 있기 때문이다. Elvis Presley와 Michael Jackson은 전통이 생겨나기에는 너무 최근에 살아서 'Elvis가 화성에서 목격되었다'와 같은 이야기를 믿는 사람이 많지 않다.

비법 적용

People get a ① thrill from passing on those stories.
☞ (부연 설명) 'those stories'는 앞에서 나온 'Spine-tingling ghost stories'를 의미하며, 그러한 이야기를 말하면서 스릴과 재미를 느낀다고 하였다.

If a rumor of a miracle gets written down in a book, the rumor becomes hard to ② believe, especially if the book is ancient.
☞ (인과) 책에 적혀 있으면, 믿을 수밖에 없다. 앞내용에 유령 이야기가 기적 이야기에도 적용된다고 한 'The same applies to miracle stories.'도 단서가 된다. 'believe'를 'challenge'로 바꾸어야 한다.

If a rumor is ③ old enough, it starts to be called a "tradition" instead, and then people believe it all the more.
☞ (인과) 주절의 '소문이 전통이 되었다(결과)'와 if절의 '그 소문이 오래되었다'는(원인) 인과 관계가 성립하고 있다.

This is rather odd because you might think they would realize that older rumors have had more time to get ④ distorted than younger rumors that are close in time to the alleged events themselves.
☞ (인과) 앞내용을 나타내는 'this'를 통해 인과 관계를 바르게 파악하도록 한다. 오래된 것은 왜곡의 가능성이 있으므로 오래될수록 더 많이 믿는 것이 이상하게 여겨질 수 있다.

Elvis Presley and Michael Jackson lived too ⑤ recently for traditions to have grown up, so not many people believe stories like "Elvis seen on Mars."
☞ (인과) 'so'가 콤마 뒤에 있으면 결과의 의미를 갖는 경우가 많다. 'Elvis의 소문을 믿는 사람이 많지 않다(결과)'는 것은 그만큼 소문이 오래되지 않았다는 것이고 'Elvis가 최근의 인물이다(원인)'라고 볼 수 있다.

오답의 모든 것

① thrill
▶ 앞내용에서 사람들이 유령 이야기를 주고 받으며 재미와 공포 등을 느낀다고 하였는데, 이것을 다른 말로 표현한 것이 'get a thrill from passing on those stories'임을 알지 못하면 고를 수 있는 오답

② believe
▶ **책에 기록되어있기 때문에 믿기 힘들다는 것은 논리적으로 어색하므로, '어려운(hard)'이라는 단어를 보았다면 고를 수 있는 정답**

③ old
▶ 전통이라 불리려면 오래된 것이어야 하므로 오답

④ distorted
▶ 'distort'의 정확한 단어 뜻을 모르거나, 'this'의 의미가 '사람들이 오래된 것일수록 더 많이 믿는다'는 것을 모르면 고를 수 있는 오답

⑤ recently
▶ 문장의 뜻을 이해하지 못하거나, 'too ~ toV'의 구조를 모른다면 선택할 수 있는 오답

주요 어휘 및 표현

spine-tingling	스릴 넘치는	alleged	(근거 없이) 주장된

라. 고난도 실전 문제

본문 75~76쪽

1. 정답 [④]

해석

Paula가 극심한 공포증을 겪는다는 것을 우리가 안다고 가정해 보자. Paula가 뱀이나 거미 둘 중 하나를 두려워한다고 추론한 다음, 그녀가 뱀을 두려워하지 않는다는 것을 규명한다면, 우리는 Paula가 거미를 두려워한다고 결론지을 것이다. 그러나 우리의 결론은 실제로 Paula의 두려움이 뱀이나 거미 둘 중 하나와 관계가 있는 경우에만 타당하다. 만약 우리가 Paula가 공포증이 있다는 것만 알고 있다면, 그녀가 뱀을 두려워하지 않는다는 사실은 그녀가 높은 곳, 물, 개, 또는 숫자 13을 두려워한다는 것과 전적으로 양립한다. 더 일반적으로는 우리에게 어떤 현상에 대한 일련의 대안적 설명이 제공되고, 그런 다음 그 설명들 중 하나를 제외하고는 모든 것이 적절하지 않다는 것을 확신한다면, 우리는 멈춰서 심사숙고해야 한다. 남아 있는 그 설명이 옳은 것이라는 것을 부정하기(→ 인정하기) 전에, 타당해 보이는 다른 선택 사항들이 무시되거나 간과되고 있는지를 고려해 보라. 잘못된 선택의 오류는, 우리가 숨어 있는 중요한 가정에 불충분하게 주의를 기울이면, 명백한 것으로 밝혀진 선택 사항들이 합리적인 대안을 고갈시키도록 오도한다.

비법 적용

If we reason that Paula is afraid either of snakes or spiders, and then ① establish that she is not afraid of snakes, we will conclude that Paula is afraid of spiders.
☞ (인과, 병렬) if(인과)와 and(병렬)의 단서가 들어있다. Paula가 '뱀'이나 '거미' 중 하나를 무서워하는데 뱀을 두려워하지 않는 것이 확실해져야(if), Paula가 거미를 두려워한다고 결론지을 수(결과) 있을 것이다.

If we know only that Paula has a phobia, then the fact that she's not afraid of snakes is entirely ② consistent with her being afraid of heights, water, dogs or the number thirteen.
☞ (인과) Paula에게 공포증이 있다는 사실만 안다면(if), 거미를 두려워하지 않는다는 것은 거미 외에 다른 것들을 두려워할 수도 있다고 추론할 수 있다. 따라서 둘의 관계는 서로 양립하는(모순이 없는) 관계이다.

More generally, when we are presented with a list of alternative explanations for some phenomenon, and are then persuaded that all but one of those explanations are ③ unsatisfactory, we should pause to reflect.

☞ (인과) 여러 개 중 하나만 만족스럽다면(when) 멈춰서 생각해야 한다는 맥락이다. 하나가 아닌 여러 개의 선택지가 있다면 당연히 멈춰 생각할 것이지만, 하나의 선택 사항만 남게 되면 우리는 깊이 생각하지 않을 것이고, 나머지 합리적일지도 모르는 선택들은 간과될 수도 있을 것이기 때문이다. 이 문장에서 'but'은 '~을 제외하고'의 의미이다.

Before ④ denying that the remaining explanation is the correct one, consider whether other plausible options are being ignored or overlooked.

☞ (병렬) 앞에서 하나의 선택 사항이 있을 때 멈춰 생각하라고 한 것과 같은 의미의 말이다. 즉, 남은 하나를 옳다고 인정하기(conceding)전에 다른 나머지 것들을 무시 혹은 간과하고 있지 않은지 고려해야 할 것이다.

The fallacy of false choice misleads when we're insufficiently attentive to an important hidden assumption, that the choices which have been made explicit exhaust the ⑤ sensible alternatives.

☞ (인과) '잘못된 선택의 오류(The fallacy of false choice)'에 대한 설명으로, 이것이 '고갈시키는(exhaust)'는 것은 '합리적 대안(the sensible alternatives)'일 것이다. '명백한 것으로 밝혀진 선택 사항들(choices which have been made explicit)'은 우리가 확실하다고 생각한 선택들을 의미한다.

오답의 모든 것

① establish

▶ 'and'를 중심으로 동사 'reason'과 'establish'가 병렬로 연결되어, 이 두 가지가 참이면(if) 뒤의 내용을 참이라 결론(conclude)지을 수 있다는 내용이므로 적절히 쓰인 오답

② consistent

▶ 공포증이 있다는 것만 알고 있다면, '뱀을 두려워하지 않는다는 것'은 '높은 곳, 물 등을 두려워할 수도 있다는 것'과 서로 일치하는 생각이므로 오답 ('However,' 'if' 등을 잘 활용하면 복잡해 보이는 내용을 이해하기 쉬울 수 있음. 'However'을 중심으로 앞내용은 거미나 뱀 둘 중 하나를 두려워하는 것이 확실한 경우이고, 뒤의 내용은 무엇에 대한 공포증인지 확실하지 않은 경우를 말하고 있음. 또한, 'If'의 인과 관계를 활용하여 'Paula가 공포증이 있다는 사실만 안다면(원인)', '거미를 두려워하지 않는다는 것은 그 외에 다른 것들을 두려워할 수도 있다(결과)'고 볼 수 있음.)

③ unsatisfactory

▶ 'but(~을 제외하고)'과 'unsatisfactory(적절하지 않은, 만족스럽지 않은)'가 결합된 이중 부정의 문장으로 긍정의 의미를 나타냄. 따라서 '하나 이외의 모든 설명이 적절치 않다'를 즉, '하나의 설명만이 적절하다'로 적절히 쓰인 오답

④ denying

▶ **'다른 선택들이 간과되지 않았는지 생각해 보라'고 말하려면 남은 하나의 설명이 옳다고 인정한 상황이어야 하므로 문맥상 어색한 정답**

⑤ sensible

▶ 앞에서 말했던 것들을 '잘못된 선택의 오류(The fallacy of false choice)'라고 반복해서 표현하고 있으므로 글의 전체 내용에 어울리는 오답 ('that' 절 뒤에 이어지는 문장은 'The fallacy of false choice(잘못된 선택의 오류)'를 수식하는 구조임. 자신이 분명하다고 생각한 선택으로 인해 고갈(exhaust)된 것이 합리적(sensible) 대안일 때 '잘못된 선택의 오류'라고 볼 수 있음. that절의 수식 구조를 놓치거나 'exhaust'의 부정적 어감만 보고 ⑤번을 선택하지 않도록 주의해야 함. 나머지 문장인 'when'과 결합해 보면 '숨은 가설에 불충분한 주의를 가설을 기울이면(when-원인)', '합리적 대안이 고갈된다(주절-결과)는 The fallacy of false choice(잘못된 선택의 오류)'에 관한 문장이 완성됨.)

주요 어휘 및 표현

phobia	공포증	overlook	간과하다
establish	규명하다, 밝히다	mislead	오도하다, 잘못 이끌다
concern	관계가 있다	assumption	가정
consistent	양립하는	explicit	명백한
unsatisfactory	적절하지 않은	exhaust	고갈시키다

2. 정답 [④]

해석

내가 여러분에게 '백곰을 생각하지 말라.'라고 말하면, 여러분은 백곰을 생각하지 않는 것이 어렵다는 것을 알게 될 것이다. 이런 식으로, '사고의 억제는 억누르고 싶은 생각을 가라앉히는 대신, 그것을 실제로 증가시킬 수 있다'. 이것의 한 가지 흔한 예는 다이어트를 하고 있어서 음식에 대해 생각하지 않으려고 노력하는 사람들이 흔히 음식에 대해 훨씬 더 많이 생각하기 시작한다는 것이다. 따라서 이 과정은 '반동 효과'라고도 알려져 있다. 그 아이러니한 결과는 관련된 두 가지 인지 과정의 상호작용에 의해 야기되는 것 같다. 우선, 이 이중 처리 체계는 의도적인 운영 과정을 포함하는데, 그것은 억제된 생각과 무관한 생각을 의식적으로 찾아내려고 한다. 다음으로, 그리고 동시에, 무의식적인 감시 과정은 운영 체계가 효과적으로 작동하고 있는지 검사한다. 감시 체계가 의도된 생각과 일치하지 않는 생각과 마주치는 경우, 그것은 의도적인 운영 과정을 자극하여 반드시 이러한 생각이 부적절한(→ 적절한) 생각에 의해 대체되도록 한다. 그러나 주장되는 바로는, 의도적인 운영 체계는 피로, 스트레스, 정서적 요인에 의해 생긴 인지 부하의 증가로 인해 작동을 멈출 수 있고, 그래서 감시 과정이 부적절한 생각을 걸러서 의식으로 스며들게 해, 그것의 접근성을 높아지게 만든다는 것이다.

비법 적용

One common example of this is that people on a diet who try not to think about food often begin to think much ① more about food.

☞ (병렬-예시) '사고의 억제(thought suppression)가 오히려 생각을 더 증가시킨다'는 내용에 관한 사례를 들고 있다. 예시는 앞내용과 동일한 의미가 사례로 나와야 하므로, '음식을 생각하지 않을수록 더 생각하게 된다'는 것은 옳은 표현이다.

The ② ironic effect seems to be caused by the interplay of two related cognitive processes.

☞ (인과) 밑줄 친 '아이러니한 결과(the ironic effect)'는 앞내용의 '반동 효과(the rebound effect)'를 뜻하는 말이다. 사고의 억제가 오히려 사고를 증가시킨다는 상황은 서로 모순된 결과를 가져왔기에 'ironic'하다고 볼 수 있다.

This dual-process system involves, first, an intentional operating process, which consciously attempts to locate thoughts ③ unrelated to the suppressed ones.

☞ (부연 설명) 반동 효과의 과정을 두 단계로 나누어 설명한 것 중 첫 번째인 'an intentional operating process'을 관계대명사로 설명하고 있다. 즉 사고를 억제하기 위해 의도적으로 관련 없는 것을 생각하려는 과정이다.

If the monitoring system encounters thoughts inconsistent with the intended ones, it prompts the intentional operating process to ensure that these are replaced by ④ inappropriate thoughts.

☞ (인과, these) 대명사 'these'는 '의도된 것과 일치하지 않은 생각(thoughts inconsistent with the intended ones)'을 가리킨다. '이러한 의도하지 않은 생각(these)'을 '적절한' 생각으로 대체하는 것이 이 시스템의 역할이므로 'inappropriate'를 'appropriate'로 바꾸어야 한다.

백곰, 음식	백곰, 음식 이외의 생각
ⓐ 억제된 생각(the suppressed ones)	ⓐ (생각하지 않으려) 의도된 생각 (the intended ones)
ⓑ 의도된 것과 일치하지 않은 생각 (thoughts inconsistent with the intended ones)	ⓑ 억제된 것과 무관한 생각 (thoughts ③ unrelated to the suppressed ones)
ⓒ 생각하면 안 되는 부적절한 생각 (④ inappropriate thoughts)	ⓒ 적절한 생각(appropriate thoughts)

However, it is argued, the intentional operating system can fail due to increased cognitive load caused by fatigue, stress and emotional factors, and so the monitoring process filters the inappropriate thoughts into consciousness, making them highly ⑤ accessible.

☞ (부연 설명) 'making them highly accessible'의 대명사 'them'은 'the inappropriate thoughts'를 의미한다. 첫 번째 과정인 의도적 운영 체계가 인지적 과부하로 인해 작동하지 못했을 경우에 어떤 결과가 발생할 수 있는지 설명하고 있다. 따라서 의도적 운영 체계의 작동 실패로 인해 부적절한 생각(백곰이나 음식)이 의식으로 스며들게 되어 오히려 접근성이 높아졌음(더 많이 생각하게 됨)을 의미한다.

오답의 모든 것

① more

▶ 'One common example of this'라는 표현을 통해 앞내용(생각을 억압하면, 오히려 더 많이 생각하게 된다)에 대한 사례임을 적용해야 하지 못하면 선택할 수 있는 오답

② ironic

▶ 'the ironic effect'는 앞의 'the rebound effect(반동 효과)' 즉, '생각을 억압하면, 오히려 더 많이 생각하게 된다'는 의미이므로 적절히 쓰인 오답

③ unrelated

▶ '의도적 운영 과정(an intentional operating process)'에 대한 설명으로 의도적으로 백곰이나 음식(억제된 생각)과 관련 없는 생각을 하려 하는 과정을 말하는 올바른 어휘이므로 오답

④ inappropriate

▶ 지문 속에서 'these(thoughts inconsistent with the intended ones)'는 문맥상 생각하지 말아야 하는 백곰과 음식과 같은 부적절한 생각이므로 적절한(appropriate) 생각으로 대체되어야 하기 때문에 잘못 표현한 정답

⑤ accessible

▶ 인지적 과부하로 인해 부적절한 생각이 의식에 스며들어 오히려 더욱 더 '생각나게(accessible)' 되었다는 반동효과에 대한 적절한 설명이므로 오답

주요 어휘 및 표현

suppression	억제, 억압	inconsistent with	~과 일치하지 않는
rebound effect	(심리학) 반동 효과	prompt	자극하다
interplay	상호작용	ensure	반드시 ~하게 하다
cognitive	인지의	replace	대체하다
dual	이중의	load	부하, 부담
intentional	의도적인	fatigue	피로
consciously	의식적으로	filter	거르다, 스며들게 하다
locate	찾아내다	inappropriate	부적절한
simultaneously	동시에	accessible	접근하기 쉬운
monitor	감시하다	encounter	마주치다

* 반동 효과(rebound effect) : 백곰을 떠올리지 말라고 요구하면 백곰만 생각하게 되는 것처럼, 의도한 것과 반대 효과가 나타나는 것

2. 어법

가. 비법 연습 문제

본문 77~82쪽

정답 **1.** 1) was 2) ones 3) are

2. 1) which 2) that

3. 1) closed 2) insulting

4. 1) smart 2) effectively

5. 1) to make 2) to remember

6. 1) sliding 2) dust

7. 1) do 2) do 3) to read 4) it

8. 1) is → are 2) which → where 3) ○ 4) depending → depend

나. 기출 연습 문제

본문 82쪽

정답 [⑤]

해석

일반적으로 민간 항공기는 물리적 구조물은 아니지만 도로와 유사한 항로로 운항한다. 항로에는 고정된 폭과 규정된 고도가 있으며, 그것들이 반대 방향으로 움직이는 통행을 분리한다. 항공기 간에 상하 간격을 둠으로써 아래에서 다른 과정이 이루어지는 동안 일부 비행기가 공항 위를 통과할 수 있게 된다. 항공 여행은 보통 장거리에 걸치며, 이륙과 착륙 시 짧은 시간의 고강도 조종사 활동과, '장거리 비행'이라고 알려진 비행 부분인, 공중에 있는 동안 긴 시간의 저강도 조종사 활동이 있다. 비행에서 장거리 비행 부분 동안 조종사들은 근처의 비행기를 탐색하는 것보다 항공기 상태를 평가하는 데 더 많은 시간을 보낸다. 이는 항공기 간의 충돌은 대개 공항 주변 지역에서 발생하는 반면 항공기 오작동으로 인한 추락은 장거리 비행 중에 발생하는 경향이 있기 때문이다.

주요 어휘 및 표현

commercial	민간의, 상업적인	airway	항로
structure	구조(물)	fixed	고정된
width	폭	define	규정하다
opposite	반대의	vertical	상하의, 수직의
aircraft	항공기 (pl. aircraft)	flight	비행(기), 항공편
intense	고강도의, 강렬한	takeoff	이륙

landing	착륙	assess	평가하다
collision	충돌	crash	(비행기의) 추락
malfunction	오작동, 고장	occur	일어나다, 발생하다

다. 실전 연습 문제

본문 84~87쪽

1. 정답 [③]

해석

나의 아버지는 음악가로 매우 늦게, 대략 새벽 3시까지 일했고, 그래서 아버지는 주말마다 늦잠을 잤다. 그 결과, 아버지가 잔디 깎기와 울타리 덤불 자르기처럼 내가 싫어했던 허드렛일을 돌보라고 계속 나에게 잔소리한 것을 제외하고는 내가 어렸을 때 우리는 많은 관계를 가지지 못했다. 그는 무책임한 아이를 다루는 책임감 있는 사람이었다. 우리가 소통했던 방식에 대한 기억들이 현재 나에게는 우스워 보인다. 예를 들어, 한번은 아버지가 나에게 잔디를 깎으라고 말했고, 나는 앞뜰만 하기로 하고 뒤뜰을 하는 것은 미루기로 결심했으나, 그러고 나서 며칠 동안 비가 내렸고 뒤뜰의 잔디가 너무 길게 자라서 나는 그것을 낫으로 베어내야만 했다. 그 일은 너무 오래 걸려서 내가 끝냈을 때쯤에는 앞뜰의 잔디가 깎기에 너무 길었고, 그런 일이 계속되었다.

비법 적용

Memories of how we interacted ③ seems funny to me today.

☞ 수일치) 'Memories (of how we interacted) seems funny to me today.'에서 볼 수 있듯이 주어를 수식하는 부분을 괄호( )로 묶으면 남는 것은 복수 주어인 'Memories이므로 동사는 복수 동사인 'seem'을 써야 한다.

오답의 모든 것

① As a result, we didn't have much of a relationship when I was young other than him constantly nagging me to take care of chores like mowing the lawn and cutting the hedges, which I hated.

▶ 관계 대명사) 동사 'hated'의 목적어가 없는 불완전한 문장이며, 선행사 'chores'를 수식하고 있는 어법상 올바른 표현이므로 오답

② He was a responsible man dealing with an irresponsible kid.

▶ 분사) 분사 'dealing'이 'a responsible man'을 수식하고 있는 능동의 관계(무책임한 아이를 다루고 있는)이므로 적절히 쓰인 오답

④ For example, one time he told me to cut the grass and I decided to do just the front yard and postpone doing the back, but then it rained for a couple days and the backyard grass became so high I had to cut it with a sickle.

▶ 동사 vs 준동사) 동사 'decided' 뒤에서 동사의 목적어 자리이며 'decide'는 to 부정사를 목적어로 취하는 동사이므로 적절히 쓰인 오답

⑤ That took so long that by the time I was finished, the front yard was too high to mow, and so on.

▶ 관계사 vs 접속사) 'so ~ that(너무 ~ 해서 ~ 하다)' 구문의 접속사 'that'절이 완전한 문장을 이루고 있어 적절히 쓰인 오답

주요 어휘 및 표현

constantly	계속해서, 끊임없이	nag	잔소리하다
chore	(하기 싫은) 잡일, 허드렛일	mow	(잔디를) 깎다
lawn	잔디	hedge	울타리 덤불
irresponsible	책임감 없는	interact	상호작용하다, 소통하다
postpone	연기하다, 미루다	backyard	뒤뜰

2. 정답 [④]

해석

비언어적 의사소통은 언어적 의사소통의 대체물이 아니다. 오히려 그것은 전달되고 있는 메시지 내용의 풍부함을 강화시키도록 도와주며, 보충으로서 기능해야 한다. 비언어적 의사소통은 말하기가 불가능하거나 부적절한 상황에서 유용할 수 있다. 여러분이 어떤 개인과 이야기하는 동안 불편한 입장에 있다고 상상해 보라. 비언어적 의사소통은 다시 편안해지도록 대화에서 잠깐 벗어날 시간을 여러분에게 달라는 메시지를 여러분이 그 사람에게 건네도록 도와줄 것이다. 비언어적 의사소통의 또 다른 장점은 여러분에게 감정과 태도를 적절하게 표현할 기회를 제공한다는 것이다. 비언어적 의사소통의 도움이 없다면 적절하게 표현되지 못할 여러분의 본성과 성격의 여러 측면들이 있다. 따라서 다시 말하면, 그것은 언어적 의사소통을 대체하는 것이 아니라 오히려 그것을 보완한다.

비법 적용

Another advantage of non-verbal communication is ④ what it offers you the opportunity to express emotions and attitudes properly.

☞ 관계사 vs 접속사) 'what'이하가 완전한 문장이며, 동사 'is'의 보어가 되는 명사절을 이루고 있으므로 접속사 'that'으로 고쳐야 한다.

오답의 모든 것

① Rather, it should function as a supplement, serving to enhance the richness of the content of the message that is being passed across.

▶ 분사) 문장의 주어인 'it(Non-verbal communication)'이 'serving'의 의미상 주어이며, 'serving'은 '~하도록 도와주면서'라는 능동의 분사구문을 이루고 있는 바른 표현이므로 오답 (1형식 자동사 'function'이 문장의 동사임.)

② Non-verbal communication can be useful in situations where speaking may be impossible or inappropriate.

▶ 관계사) 관계 부사 'where' 뒤의 문장이 완전한 구조이며, 'situation'을 선행사로 받고 있는 올바른 표현이므로 오답 (관계 부사 'where'은 추상적 의미의 공간 개념을 선행사로 받을 수 있음.)

③ Non-verbal communication will help you get the message across to him or her to give you some time off the conversation to be comfortable again.

▶ to 부정사) 'help'는 준 사역동사로 목적보어 자리에 to 부정사 혹은 동사원형을 모두 취할 수 있으므로 적절히 쓰인 오답

⑤ So, again, it does not substitute verbal communication but rather complements it.

▶ 병렬 구조) 'not A but B'로 이루어진 형태로, 주어인 'it' 뒤에서 'does'와 병렬구조를 이루고 있어 적절히 쓰인 오답

주요 어휘 및 표현

verbal	언어적인	substitute	대체하다; 대체물
function as ~	~로서 기능하다	supplement	보충
enhance	강화하다	content	내용
inappropriate	부적절한	advantage	유리함, 장점
attitude	태도	properly	적절하게
aid	도움	aspect	측면
personality	성격, 개성	adequately	적절하게

3. 정답 [⑤]

해석

모든 것을 당신 스스로 생산하려고 노력하는 것은 당신이 고비용 공급자가 되는 많은 것들을 생산하기 위해 당신의 시간과 자원을 사용하고 있다는 것을 의미한다. 이것은 더 낮은 생산과 수입으로 해석될 수 있다. 예를 들면, 비록 대부분의 의사가 자료 기록과 진료 예약을 잡는 데 능숙할지라도, 이러한 서비스를 수행하기 위해 누군가를 고용하는 것은 일반적으로 그들에게 이익이 된다. 기록을 하기 위해 의사가 사용하는 시간은 그들이 환자를 진료하면서 보낼 수 있었던 시간이다. 그들이 환자와 보내게 되는 시간은 많은 가치를 가지기 때문에 의사들에게 자료 기록을 하는 기회비용은 높을 것이다. 따라서 의사는 자료 기록을 하고 그것을 관리하기 위해 누군가 다른 사람을 고용하는 것이 이득이라는 것을 거의 항상 알게 될 것이다. 더군다나 의사가 진료 제공을 전문으로 하고,

자료 기록에 비교 우위를 가지고 있는 사람을 고용하면, 그렇게 하지 않으면 얻을 수 있는 것보다 그 비용은 더 낮아질 것이고 공동의 결과물이 더 커질 것이다.

비법 적용

Moreover, when the doctor specializes in the provision of physician services and ⑤ hiring someone who has a comparative advantage in record keeping, costs will be lower and joint output larger than would otherwise be achievable.

☞ 병렬 구조) 대등 접속사 'and' 뒤에서 주어 'the doctor'의 동사인 'specializes'와 병렬 구조이므로 동사인 'hires'가 되어야 한다.

오답의 모든 것

① Trying to produce everything yourself would mean you are using your time and resources to produce many things for which you are a highcost provider.

▶ 관계사) 전치사+관계대명사인 'for which' 뒤의 구조가 완전한 문장으로 적절히 쓰인 오답

② For example, even though most doctors might be good at record keeping and arranging appointments, it is generally in their interest to hire someone to perform these services.

▶ 대명사) 진주어 'to hire' 뒤를 받는 가주어 'it'은 적절히 쓰인 오답

③ Because the time spent with their patients is worth a lot, the opportunity cost of record keeping for doctors will be high.

▶ 분사) 과거 분사 'spent'가 'time'을 수식하여 '보내어진 시간'이라는 수동의 의미를 나타내는 구조이며, 접속사 'because'의 동사 'is'가 이미 존재하고 있으므로 적절히 쓰인 오답

④ Thus, doctors will almost always find it advantageous to hire someone else to keep and manage their records.

▶ 형용사 vs 부사) 가목적어 'it' 뒤의 목적보어 자리에 위치하고 있어 형용사 'advantageous'는 적절히 쓰인 오답 (to hire 이하가 진목적어임.)

주요 어휘 및 표현

translate into ~	~으로 해석되다	joint	공동의
hire	고용하다	worth	~의 가치가 있는
opportunity cost	기회 비용	advantageous	이로운, 이득이 되는

provision	제공	physician	(내과) 의사
comparative advantage	비교 우위	arrange an appointment	약속 시간을 잡다
outcome	결과	achievable	성취 가능한, 얻을 수 있는

4. 정답 [③]

해석

야외에서 곤충의 성공적인 생존의 열쇠 중 하나는 그들의 작은 몸이 탈수가 되는 것을 막도록 돕는 단단한 밀랍 같은 층인 외피에 있다. 그들은 공기로부터 산소를 흡수하기 위해 몸의 마디에 있는 좁은 호흡구들을 사용하는데, 이들은 공기를 수동적으로 흡입하고 필요로 될 때 열리고 닫힐 수 있다. 혈관 내 담긴 피 대신 그들은 자유롭게 흐르는 혈림프를 갖고 있는데, 이는 그들의 몸이 단단하게 유지되도록 돕고 움직임을 거들고 영양분과 노폐물이 적절한 몸의 부위로 이동하는 것을 도와준다. 신경 체계가 모듈식으로 되어 있는데, 어떤 의미에서는 각각의 몸의 마디가 그 자체의 개별적이고 자율적인 뇌를 갖고 있으며, 몇몇 다른 몸의 체계가 유사한 모듈화를 보여 준다. 이것들은 곤충의 몸이 우리의 것과는 완전히 다르게 구조화되어 있고 기능하는 많은 방식들 중 몇 가지일 뿐이다.

비법 적용

Instead of blood ③ <u>containing</u> in vessels,

☞ 분사) 전치사 'instead of' 뒤에서 '혈관내에 담겨진 피 대신에'라는 수동의 의미가 되어야 하므로 과거 분사인 '<u>contained</u>'가 올바른 표현이다.

오답의 모든 것

① One of the keys to insects' successful survival in the open air <u>lies</u> in their outer covering — a hard waxy layer that helps prevent their tiny bodies from dehydrating.

▶ 수일치) 주어가 단수 'one'이므로 단수동사 'lies'는 적절히 쓰인 오답

② To take oxygen from the air, they use narrow breathing holes in the body-segments, which take in air <u>passively</u> and can be opened and closed as needed.

▶ 형용사 vs 부사) '수동적으로 흡입하다'는 의미로 동사 'take'를 수식하는 부사의 자리이므로 적절히 쓰인 오답

④ The nervous system is modular — in a sense, each of the body segments has <u>its</u> own individual and autonomous brain — and some other body systems show a similar modularization.

▶ 수일치) 대명사 'its'가 대신해 주는 명사는 주어인 'each of the body segments'의 'each' 즉, 단수이므로 적절히 쓰인 오답

⑤ These are just a few of the many ways in which insect bodies are structured and function completely differently from our own.
▶ 관계사) 전치사 + 관계대명사의 형태로 뒤 문장이 완전한 문장을 이루고 있으므로 적절히 쓰인 오답

주요 어휘 및 표현

lie in	~에 있다	outer covering	(동물의) 외피, 겉껍데기
waxy	밀랍 같은, 밀랍으로 만든	dehydrate	탈수 상태가 되다
breathing hole	(동물의) 숨구멍, 공기 구멍	segment	부분, 마디
passively	수동적으로	vessel	(동물의) 혈관
hemolymph	혈림프	rigid	단단한
transportation	이동, 운송	modular	모듈식의 (여러 개의 개별 단위로 되어 있는)
autonomous	자율적인	structure	구조화하다
function	(제대로) 기능하다	completely	완전히

라. 고난도 실전 문제

본문 88~89쪽

1. 정답 [⑤]

해석

Baylor 대학의 연구자들은 다양한 종류의 글쓰기가 사람들을 편하게 하여 잠들도록 해 줄 수 있는지 아닌지를 조사하였다. (그것을) 알아보려고, 그들은 57명의 젊은 성인들에게 잠자리에 들기 전 5분간 앞으로 며칠 동안 해야 할 일의 목록과 지난 며칠 동안 끝낸 일들의 목록 중 하나를 쓰도록 했다. 그 결과는 잠들기 전 글쓰기가 모두 똑같이 만들어지지는 않는다는 것을 확인해 준다. 해야 할 일의 목록을 잠자리에 들기 전에 만드는 사람들은 지나간 일에 관해 쓰는 사람들보다 9분 더 빨리 잠들 수 있었다. 목록의 질 또한 중요했는데, 과업이 더 많을수록 그리고 해야 할 일의 목록이 더 구체적일수록, 글을 쓴 사람들은 더 빨리 잠들었다. 그 연구의 저자들은 미래의 과업을 적으면 생각을 내려놓게 되므로 여러분은 그것을 곰곰이 생각하는 것을 멈출 수 있다고 결론짓는다. 여러분은 자신의 뇌에게 그 과업이 처리될 것인데 단지 지금 당장은 아니라고 말하고 있는 것이다.

비법 적용

The study authors figure that writing down future tasks ⑤ unloading the thoughts so you can stop turning them over in your mind.
☞ 준동사 vs 동사) 하나의 절 안에 동사가 반드시 하나는 있어야 하는데 접속사 'that'절 이하에 동사가 없으므로 'unloads'로 고쳐야 올바른 표현이다.

오답의 모든 것

① Baylor University researchers investigated whether different types of writing could ease people into sleep.
▶ 관계사 vs 접속사) 접속사 'whether'는 'investigated'의 목적어 자리에서 '~인지 아닌지'의 의미를 갖는 명사절로 쓰였으므로 적절히 쓰인 오답

② To find out, they had 57 young adults spend five minutes before bed writing either a todo list for the days ahead or a list of tasks they'd finished over the past few days.
▶ 준동사 vs 동사) 'spend'는 사역동사 'had'의 목적보어이며, 'spend 시간/돈 ~ing' 구문으로 적절히 쓰인 오답

③ Those who made todo lists before bed were able to fall asleep nine minutes faster than those who wrote about past events.
▶ 수일치) 수식하는 관계사절을 (　)로 묶어보면 문장의 주어는 'those'이므로 복수동사인 'were'는 적절히 쓰인 오답

④ The quality of the lists mattered, too; the more tasks and the more specific the todo lists were, the faster the writers fell asleep.
▶ 형용사 vs 부사) 'the to-do lists were'의 보어 자리에 오는 형용사 'specific'이 'the 비교급 SV, the 비교급 SV' 표현으로 인해 앞부분으로 도치된 형태로 적절히 쓰인 오답

주요 어휘 및 표현

investigate	조사하다	ease	편안하게 만들다
todo list	해야 할 일 목록	task	일, 과업
confirm	확인해 주다	presleep	잠들기 전
matter	중요하다	specific	구체적인, 상세한
author	저자, 필자	figure	결론짓다, 생각하다, 이해하다
unload	짐을 내려놓다, 부담을 덜다	turn ~ over in one's mind	~을 곰곰이 생각하다

2. 정답 [⑤]

해석

인간 피험자에 관한 과학 실험을 다루는 규정은 엄격하다. 피험자는 충분한 설명에 입각한 서면으로 된 동의를 해야 하고, 실험자는 자신들의 계획된 실험을 제출해 감독 기관에 의한 철저한 정밀 조사를 받아야 한다. 자신을 실험하는 과학자들은, 법률적으로는 아니지만, 기능적으로는 다른 사람을 실험하는 것과 관련된 규제를 피할 수 있다. 그들은 또한 관련된

윤리적인 문제도 대부분 피할 수 있다. 실험을 고안한 과학자보다 그것의 잠재적인 위험을 더 잘 알고 있는 사람은 아마 없을 것이다. 그럼에도 불구하고, 자신을 실험하는 것은 여전히 문제가 심각하다. 한 가지 명백한 문제점은 (실험에) 수반되는 위험이다. 위험이 존재한다는 것을 안다고 해서 위험이 줄어드는 것은 결코 아니다. 덜 명백한 문제점은 실험이 만들어 낼 수 있는 데이터의 제한된 범위이다. 인체의 해부학적 구조와 생리는 성별, 나이, 생활 방식, 그리고 기타 요인에 따라 사소하지만, 의미 있는 방식으로 각기 다르다. 따라서, 단 한 명의 피험자로부터 얻어진 실험 결과는 가치가 제한적이며, 피험자의 반응이 집단으로서의 인간 반응의 전형적인 것인지 이례적인 것인지 알 방법이 없다.

비법 적용

~ there is no way to know ⑤ what the subject's responses are typical or atypical of the response of humans as a group.

☞ 관계사 vs 접속사) 'to know'의 목적어 역할을 하는 명사절 자리로 완전한 형태의 문장이 이어지기 때문에 관계대명사 what은 들어갈 수 없으며 문맥상 or과 함께 쓰여 '~인지 아닌지'의 뜻을 나타내고 있으므로 what을 'whether'로 고쳐야 한다.

오답의 모든 것

① Scientists who experiment on themselves can, functionally if not legally, avoid the restrictions associated with experimenting on other people.

▶ 분사) 'restrictions'를 수식하는 형용사 자리로 '관련된 규제'라는 수동의 뜻을 나타내므로 과거 분사인 'associated'는 적절히 쓰인 오답

② They can also sidestep most of the ethical issues involved: nobody, presumably, is more aware of an experiment's potential hazards than the scientist who devised it.

▶ 수일치) 앞에 나오는 'an experiment'를 대신하는 대명사이므로 단수 대명사인 'it'은 적절히 쓰인 오답

③ Nonetheless, experimenting on oneself remains deeply problematic.

▶ 형용사 vs 부사) 동사 'remain'의 보어인 형용사 'problematic'을 수식하는 부사 자리이므로 deeply는 적절히 쓰인 오답 (deep은 '깊은', '깊게'의 뜻으로 형용사, 부사의 역할을 모두 할 수 있으며, 'deeply'는 '매우'라는 부사의 뜻을 가짐.)

④ One obvious drawback is the danger involved; knowing that it exists does nothing to reduce it.

▶ 수일치) 문장의 주어인 동명사 'knowing'은 단수 동사로 받으므로 문장의 동사로 쓰인 'does'는 적절히 쓰인 오답

주요 어휘 및 표현

regulation	규정, 규제	strict	엄격한
consent	동의	oversee	감독하다
functionally	기능적으로	restriction	규제, 제한
associated	관련된	sidestep	피하다
presumably	아마, 짐작건대	potential	잠재적인
hazard	위험	devise	고안하다, 생각해 내다
drawback	문제점, 결점	generate	만들어 내다, 발생시키다
anatomy	(해부학적) 구조	physiology	생리적 현상
derive	얻다, 끌어내다	atypical	이례적인

IV 파이널 모의고사

1. 파이널 모의고사 1회

본문 92쪽

1. 정답 [⑤]

해석

텔레비전에서 시간이 압축되는 방식은 상호 작용의 타이밍과는 다르다. 구체적으로 말하자면, 일상을 특징짓는 짧은 멈춤과 지연은 편집을 통해 제거되고, 새로운 특색, 즉 웃음 트랙이 더해진다. (C) 수 시간, 심지어 수 일(日)을 수 분(分)으로, 그리고 수 분(分)을 수 초(秒)로 압축시키면서 행동이 빠르고 수월하게 흘러가는 압축된 사건이 그것의 익숙한 결과이다. 일상에서는 흔한 기다림을 시청자들이 경험하지 않아도 된다. 이러한 시간의 사용은 일반적인 의미로는 부자연스럽게 보일 수 있으나, 텔레비전 시청자들은 그것을 기대하게 되었고, 비평가들은 그것을 요구한다. (B) 더 중요하게는, 텔레비전 연기자들, 혹은 정치가들처럼 텔레비전에 의존하는 사람들은 순간을 포착하는 한 문장으로 생생하게 표현된 말 혹은 비유적 표현과 같은 시간 압축 요건을 충족할 수 있는 그들의 능력으로 시청자(유권자)들에 의해 평가를 받는다. (A) 신문과 잡지 기사에서 굵은 활자로 인쇄되거나 네모 표시된 삽입란에 들어가는 것이 그러한 말이다. 그렇기 때문에, 압축 기술은 텔레비전이 가진 시간의 또 다른 중요한 특성인 리듬과 속도를 강조한다.

비법 적용

Distinct from the timing of interaction is the way in which time is compressed on television. Specifically, the pauses and delays that characterize everyday life are removed through editing, and new accents are added—namely, a laugh track.

☞ 매일의 일상적인 시간과 구별되는 '텔레비전의 시간 압축 방식'에 대해 구체적으로 설명하고 있다.

(A) It is the statement that is in bold print or the boxed insert in newspaper and magazine articles. As such, compression techniques accentuate another important temporal dimension of television—rhythm and tempo.

☞ (the+명사) 신문과 잡지 기사에 실리는 '그 말(the statement)'에 해당하는 것이 (A)의 앞내용에 먼저 언급되어야 한다. 여기서 '그 말'은 (B)의 'one sentence graphic statement or metaphor to capture the moment'를 의미한다.

☞ (another) 'another+명사' 형태인 '텔레비전이 가진 시간의 또 다른 중요한 특성(another important temporal dimension of television)'을 통해 앞내용에 '명사'에 해당하는 '텔레비전 시간의 다른 특성'이 먼저 언급되어야 함을 알 수 있다.

(B) More important, television performers, or people who depend on television, such as politicians, are evaluated by viewers (voters) on their ability to meet time compression requirements, such as the one sentence graphic statement or metaphor to capture the moment.

☞ 'more important' 뒤에서 시간 압축에 관한 더 중요한 내용을 언급하고 있으므로, 시간 압축에 관한 다른 중요성이나 필요성이 (B) 앞에 먼저 언급되어야 한다.

☞ 시간 압축의 중요성으로 텔레비전 연기자들이나 정치인들은 시간 압축이 가능한 '생생한 말이나 비유(one sentence graphic statement or metaphor)'가 시청자(유권자)들에게 좋은 평가를 받게 할 수도 있다고 언급하고 있다. 여기서 말하는 '생생한 말이나 비유'는 (A)의 'the statement'이다

(C) The familiar result is a compressed event in which action flows with rapid ease, compacting hours or even days into minutes, and minutes into seconds. Audiences are spared the waiting common to everyday life. Although this use of time may appear unnatural in the abstract, the television audience has come to expect it, and critics demand it.

☞ 시간을 압축하여 빠르게 흘러가는 '압축된 사건(a compressed event)'이 '익숙한 결과(The familiar result)'라고 말하고 있다. 앞내용에는 이에 대한 원인이 언급되어야 한다.

☞ 'action flows with rapid ease, compacting hours or even days into minutes, and minutes into seconds'의 의미는 주어진 글에서 말하는 멈춤과 지연이 편집되는 '시간 압축(time is compressed)'과 동일한 의미를 가진다.

☞ (C)의 마지막 문장에서 시간의 압축을 기대하고 요구하는 시청자와 비평가들에 관한 내용은 시간 압축의 필요성 및 중요성에 해당하는 말이므로 (B)의 앞에 오기에 적절한 내용하다.

오답의 모든 것

(1) 첫 번째 문단 찾기

▶ **(C)의 'The familiar result'인 '압축된 사건'에 해당하는 것은 문맥상 주어진 글에서 말하는 '텔레비전의 시간 압축'으로 결과를 의미하므로 주어진 글 뒤에 (C)는 정답**

▶ (A)의 'the statement'가 주어진 글에서 언급되지 않았으므로 (A)는 오답

▶ (B) 뒤에서 시간 압축의 추가적인 중요성에 대해 말하고 있으나, 주어진 글에서는 '시간 압축'의 방식만을 언급하고 있으므로 (B)는 오답

(2) 두 번째 문단 찾기

▶ **(C)에서 언급한 시청자들과 비평가들 이외에도 (B)의 연기자나 정치가들이 텔레비전의 시간 압축에 의존한다는 내용이 자연스러우므로 (B)가 정답**

▶ (A)의 'the statement'가 (C)에서 언급되지 않았으므로 (A)는 오답

(3) 세 번째 문단 찾기

▶ **(B)의 'one sentence graphic statement or metaphor to capture the moment'에 해당하는 것이 (A)의 'the statement'를 의미하므로 (B) 뒤에 (A)는 정답**

주요 어휘 및 표현

distinct from	~와 구별되는	compress	압축하다
insert	삽입하다	accentuate	강조하다
temporal	시간적인	metaphor	비유
graphic	시각적인	compact	압축된
abstract	추상적인	critic	비평가

본문 93쪽

2. 정답 [⑤]

해석

카카오 열매 안이나 냄비 안, 혹은 어디에 있든, 당 분자가 가열되었을 때 갈색으로 변하는 이유는 탄소의 존재와 관련이 있다. (C) 당은 탄수화물인데, 이것은 당이 탄소("carbo"), 수소("hydr") 그리고 산소("ate") 원자로 이루어졌다는 것을 의미한다. 가열되었을 때, 이 긴 분자는 더 작은 단위로 분해되고, 이 중 일부는 너무 작아서 증발한다(이것은 좋은 냄새가 나는 이유를 설명해 준다). (B) 대체로, 더 큰 것이 탄소가 풍부한 분자라서, 이것이 남게 되고, 이 안에는 탄소탄소 이중 결합이라고 불리는 구조가 있다. 이 화학 구조는 빛을 흡수한다. 적은 양일 때 그것은 캐러멜화된 당에 황갈색을 띠게 한다. (A) 더 로스팅하면 일부의 당이 (사방에 이중 결합이 있는) 순수 탄소가 되는데, 그것은 탄맛과 진갈색을 만들어낸다. 완전히 로스팅하면 숯이 된다. 즉 모든 당이 탄소가 되고, 검은색이 된다.

비법 적용

The reason why any sugar molecule—whether in cocoa bean or pan or anywhere else—turns brown when heated is to do with the presence of carbon.
☞ 당 분자를 가열하면 탄소로 인해(원인) 갈색으로 변한다(결과)고 말하고 있다.

(A) Further roasting will turn some of the sugar into pure carbon (double bonds all round), which creates a burnt flavor and a dark-brown color. Complete roasting results in charcoal: all of the sugar has become carbon, which is black.
☞ 'further roasting'이라는 표현을 통해 앞에서 먼저 가열 과정이 있었음을 예상할 수 있다. 또한 '이중 결합(double bonds)'이 무엇인지에 대한 설명이 (A) 앞에 먼저 와야 한다.
☞ 색깔 변화(yellow brown → dark brown → black)도 단서가 될 수 있다.

(B) On the whole, it is the carbonrich molecules that are larger, so these get left behind, and within these there is a structure called a carbon-carbon double bond. This chemical structure absorbs light. In small amounts it gives the caramelizing sugar a yellow-brown color.
☞ '더 큰(larger)' 부분이 남는다고 말하려면 앞에서 '작은', 또는 크기를 비교할만한 대상이 (B)의 앞에 먼저 언급되어야 한다.
☞ '탄소-탄소 이중결합(a carbon-carbon double bond)'이라는 말이 처음 언급되었으며, 색깔의

변화를 설명하고 있음에 주목한다.

(C) Sugars are carbohydrates, which is to say that they are made of carbon ("carbo-"), hydrogen ("hydr"), and oxygen ("ate") atoms. When heated, these long molecules disintegrate into smaller units, some of which are so small that they evaporate (which accounts for the lovely smell).
☞ 당의 구성 성분으로 탄소, 수소, 산소에 대해 언급하고 있다. 가열하면 이들은 더 작은 단위로 분해된다고 말하고 있다.

오답의 모든 것

(1) 첫 번째 문단 찾기

▶ **주어진 글에서 당 분자를 가열하면 탄소로 인해 색깔이 변한다고 말한 뒤에, 이러한 과정을 설명하기 위해 당 분자에 탄소가 포함되어 있다고 먼저 말하는 것이 자연스러우므로 (C)가 정답**

▶ 주어진 글에서 크기를 비교할 만한 대상이 언급되지 않았으므로 (B)는 오답

▶ (A)의 'further roasting'과 색깔 변화 내용은 (B)와 (C)에서 말하는 가열 과정과 색깔 변화 뒤에 나오는 것이 자연스러우므로 주어진 글 뒤에 (A)는 오답

(2) 두 번째 문단 찾기

▶ **(C)에서 가열했을 때 크기가 작은 분자들로 분해 및 증발 된다고 언급한 뒤에, (B)에서 더 큰 탄소 분자는 남아있다고 말하는 것이 자연스러우므로 (B)가 정답**

▶ (A)의 'double bonds'에 대한 설명과 색깔 변화가 (C)에서 아직 언급되지 않았으므로 (A)는 오답

(3) 세 번째 문단 찾기

▶ **(A)에서 말하는 추가 가열, 색깔 변화, 'double bonds'에 대한 설명이 (B)에서 모두 언급되었으므로 (B)뒤에 (A)는 정답**

주요 어휘 및 표현

molecule	분자	carbon	탄소
roasting	가열, 굽기	burnt	탄
charcoal	숯	caramelize	카라멜로 만들다
hydrogen	수소	disintegrate	분해되다

본문 94쪽

3. 정답 [②]

해석

듣는 것보다 보는 것과 관련된 어떤 분야가 있다면, 그것은 과학이다. 서양 문화의 시각적 편향을 강조하는 학자들은 자신들이 가장 선호하는 예로 과학을 지적하기조차 한다. 이미지, 그래프, 그리고 도표를 사용하지 않고 연구를 하는 것이 불가능한 것처럼 보이기 때문에, 그들의 관점에서 과학은 최상의 시각적 노력이다. 과학 역사학자들과 사회학자들은 보는 것 외에 듣는 것을 포함한 감각들이 지식의 발전에 있어 얼마나 중요했는지를 보여 주면서 이러한

주장을 최근에 바로잡았는데, (그것은) 특히 실험실 안에서 두드러졌다. 그들은 과학적 연구가 시각적 관찰 그 이상의 것을 포함한다는 점을 강조한다. 결과를 판독하는 것, 그래서 보는 것을 요구하는 것처럼 보일 뿐인 측정 도구의 도입은 과학자들의 다른 감각 사용을 배제하지 않았다. 도리어, 실험 환경에서의 과학적 연구는 흔히 신체 능력들을 필요로 하는데, 그것들 중 하나는 듣는 것이다. 그러나 과학 그 자체의 세계는 여전히 듣는 것을 보는 것보다 지식 생산으로 들어가는 덜 객관적인 입구로 여긴다.

비법 적용

Historians and sociologists of science have recently corrected this claim by showing how senses other than seeing, including listening, have been significant in the development of knowledge, notable in the laboratory.

☞ (this+명사) 'this claim'이라는 단서를 통해 앞내용 예상하기

☞ 'corrected this claim'이라는 표현을 통해 앞내용에 '이 주장(this claim)'에 해당하는 언급이 먼저 나오고 이것에 반대하는 새로운 주장이 나오는 지점임을 알 수 있다.

☞ 'how senses other than seeing, including listening, have been significant'라는 표현을 통해 앞내용에는 시각의 중요성이, 뒷부분에는 듣기와 같은 시각 이외의 감각 기관의 중요성이 언급될 것이라 예상해 볼 수 있다. 'other than'은 '~이외의' 의미이다.

If there is any field that is associated with seeing rather than with hearing, it is science. Scholars who emphasize the visual bias in Western culture even point to science as their favorite example.

☞ '보는 것(seeing)'과 관련된 '과학'이라는 분야와 서양 문화의 '시각적 편향(the visual bias)'에 대해 언급하고 있다. '편향'이라는 단어를 통해 '시각'을 비판하는 내용의 글이라 예상해 볼 수 있다.

① Because doing research seems impossible without using images, graphs, and diagrams, science is – in their view – a visual endeavor par excellence.

☞ 과학이 '최상의 시각적 노력(a visual endeavor par excellence)'이라는 기존의 관점을 다시 한번 강조하고 있다.

② They stress that scientific work involves more than visual observation.

☞ (they) 'They'가 의미하는 것이 앞에서 무엇 혹은 누구를 가리키는지 확인한다. 동사인 '강조하다(stress)'를 보면 'They'가 사람을 언급하고 있음을 알 수 있으며, 앞 문장에는 이를 가리킬만한 복수 명사가 없으므로 'They'에 관련된 인물이 추가적으로 필요하다. 또한 과학적 연구가 '시각적 관찰 그 이상의 것(more than visual observation)'과 관련된다는 말은 앞에서 말하는 '시각적 편향'과 논리적으로 어울리지 않는 표현이다.

③ The introduction of measurement devices that merely seem to require the reading of results and thus seeing has not ruled out the deployment of the scientists' other senses.

☞ 결과를 보고 읽어야 하는 것처럼 보이는 측정 도구가 도입되었으나, 이로 인해 과학자들의 시각 이외의 다른 감각 사용이 배제된 것은 아니다(not ruled out the deployment of the scientists' other senses)'라는 말의 의미는 시각 이외의 다른 감각의 필요성을 의미한다.

④ On the contrary, scientific work in experimental settings often calls for bodily skills, one of which is listening.
☞ (on the contrary) 여기서 'On the contrary'는 앞 문장의 'not' 과 결합하여, 'not A but B'의 'but'과 같은 의미를 갖는다. 과학적 연구는 앞 문장에서 말한 '다른 감각이 배제'되는 것이 아니라 듣기와 같은 신체 능력을 필요로 한다고 말하고 있다.

⑤ The world of science itself, however, still considers listening a less objective entrance into knowledge production than seeing.
☞ (however) 역접의 연결사 뒤에서 여전히 시각에 대해 강조하는 과학 세상에 대해 언급하고 있다.

오답의 모든 것

① Because doing research seems impossible without using images, graphs, and diagrams, science is – in their view – a visual endeavor par excellence.
▶ 과학 연구에서 강조하는 시각의 중요성이 언급되고 있으므로 오답

② They stress that scientific work involves more than visual observation.
▶ **문맥상 'They'가 가리키는 것이 사람인데, 앞 문장에는 지칭할 대상이 없다. 또한 시각적 관찰 이상의 것을 강조한다는 말은 앞 문장과 상충되기 때문에 정답 ('They'는 주어진 문장의 'Historians and sociologists'을 의미함.)**

③ The introduction of measurement devices that merely seem to require the reading of results and thus seeing has not ruled out the deployment of the scientists' other senses.
▶ 측정 장치의 도입이 시각에 대한 중요성을 의미하는 것으로 잘못 이해하여 고를 수 있는 오답

④ On the contrary, scientific work in experimental settings often calls for bodily skills, one of which is listening.
▶ 'On the contrary'라는 대조의 연결사가 앞의 내용을 부정하는 내용으로 잘못 생각하여 고를 수 있는 오답 (앞 문장의 내용을 강조하는 역할로 쓰임.)

⑤ The world of science itself, however, still considers listening a less objective entrance into knowledge production than seeing.
▶ 듣는 능력이 중요하지만, 여전히 과학의 세계가 '듣는 것'을 경시하고 있다는 의미이므로 오답

주요 어휘 및 표현

sociologist	사회학자	correct	바로잡다
claim	주장	significant	중요한
notable	두드러진	laboratory	실험실
bias	편향, 편견	endeavor	노력
par excellence	최상의	stress	강조하다

measurement	측정	rule out	~을 배제하다
experimental	실험의	bodily	신체의

본문 95쪽

4. 정답 [④]

해석

영화에는 문법이 없다. 그러나 영화 언어 사용에 관한 어렴풋이 정의된 몇 가지 규칙이 있고, 영화의 문법, 즉 그것의 체계적인 (처리) 방식은 이러한 규칙들을 정리하고 그것들 사이의 관계를 보여준다. 문어와 구어에서와 마찬가지로, 영화의 문법은 그것(영화)에서의 사용의 결과물이지 그것의 결정 요인은 아니라는 것을 기억하는 것이 중요하다. 영화 문법에 관해 미리 정해진 것은 아무것도 없다. 오히려, 그것은 특정 방법이 실제로 운용할 수 있고 유용하다는 것이 밝혀지면서 자연스럽게 발전했다. 문어와 구어의 문법처럼, 영화의 문법은 자연스럽게 성장한 것으로 규범적이지 않고 기술적이고, 여러 해에 걸쳐 상당히 변화했다. '할리우드 문법'은 지금은 웃기는 것처럼 들릴지 모르지만, 30년대, 40년대, 50년대 초반에는 할리우드 영화의 제작 방식의 정확한 모델이었다.

비법 적용

Rather, it evolved naturally as certain devices were found in practice to be both workable and useful.
☞ (rather) 연결사 'Rather'을 이용해 앞내용을 예상해 본다.
☞ 앞내용에 'it'이 가리키는 단수 명사가 무엇인지 생각하며 읽는다.
☞ 'rather'는 '~이 아니다'라는 말 뒤에 나와야 한다. 주어진 문장에서 '그것이 자연스럽게 발전했다(it evolved naturally)'라고 하였으므로 주어진 문장 앞에는 '인위적이지 않다', '고정된 것이 아니다'라는 의미가 먼저 나오고, 뒷부분은 자연스럽게 발전했다는 내용이 나올 것으로 예상해 볼 수 있다.

Film has no grammar.
☞ '영화에는 문법이 없다'라는 주제가 제시되었다.

① There are, however, some vaguely defined rules of usage in cinematic language, and the syntax of film – its systematic arrangement – orders these rules and indicates relationships among them.
☞ 연결사 'however' 뒤에서 (문법은 없지만) 영화에서 언어 사용의 어렴풋한 규칙이 존재한다고 말하고 있다.

② As with written and spoken languages, it is important to remember that the syntax of film is a result of its usage, not a determinant of it.
☞ 영화의 문법은 '영화 사용의 결과물일 뿐이지 영화를 결정짓는 요소가 아니다(a result of its usage, not a determinant of it)'라는 내용으로 보아 영화에 문법이 없음을 알 수 있다.

③ There is nothing preordained about film syntax.

☞ 앞에서 언급한 말을 '영화 문법은 미리 정해진 규칙이 없다(nothing preordained about film syntax)'는 말로 다시 한번 강조하고 있다.

④ Like the syntax of written and spoken language, the syntax of film is an organic development, descriptive rather than prescriptive, and it has changed considerably over the years.
☞ 주어진 문장에서 언급된 'it evolved naturally'라는 표현을 유사한 의미의 'an organic development', 'it has changed considerably over the years'로 다시 한번 반복하고 있다.

⑤ "Hollywood Grammar" may sound laughable now, but during the thirties, forties, and early fifties it was an accurate model of the way Hollywood films were constructed.
☞ '30년대, 40년대, 50년대 초반(during the thirties, forties, and early fifties)'동안 구축되었다는 표현은 앞 문장의 오랜 시간에 걸쳐 변화해 왔다(it has changed considerably over the years)는 내용과 자연스럽게 연결되고 있다.

오답의 모든 것

① There are, however, some vaguely defined rules of usage in cinematic language, and the syntax of film – its systematic arrangement – orders these rules and indicates relationships among them.
▶ 역접 뒤에서 문법은 없지만 규칙이 존재한다는 말이 자연스러우므로 오답

② As with written and spoken languages, it is important to remember that the syntax of film is a result of its usage, not a determinant of it.
▶ 영화에 문법이 없다는 내용이 자연스럽게 이어지고 있으므로 오답

③ There is nothing preordained about film syntax.
▶ 영화에 정해진 문법이 없다는 내용이 반복되며 자연스럽게 이어지고 있으므로 오답

④ Like the syntax of written and spoken language, the syntax of film is an organic development, descriptive rather than prescriptive, and it has changed considerably over the years.
▶ 앞내용은 주어진 문장을 통해 예상한 '인위적이지 않다', '고정된 것이 아니다'라는 의미이며, '자연스러운 성장, 변화' 등의 표현이 주어진 문장의 의미와 문맥상 동일하므로 정답(주어진 문장의 'it'은 ③번의 'film syntax'을 의미함.)

⑤ "Hollywood Grammar" may sound laughable now, but during the thirties, forties, and early fifties it was an accurate model of the way Hollywood films were constructed.
▶ 영화 문법이 오랜 기간에 걸쳐 변화해 오고 있다는 앞 문장의 구체적인 사례로서, 'rather'와 어울리는 표현이 앞 문장에 없으므로 오답

주요 어휘 및 표현

vaguely	어렴풋이	cinematic	영화의
syntax	문법, 통사론	determinant	결정 요인
evolve	발전하다	device	방법, 장치
workable	운용할 수 있는	organic	자연스러운, 서서히 생기는
descriptive	기술적인	prescriptive	규범적인
accurate	정확한	construct	제작하다

본문 96쪽

5. 정답 [①]

해석

작은 것에서 큰 것으로 규모가 커지는 것은 기본적인 요소가 변하지 않거나 보존되도록 유지하면서 흔히 단순함에서 복잡함으로의 진화를 수반한다. 이것은 공학, 경제학, 회사, 도시, 유기체, 그리고 어쩌면 가장 극적으로는 진화 과정에서 흔하다. 예를 들어, 대도시의 고층 건물은 소도시의 보통 가정집보다 상당히 더 복잡한 물체이지만, 역학의 문제, 에너지와 정보의 분배, 전기 콘센트, 수도꼭지, 전화기, 노트북 컴퓨터, 문 등의 크기를 포함한 건축과 디자인의 기본 원리는 모두 건물의 규모와 상관없이 거의 똑같이 유지된다. 마찬가지로, 유기체는 대단히 다양한 크기 그리고 놀랄 만큼 다양한 형태와 상호 작용을 가지도록 진화했는데, 그것은 흔히 증가하는 복잡성을 반영하지만, 세포, 미토콘드리아, 모세관, 그리고 심지어 나뭇잎과 같은 근본적인 구성 요소는 몸체의 크기, 혹은 그것들이 속한 체계 부류의 복잡함이 증가함에 따라 눈에 띄게 변하지는 않는다.

비법 적용

〈빈칸에서 묻는 말 파악하기〉

Scaling up from the small to the large is often accompanied by an evolution from simplicity to complexity while ______________________________.

☞ '작은 것에서 큰 것으로 규모가 커지는 것(Scaling up from the small to the large)'에 대해 묻고 있다.

☞ 빈칸 문장이 예시 앞에 위치하고 있으므로 주제문에 해당하며, 빈칸 뒤에서 두 개의 사례가 제시되었기 때문에 예시의 공통점을 찾아 빈칸을 완성해야 한다.

This is familiar in engineering, economics, companies, cities, organisms, and, perhaps most dramatically, evolutionary process.

☞ 'This'는 앞 문장의 내용을 의미하며, 이것이 많은 곳에서 일어나는 일반적인 현상이라고 말하고 있다.

For example, a skyscraper in a large city is a significantly more complex object than a modest family dwelling in a small town, but the underlying principles of construction and design, including questions of mechanics, energy and information distribution, the size of electrical outlets, water faucets, telephones, laptops, doors, etc., all remain approximately the same independent of the size of the building.

☞ 대도시의 큰 빌딩과 작은 마을의 집을 예시로 설명하고 있다. 건물의 규모는 다르지만, 'but' 뒤에서 적용되는 '건축과 디자인의 기본 원리(the underlying principles of construction and design)'는 '동일하다(all remain approximately the same independent of the size of the building)'고 말하고 있다. '규모가 커졌다, 복잡하다'는 빈칸 문장의 'Scaling up from the small to the large', 'an evolution from simplicity to complexity'를 의미한다.

Similarly, organisms have evolved to have an enormous range of sizes and an extraordinary diversity of morphologies and interactions, which often reflect increasing complexity, yet fundamental building blocks like cells, mitochondria, capillaries, and even leaves do not appreciably change with body size or increasing complexity of the class of systems in which they are embedded.

☞ 'Similarly' 뒤에서 앞내용과 유사한 사례를 제시하고 있다.

☞ 앞의 사례와 동일하게 연결사 'yet'의 앞에는 유기체의 진화를 '규모가 커졌다, 복잡하다' 등으로 설명하였으며, 뒷부분에서는 '근본적인 구성 요소(fundamental building blocks)'는 '눈에 띄게 변하지는 않는다(do not appreciably change with body size or increasing complexity of the class of systems)'고 설명하고 있다.

오답의 모든 것

① 기본적인 요소가 변하지 않거나 보존되도록 유지하면서
▶ **크기와 상관없이 기본 요소들이 변하지 않거나 유지된다는 것이 두 사례의 공통점이므로 정답**

② 구조적인 성장을 위한 에너지를 최적화하면서
▶ 구조적인 성장을 위한 에너지 사용을 최적화한다는 내용은 언급되지 않았으므로 오답

③ 이미 존재하는 요소들에 새로운 기능을 부여하면서
▶ 이미 존재하는 요소에 새로운 기능들을 할당한다는 내용은 언급되지 않았으므로 오답

④주변으로부터 새로운 요소들을 통합하면서
▶ 주변 환경으로부터 새로운 요소들을 통합한다는 내용은 언급되지 않았으므로 오답

⑤ 필요 없는 부분들의 제거를 가속화하면서
▶ 필요 없는 부분들의 제거를 가속화시킨다는 내용은 언급되지 않았으므로 오답

주요 어휘 및 표현

scale up	(크기나 규모가) 커지다	be accompanied by	~을 수반하다
evolution	진화, 발전	simplicity	단순함
complexity	복잡함	organism	유기체

dramatically	극적으로	skyscraper	고층건물, 마천루
modest	보통의, 수수한	underlying principle	기본원리
construction	건축, 건설	mechanics	역학, 기계학
distribution	분배, 분포	outlet	콘센트, 출구
water faucet	수도꼭지	approximately	거의
similarly	마찬가지로, 비슷하게	extraordinary	놀랄 만한, 대단한
reflect	반영하다, 반사하다	fundamental	근본적인
building block	구성 요소	appreciably	눈에 띄게, 상당히

본문 97쪽

6. 정답 [②]

해석

작가가 누구인지, 그리고 글이나 예술 작품을 창작할 때 그 사람이 가졌을 법한 의도가 무엇인지를 아는 것은 우리 대부분에게 엄청나게 중요하다. 어떤 예술 작품을 누가 썼는지, 혹은 창작했는지 알지 못하는 것은 흔히 심하게 좌절감을 준다. 우리의 문화는 화자, 작가, 예술가의 정체성에 가치를 크게 둔다. 어쩌면 '작가 정체성'의 가장 중요한 하나의 측면은, 명의상의 작가 정체성이 제공한다고 여겨지는, 막연하게 이해되는 인간의 창조성, 개성, 그리고 권위의 존재이다. 미술관의 방문객이 개별 화가의 이름도 알지 못한 채 한 방 가득한 그림들에 감탄하는 것, 혹은 독자가 자신이 읽고 있는 소설의 작가가 누구인지 알지 못하는 것은 거의 생각할 수 없다. 출판사들은 그들 도서의 표지, 책등, 그리고 속표지에 자랑스럽게 작가의 이름을 보여 준다. 'The New York Review of Books'와 'The New York Times Book Review'에 실리는 책 광고는 보통은 작가의 사진을 포함하고 작가가 자신의 작품에 관해 이야기할 때 한 말을 인용하는데, 이 두 가지는 모두 우리의 관심이 그들의 책만큼이나 작가에게도 있다는 것을 보여 준다.

비법 적용

〈빈칸에서 묻는 말 파악하기〉

Book advertisements in The New York Review of Books and The New York Times Book Review regularly include pictures of authors and quote authors as they talk about their work, both of which show that ______________________.

☞ 빈칸에서는 'both of which(책 광고에 실린 저자의 사진의 저자의 말)'이 무엇을 시사하는지 묻고 있다.

Knowing who an author is and what his or her likely intentions are in creating text or artwork is tremendously important to most of us. Not knowing who wrote, or created, some artwork is often very frustrating.

☞ '작가가 누구인지와 작품을 만든 의도를 아는 것(Knowing who an author is and what his or her likely intentions are in creating text or artwork)'이 중요하다고 말하고 있다.

Our culture places great worth on the identity of speakers, writers, and artists. Perhaps the single most important aspect of "authorship" is the vaguely apprehended presence of human creativity, personality, and authority that nominal authorship seems to provide.
☞ 앞에서 말한 '작가가 누구인가'에 대한 것을 'the identity', 'authorship' 등으로 표현하였다.
☞ 앞 문장과 마찬가지로 작품의 작가를 아는 것이 매우 중요하다는 이야기를 반복하고 있다.

It is almost unthinkable for a visitor to an art museum to admire a roomful of paintings without knowing the names of the individual painters, or for a reader not to know who the writer is of the novel she is reading.
☞ 작가가 누구인지 아는 것이 매우 중요함을 또 다시 반복하여 이야기한다.

Publishers proudly display authors' names on the jackets, spines and title pages of their books.
☞ 출판사에서 그들의 책에서 작가에 대한 정보를 자랑스럽게 보여준다고 하였는데, 이것은 작품을 쓴 작가가 누구인지가 중요하다는 것을 의미한다.

Book advertisements in The New York Review of Books and The New York Times Book Review regularly include pictures of authors and quote authors as they talk about their work, both of which show that ________________.
☞ 'both of which'는 책 광고에 실린 저자의 사진과 저자의 말을 의미하며, 이것은 작가의 정체성, 즉 작가가 누구인지를 아는 것이 우리에게 얼마나 중요한지를 보여주고 있다.

오답의 모든 것

① 책을 홍보하는 방식이 다양화되고 있다
▶ 작가의 정체성이 중요하기 때문에 작가에 관한 정보를 광고에 싣는다는 것일 뿐, 광고 전략이 다양하다는 의미가 아니므로 오답

② 우리의 관심이 그들의 책만큼이나 작가에게도 있다
▶ 작가가 누구인지 즉, 작가의 정체성에 관심이 있다는 말이므로 정답

③ 작가들은 당대의 유명한 작품들의 영향을 받는다
▶ 작가가 당대의 인기 있는 작품들에 의해 영향을 받는다는 말은 언급된 적 없으므로 오답

④ 책의 표지가 타겟 독자층을 보여준다
▶ 주요 독자층이 아닌 작가의 정체성에 관한 글이므로 오답

⑤ 책 저술이 점점 더 책 마케팅에 의해 좌우되고 있다
▶ 책의 마케팅 방식이 책 저술에 영향을 주는 것이 아니라, 작가의 정체성이 중요하기 때문에 작가에 관한 정보를 광고에 넣는다는 의미이므로 오답

주요 어휘 및 표현

author	작가, 저자	intention	의도
tremendously	엄청나게	frustrating	좌절감을 주는
place worth on	~에 가치를 두다	vaguely	막연하게, 애매하게
apprehend	이해하다, 파악하다	presence	존재, 실재
nominal	명의상의, 이름의	unthinkable	생각할 수 없는
admire	감탄하다	jacket	(책의) 표지
spine	(책의) 등	title page	(책의) 속표지
regularly	보통은, 자주	quote	~의 말을 인용하다

본문 98쪽

7. 정답 [④]

해석

장르 영화는 영화 제작뿐 아니라 영화 시청도 단순화한다. 서부 영화에서, 외모, 복장, (행동) 방식의 관례 때문에 우리는 주인공, 조수, 악당 등을 보자마자 알아차리고 그들의 관례적 역할에 관한 우리의 기대를 그들이 저버리지 않을 것이라고 생각한다. ① 우리가 그 장르에 대해 갖는 익숙함은 시청을 더 쉽게 해 줄 뿐만 아니라 어떤 면에서는 더 즐겁게 해 준다. ② 우리가 모든 관례를 알고 그것에 익숙하기 때문에, 우리는 각각의 등장인물, 각각의 이미지, 각각의 익숙한 장면을 알아보는 데에서 즐거움을 얻는다. ③ 관례가 확립되어 반복된다는 사실은 또 다른 종류의 즐거움을 강화한다. ④ 장르 혼합은 지난 몇 십 년의 혁신이 아니라, 고전 영화 시대에 이미 영화 산업의 필수 불가결한 일부였다. ⑤ 우리의 기본적 기대를 충족한 채로 편안한 장르 속에 자리를 잡고서, 우리는 영화를 신선하고 독창적으로 보이게 만드는 창의적 변형, 정제, 그리고 복잡한 것들을 더 예민하게 인식하게 되고 그것들에 반응하게 되며, 그리고 우리의 기대를 넘어섬으로써 각각의 혁신은 흥미진진한 놀라움이 된다.

비법 적용

The genre film simplifies film watching as well as filmmaking. In a western, because of the conventions of appearance, dress, and manners, we recognize the hero, sidekick, villain, etc., on sight and assume they will not violate our expectations of their conventional roles.

☞ 글의 주제 : 장르 영화는 영화 제작과 영화 시청을 단순하게 해준다.
글의 핵심 소재 : The genre film, simplifies film watching

① Our familiarity with the genre makes watching not only easier but in some ways more enjoyable.

☞ '장르 영화에 대한 친숙함(Our familiarity with the genre)'이란 앞에서 언급한 단순화에서 나오는 '익숙함, 친숙함'을 의미하며 이것이 영화 시청에 즐거움을 준다고 말하고 있다.

② Because we know and are familiar with all the conventions, we gain pleasure from recognizing each character, each image, each familiar situation.

☞ 장르 영화의 '모든 관례(all the convention)가 주는 친숙함'이 영화 시청에 즐거움을 준다는 내용이 계속되고 있다.

③ The fact that the conventions are established and repeated intensifies another kind of pleasure.
☞ 'The fact that the conventions are established and repeated'는 영화가 주는 익숙함을 의미하여 동일한 맥락을 유지하고 있다.

④ Genre mixing is not an innovation of the past few decades; it was already an integral part of the film business in the era of classical cinema.
☞ 비법 1, 2 오류) '장르 혼합(Genre mixing)'이라는 새로운 소재에 대해 무관한 내용이 언급되고 있다.

⑤ Settled into a comfortable genre, with our basic expectations satisfied, we become more keenly aware of and responsive to the creative variations, refinements, and complexities that make the film seem fresh and original, and by exceeding our expectations, each innovation becomes an exciting surprise.
☞ 'Settled into a comfortable genre'는 장르 영화에 대한 익숙함을 나타내는 말이며, 이것이 신선하고 창의적인 것에 더 민감하게 반응하여 '흥미진진한 놀라움(an exciting surprise)'을 준다는 주제를 일관성 있게 유지하고 있다.

오답의 모든 것

① Our familiarity with the genre makes watching not only easier but in some ways more enjoyable.
▶ 장르 영화가 주는 익숙함이 즐거움을 준다는 핵심 소재와 주제가 일관성이 유지되고 있으므로 오답

② Because we know and are familiar with all the conventions, we gain pleasure from recognizing each character, each image, each familiar situation.
▶ 'the conventions'은 장르 영화의 관례를 의미하며 이것의 익숙함이 즐거움을 준다는 핵심 소재와 주제가 일관성이 유지되고 있으므로 오답

③ The fact that the conventions are established and repeated intensifies another kind of pleasure.
▶ 'The fact that the conventions are established and repeated'는 장르 영화가 주는 익숙함을 의미하며, 이것이 즐거움을 준다는 주제와 일치하는 내용이므로 오답

④ Genre mixing is not an innovation of the past few decades; it was already an integral part of the film business in the era of classical cinema.
▶ 핵심 소재나 주제와 관련 없는 무관한 문장이므로 정답 (genre mixing을 장르 영화로 혼동하지 않도록 주의)

⑤ Settled into a comfortable genre, with our basic expectations satisfied, we become more keenly aware of and responsive to the creative variations, refinements, and complexities that make the film seem fresh and original, and by exceeding our expectations, each innovation becomes an exciting surprise.
▶ 'Settled into a comfortable genre'는 장르 영화에 익숙한 상태를 의미하며 즐거움을 준다는 핵심 소재와 주제가 일관되므로 오답

주요 어휘 및 표현

simplify	단순화하다	western	서부 영화, 서부극
convention	관례	appearance	외모
manner	(행동) 방식	sidekick	조수, 동료
villain	악당, 악역	on sight	보자 마자, 발견하는 대로
assume	생각하다, 추정하다	violate	저버리다, 위반하다
familiarity	익숙함	establish	확립하다
intensify	강화하다	innovation	혁신
integral	필수 불가결한	keenly	예민하게, 열심히
responsive	반응하는, 대답하는	refinement	정제, 순화
original	독창적인	exceed	넘어서다, 능가하다

본문 99쪽

8. 정답 [④]

해석

가장 널리 퍼져있고 아쉽게도 잘못된, 환경에 대한 근거 없는 통념 중 하나는 시골이나 잎이 우거진 교외에서 '자연과 가까이' 사는 것이 최고의 '친환경적인' 생활 방식이라는 것이다. 반면에 도시들은 귀중한 자원을 빨아먹는 인공적이고 혼잡한 장소로서 자주 생태 파괴의 주요 원인으로 비난받는다. 그러나 사실들을 살펴보면, 그것은 전혀 진실이 아니다. ① 시골과 대부분의 교외의 생활양식은 출근하고, 식료품을 사고, 아이들을 학교와 활동에 데리고 가기 위해 연료를 소모하고 배기가스를 뿜어내면서 매주 자동차 안에서 오랜 시간 동안 있는 것을 포함한다. ② 반면에 도시 거주자들은 일터, 상점, 학교로 걸어가거나 대중교통을 선택할 수 있다. ③ 도시 밖에서 발견되는 더 큰 마당과 집들도 또한 에너지 사용, 물 사용, 토지 사용 측면에서 환경적인 대가를 치르게 한다. ④ 이는 대부분의 도시 거주자들이 도시 생활에 지쳐서 시골에서 정착하기로 하는 경향을 보여준다. ⑤ 지구의 미래가 더 많은 사람들이 밀집한 공동체들 속에 모이는 것에 달린 것은 분명하다.

비법 적용

One of the most widespread, and sadly mistaken, environmental myths is that living "close to nature" out in the country or in a leafy suburb is the best "green" lifestyle. Cities, on the other hand, are often blamed as a major cause of ecological destruction — artificial, crowded places that suck up precious resources. Yet, when you look at the facts, nothing could be farther from the truth.

☞ 글의 주제 : '친환경적인' 생활 방식에 대한 통념
글의 핵심 소재 : living close to nature, green lifestyle

① The pattern of life in the country and most suburbs involves long hours in the automobile each week, burning fuel and pumping out exhaust to get to work, buy groceries, and take kids to school and activities.
☞ 앞에서 언급하였듯이 '시골과 교외의 생활 양식(The pattern of life in the country and most suburbs)'이 오히려 환경에 해롭다고 말하며 기존의 통념이 잘못되었음을 말하고 있다.

② City dwellers, on the other hand, have the option of walking or taking transit to work, shops, and school.
☞ 연결사 'on the other hand' 뒤에서 시골에서의 삶과는 대조적인 도시 거주자가 오히려 더 친환경적임을 강조하고 있다.

③ The larger yards and houses found outside cities also create an environmental cost in terms of energy use, water use, and land use.
☞ 'The larger yards and houses found outside cities'은 핵심 소재인 시골 생활을 의미하며, 이 역시 '환경적 대가(an environmental cost)'를 치르게 한다는 내용으로 주제와 일관성을 유지하고 있다.

④ This illustrates the tendency that most city dwellers get tired of urban lives and decide to settle in the countryside.
☞ 비법 2, 3 오류) 문맥상 'This' 뒤에서 도시 거주자들이 시골에 정착하고 싶어 한다는 앞 문장과 무관한 내용이 전개되고 있다.

⑤ It's clear that the future of the Earth depends on more people gathering together in compact communities.
☞ '지구의 미래(the future of the Earth)'가 도시에서의 삶을 의미하는 'more people gathering together in compact communities'에 달려있다고 말하고 있으므로 주제 전체에 부합하는 문장이다.

오답의 모든 것

① The pattern of life in the country and most suburbs involves long hours in the automobile each week, burning fuel and pumping out exhaust to get to work, buy groceries, and take kids to school and activities.
▶ '시골과 교외에서 사는 사람들의 친환경적이지 못한 삶'이라는 주제와 일치하고 있으므로 오답

② City dwellers, on the other hand, have the option of walking or taking transit to work, shops, and school.
▶ 시골이나 교외에 사는 사람들과 달리 걷기나 대중교통을 이용하는 도시 거주자들이 오히려 친환경적이라는 주제와 일치하는 내용이므로 오답

③ The larger yards and houses found outside cities also create an environmental cost in terms of energy use, water use, and land use.
▶ 도시 밖의 삶인 시골과 교외의 삶이 친환경적이지 않다는 내용이므로 주제와 일치하는 오답

④ This illustrates the tendency that most city dwellers get tired of urban lives and decide to settle in the countryside.
▶ **도시인들의 시골 정착에 관한 주제와 관련 없는 내용이므로 정답**

⑤ It's clear that the future of the Earth depends on more people gathering together in compact communities.
▶ 더 많은 사람이 밀집해서 도시에 사는 것이 오히려 지구의 미래에 이롭다는 내용으로 주제와 일치하는 오답

주요 어휘 및 표현

mistaken	틀린, 잘못된	myth	근거 없는 믿음, 통념, 신화
ecological	생태계[학]의, 생태상의	suck up	~을 빨아먹다[빨아들이다]
exhaust	배기가스	dweller	거주자
transit	대중교통	in terms of	~의 측면에서
illustrate	보여주다	settle	정착하다

본문 100쪽

9. 정답 [②]

해석

때로는 신뢰를 얻지 못한다는 인식이 자기 성찰에 필요한 동기를 제공할 수 있다. 직장에서 자신의 동료들이 공유된 책무를 자신에게 (믿고) 맡기지 않고 있다는 사실을 깨달은 직원은 성찰을 통해 자신이 지속적으로 다른 사람들을 실망하게 했거나 이전의 약속들을 이행하지 못했던 분야를 찾아낼 수 있다. 그러면 그녀에 대한 다른 사람들의 불신은, 그녀가 그들의 신뢰를 받을 만한 자격이 더 생기게 해 주는 방식으로 그녀가 직무의 자기 몫을 수행하지 못하게 할(→하도록 동기를 부여할) 수 있다. 하지만 신뢰할 만하고 믿을 만한 사람이 되려는 노력을 성실하게 하는 사람에 대한 불신은 혼란스럽게 할 수 있고, 그녀로 하여금 자신의 인식을 의심하고 자신을 불신하게 할 수 있다. 예를 들어 밤에 외출할 때 의심하고 믿지 않는 부모를 가진 십 대 소녀를 생각해 보라. 비록 그녀가 자신의 계획에 대해 솔직해 왔고 합의된 규칙은 어떤 것도 어기고 있지 않을지라도, 존경할 만한 도덕적 주체로서의 그녀의 정체성은 속임수와 배신을 예상하는 널리 스며 있는 부모의 태도에 의해 손상된다.

비법 적용

Sometimes the awareness that one is distrusted can provide the necessary incentive for self-reflection.
☞ 자신이 신뢰받지 못한다는 사실을 알면 자기 성찰의 계기가 될 수 있다고 하였다. (자신에 대한 타인의 불신은 자기 성찰로 이어져 타인의 신임을 받을 만한 자격이 생기도록 노력하게 된다는 의미)

An employee who ① realizes she isn't being trusted by her co-workers with shared responsibilities at work might, upon reflection, identify areas where she has consistently let others down or failed to follow through on previous commitments.

☞ (병렬-예시) 다른 사람들을 실망시켰거나 약속을 이행하지 않아 신뢰받지 못하는 '한 직원(an employee)'의 예시이다. 'an employee'와 같이 'a(n) 사람'의 형태도 예시의 일종이므로 앞 문장의 내용과 동일한 의미의 문장이 되어야 한다. 앞 문장의 '신뢰를 얻지 못한다는 인식(the awareness that one is distrusted)'은 '신뢰받지 못하고 있음을 안다(① realizes she isn't being trusted)'와 같은 의미이다.

Others' distrust of her might then ② forbid her to perform her share of the duties in a way that makes her more worthy of their trust.
☞ (병렬-예시) 앞의 예시에 등장한 'an employee'를 지칭하는 'her'에 대한 설명이 이어지고 있다. 앞에서 신뢰받지 못한다는 사실을 알면 자기 성찰의 계기로 이어진다고 하였으므로, '그녀에 대한 다른 사람들의 불신(Others' distrust of her)'은 그녀가 자기 성찰을 통해 신뢰받을 가치가 있는 행동을 하게 만든다는 의미가 되어야 한다.

	신뢰를 얻지 못한다는 인식	자기 성찰
첫 번째 문장	the awareness that one is distrusted	provide the necessary incentive for self-reflection
두 번째 문장	realizes she isn't being trusted	upon reflection, identify areas where she has consistently let others down or failed to follow through on previous commitments
세 번째 문장	Others' distrust of her	perform her share of the duties in a way that makes her more worthy of their trust

But distrust of one who is ③ sincere in her efforts to be a trustworthy and dependable person can be disorienting and might cause her to doubt her own perceptions and to distrust herself.
☞ (역접) 역접 뒤에서 앞내용과는 상반된 사례를 보여주고 있다. 앞에서는 다른 이를 실망시킨 사람에 대한 불신이 언급되었으므로 이와 상반되는 신뢰받기 위해 노력하는 성실한 사람에 대한 불신의 사례가 나와야 한다.

Consider, for instance, a teenager whose parents are ④ suspicious and distrustful when she goes out at night
☞ (예시,병렬) 앞에서 언급한 성실한 사람에 대한 불신의 사례이다. A and B의 병렬 구조를 이루고 있으며, 부모의 불신을 받고 있는 십대의 사례를 보여주고 있다.

; even if she has been forthright about her plans and is not ⑤ breaking any agreed-upon rules, her identity as a respectable moral subject is undermined by a pervasive parental attitude that expects deceit and betrayal.
☞ (병렬) A and B의 병렬 구조를 이루고 있으므로, 'she has been forthright about her plans'와 'is not ⑤ breaking any agreed-upon rules'는 유사한 의미가 되어야 한다.

오답의 모든 것

① realizes
▶ '신뢰받지 못한다는 것을 알고 있다'는 앞내용의 사례이며, 앞 문장의 'awareness'와 동일한 의미로 적절히 쓰인 오답

② forbid
▶ **신뢰받지 못하는 것을 알면 '자기성찰을 통해 신뢰받을 행동을 하려 노력한다'는 앞내용에 대한 사례이므로 이와 동일한 의미의 문장이 되어야 하는데, 해당 어휘는 '신뢰받을 행동을 하지 못하게 한다'는 의미가 되므로 적절하지 않은 정답 (motivate로 바꿔야 함.)**

③ sincere
▶ 역접 뒤에서 신뢰받기 위해 노력하는 성실한 사람에 대한 불신의 의미가 되어야 하므로 적절히 쓰인 오답

④ suspicious
▶ 신뢰받기 위해 노력하지만 부모님에게 불신받는 십대의 예시이며 'distrustful'과 병렬 관계를 이루는 적절히 쓰인 오답

⑤ breaking
▶ 앞과 동일하게 자신의 계획에 대해 솔직하고 합의된 규칙을 깨지 않고 신뢰받기 위해 노력하는 십대의 예시로 A and B의 병렬 관계가 적절히 쓰인 오답

주요 어휘 및 표현

self-reflection	자기 성찰	identify	찾다, 발견하다
consistently	지속적으로	let down	~을 실망하게 하다
follow through on	~을 이행하다	commitment	약속, 전념
disorienting	혼란스럽게 하는	perception	인식
suspicious	의심하는	agreed-upon	합의된
undermine	손상시키다	deceit	속임수
respectable	존경할 만한	betrayal	배신

본문 101쪽

10. 정답 [⑤]

해석

편승 효과가 어떻게 발생하는지는 빛의 속력 측정의 역사로 입증된다. 이 빛의 속력은 상대성 이론의 기초이기 때문에, 과학에서 가장 빈번하고 면밀하게 측정된 물리량 중 하나이다. 우리가 아는 한, 빛의 속력은 시간이 흘러도 이제껏 아무런 변함이 없었다. 그러나 1870년부터 1900년까지 모든 실험에서 너무 높은 속력이 발견되었다. 그러고 나서, 1900년부터

1950년까지 그 반대 현상이 일어나, 모든 실험에서 너무 낮은 속력이 발견되었다! 결과치가 항상 실제 값의 어느 한쪽에 있는 이런 형태의 오류를 '편향'이라고 한다. 그것은 아마 시간이 지나면서 실험자들이 자신들이 발견할 것이라 예상한 것과 일치하도록 잠재의식적으로 결과를 조정했기 때문에 생겨났을 것이다. 결과가 그들이 예상한 것과 부합하면, 그들은 그것을 유지했다. 결과가 부합하지 않으면, 그들은 그것을 버렸다. 그들은 의도적으로 부정직한 것은 아니었고, 단지 일반 통념에 의해 영향을 받았을 뿐이었다. 그 패턴은 누군가가 예상된 것 대신에 실제로 측정된 것을 보고할 용기가 부족했을(→ 있었을) 때가 되어서야 바뀌었다.

비법 적용

How the bandwagon effect occurs is demonstrated by the history of measurements of the speed of light.
☞ '편승 효과(the bandwagon effect)'에 관한 내용을 속력 측정을 통해 설명하려고 하고 있다.

Because this speed is the basis of the theory of relativity, it's one of the most frequently and carefully measured ① quantities in science.
☞ (인과) 밑줄 친 어휘는 주어인 대명사 'it'에 대한 설명이며, 'it'은 상대성 이론을 기초로 하는 'this speed'를 의미한다. 따라서 이러한 속도는 빈번하고 면밀히 측정되는 물리량 중 하나라 볼 수 있다.

As far as we know, the speed hasn't changed over time. However, from 1870 to 1900, all the experiments found speeds that were too high. Then, from 1900 to 1950, the ② opposite happened – all the experiments found speeds that were too low!
☞ (역접) 밑줄 친 어휘인 'opposite'은 앞·뒤 내용이 서로 상반된 내용임을 뜻한다. 'too high'와 'too low'는 서로 반대 의미이다.

This kind of error, where results are always on one side of the real value, is called "bias." It probably happened because over time, experimenters subconsciously adjusted their results to ③ match what they expected to find.
☞ (인과) 밑줄 친 어휘는 주어인 'It' 즉, '편향(bias)'이 발생하는 원인에 대한 설명 부분이다. '편향(bias)의 의미를 관계부사 'where' 뒤에서 '실제 값의 어느 한쪽에(results are always on one side of the real value)' 치우친 상태라고 표현하였으므로, 실험 결과를 자신의 예상에 일치시키려 할 때 편향이 발생한다고 볼 수 있다. 다음 문장의 'If'로 시작하는 문장의 'fit', 'keep'이라는 단어를 통해서도 단서를 얻을 수 있다.

If a result fit what they expected, they kept it. If a result didn't fit, they threw it out. They weren't being intentionally dishonest, just ④ influenced by the conventional wisdom.
☞ (부연 설명) 자신의 기대에 결과를 맞추려고 하는 'bias'에 대한 구체적인 설명이다. 이러한 편향은 '부정직'의 영향이 아닌 통념의 영향임을 말하고 있다. (속도를 측정한 뒤, 그 당시에 자주 발견되는 결과 값만 취하고 그렇지 않은 결과 값은 버렸다고 하였다. 때문에 시대별로 너무 높거나, 너무 낮은 상반된 측정값은 통념의 영향으로 볼 수 있을 것이다.)

The pattern only changed when someone ⑤ lacked the courage to report what was actually measured instead of what was expected.
☞ (인과) 이러한 통념의 영향으로 인해 편향의 '패턴이 바뀌는(The pattern only changed)' 결과를 얻으려면, 예상한 것과 다른 실제 측정한 것을 보고할 용기가 '있어(had)야' 가능할 것이다.

오답의 모든 것

① quantities
▶ 속도 측정에 관한 설명으로 '양적(물리량)'이라는 표현은 적절하므로 오답

② opposite
▶ 두 시기 사이의 속도가 'too high'와 'too low'로 서로 상반된 모습을 보이고 있으므로 오답

③ match
▶ 편향의 원인은 자신이 발견한 결과를 자신의 기대와 일치시키기 때문에 발생하므로 오답

④ influenced
▶ 편향이라는 것은 부정직해서가 아니라, 통념의 영향이라는 부연 설명이므로 오답

⑤ lacked
▶ 이러한 편향의 패턴이 바뀌려면 자신이 측정한 결과가 기대와 달랐음을 보고할 용기가 필요하므로 적절하지 않은 정답 (had로 바꿔야 함.)

주요 어휘 및 표현

demonstrate	입증하다, 보여 주다	measurement	측정, 치수, 크기
relativity	상대성	subconsciously	잠재의식적으로
adjust	조정하다	match	일치하다
intentionally	의도적으로	conventional wisdom	일반 통념

본문 102쪽

11. 정답 [⑤]

해석

아이들이 어릴 때, 일의 많은 부분은 아이들이 정말로 통제권을 가지고 있음을 그들에게 보여 주는 것이다. 20년간 부모 교육자로 일했던 우리의 현명한 친구 한 명은 취학 전 연령의 아이들에게 달력을 주고 아이들 생활에서 중요한 모든 일들을 적어 보라고 조언하는데, 이는 부분적으로 아이들이 시간의 흐름을 더 잘 이해하도록, 그리고 자신들의 하루하루가 어떻게 펼쳐질지 이해하도록 도움을 주기 때문이다. 아이들이 자신의 하루를 통제하고 있다고 느끼도록 돕는 데 있어 달력이라는 도구의 중요성은 아무리 과장해도 지나치지 않다. 요일들에 다가가면서, 아이들이 그 요일들을 지워가도록 하라. 가능한 경우마다 그 일정에 대해 아이들에게 선택권을 주면서 그날의 일정을 검토하는 데 시간을 보내라. 이러한 의사소통은 존중을 보여 주어, 아이들이 자신들이 그저 여러분의 하루와 여러분의 계획에 붙어서 따라다니는 사람이 아니라는 것을 알게 되고, 어떤 일이 언제, 왜 일어나게 될지 이해하게 된다. 아이들은 나이가 더 들어감에 따라, 그 다음에는 스스로 중요한 일들을 적어 넣기 시작할 것이며, 그것은 나아가 그들이 자신의 통제감을 발달시키는 데 도움을 준다.

비법 적용

As they get older, children will then start to write in important things for themselves, ⑤ it further helps them develop their sense of control.

☞ 대명사 vs 관계대명사) 'children will then start ~ for themselves'와 'it further helps ~ their sense of control'의 두 개의 문장이 이어질 때, 접속사가 필요하므로 대명사 it이 아닌 관계사 'which'가 적절하다.

오답의 모든 것

Some of the best evidence for this ① comes from the field of musical performance.

▶ 수일치) 부분을 가리키는 대명사 'some'은 'of' 뒤의 내용을 통해 수일치가 결정되므로 단수 명사인 'the best evidence'에 맞추어 적절히 쓴 단수 동사 'comes'는 오답

One wise friend of ours who was a parent educator for twenty years ② advises giving calendars to preschoolage children and writing down all the important events in their life, in part because it helps children understand the passage of time better, and how their days will unfold.

▶ 수일치) 'of ours ~ years' 부분을 괄호로 묶고 남는 부분인 'One wise friend'는 단수이므로 단수 동사인 advises는 적절히 쓰인 오답

Have them ③ cross off days of the week as you come to them.

▶ 사역동사) 문장의 본동사가 사역동사 'Have'이므로, 목적격보어 자리에 동사원형이 적절히 쓰인 오답

Spend time going over the schedule for the day, giving them choice in that schedule wherever ④ possible.

▶ 형용사 vs 부사) wherever이하에 it is 가 생략된 구조이며, is 뒤에 들어갈 보어로 쓰인 형용사 'possible'은 적절히 쓰인 오답

주요 어휘 및 표현

demonstrate	보여주다	educator	교육자
advise	조언하다	preschoolage	취학 전 연령의
in part	부분적으로	overstate	과장하다
cross off	지우다	tagalong	뒤를 따라다니는

12. 정답 [④]

해석

심적 표상은 감각에 실제로 존재하지 않는 것들에 대한 심상이다. 일반적으로, 심적 표상은 우리가 학습하는 데 도움을 줄 수 있다. 이에 대한 최고의 증거 중 몇몇은 음악 연주 분야에서 온다. 여러 연구자들은 최고의 음악가들과 실력이 더 낮은 음악가들을 무엇이 구분 짓는가를 조사해 왔으며, 주요한 차이점들 중 하나가 최고의 음악가들이 만드는 심적 표상의 질에 있다. 새로운 작품을 연습할 때 상급 음악가들은 작품에 대한 자신의 연습, 궁극적으로 자신의 연주를 이끌기 위해 사용하는 음악에 대한 매우 정밀한 심적 표상을 가지고 있다. 특히, 그들은 자신이 그 작품을 제대로 이해하는 것에 얼마나 근접했는지와 그들이 향상하기 위해 무엇을 다르게 할 필요가 있는지를 알 수 있도록 심적 표상을 자기 자신의 피드백을 제공하기 위해 사용한다. 초급 및 중급학생들은 예를 들어 자신이 언제 틀린 음을 쳤는지 알게 해주는 음악에 대한 투박한 표상을 가질 수도 있겠으나, 더 미묘한 실수와 약점을 알아내기 위해서는 자기 선생님의 피드백에 의존해야 한다.

비법 적용

In particular, they use their mental representations to provide their own feedback so that they know how ④ closely they are to getting the piece right and what they need to do differently to improve.

☞ 형용사 vs 부사) 'how closely they are'에서 'they are' 뒤에 들어갈 보어가 필요하므로 'closely'가 아닌 형용사 'close'가 적절하다.

오답의 모든 것

When children are young, much of the work is demonstrating to them that they ① do have control.

▶ 동사의 강조) 'that' 절의 본동사 'have'를 강조하는 의미로 복수 주어인 'they'에 맞게 수일치까지 적절히 쓰인 정답

Several researchers have examined ② what differentiates the best musicians from lesser ones, and one of the major differences lies in the quality of the mental representations the best ones create.

▶ 관계사) 'what' 앞에 선행사가 없고 뒤에는 주어가 없는 불완전한 구조이므로 적절히 쓰인 오답

When ③ practicing a new piece, advanced musicians have a very detailed mental representation of the music they use to guide their practice and, ultimately, their performance of a piece.

▶ 분사) 분사구문에서 접속사를 생략하지 않은 형태이며, 'practicing'의 생략된 주어인 'advanced musicians'가 '연습하다(practice)'는 의미이므로 'practicing'은 적절히 쓰인 오답

The beginners and intermediate students may have crude representations of the music ⑤ that allow them to tell, for instance, when they hit a wrong note, but they must rely on feedback from their teachers to identify the more subtle mistakes and weaknesses.

▶ 관계사) 'that' 절 뒤의 문장이 주어가 없는 불완전한 구조이며, 선행사가 'representations of the music' 이므로 관계사 'that'은 적절히 쓰인 오답

주요 어휘 및 표현

mental	심적인, 정신의	representation	표현, 표상
differentiate	구별하다	ultimately	궁극적으로
intermediate	중급의	crude	투박한

1. 파이널 모의고사 2회

본문 106쪽

1. 정답 [②]

해석

1980년대와 90년대에, 일부 환경보호 활동가들은 오랑우탄이 20년 혹은 30년 이내에 야생에서 멸종할 것으로 예측했다. 다행히 그런 일은 발생하지 않았다. 밀레니엄의 전환기에 인지된 것보다 수천 마리나 더 많은 오랑우탄이 현존하는 것으로 알려져 있다. (B) 이것은 오랑우탄의 세계에서 아무문제가 없다는 의미가 아니다. 더 높은 그 수치는 실제 개체 수가 증가했기 때문이 아니라, 향상된 조사 기법들과 이전에 알려지지 않았던 개체들이 발견된 덕분에 나온 것이다. (A) 사실, 전체 오랑우탄 개체 수는 지난 75년간 적어도 80퍼센트 감소했다. 과학자인 Erik Meijaard가 40,000마리에서 100,000마리 사이의 오랑우탄이 보르네오섬에 살고 있다고만 말하는 것을 개의치 않는 것은 오랑우탄 연구의 어려움을 시사한다. 수마트라섬의 환경보호 활동가들은 단지 14,000마리만 그곳에서 생존하고 있다고 추측한다. (C) 이러한 감소의 상당 부분은 벌목으로 인한 서식지 파괴와 요리 및 많은 식품에 사용되는 기름을 만들기 위해 판매되는 열매를 맺는 기름 야자나무의 광대한 재배 농장이 급속도로 널리 퍼진것 때문에 초래되었다.

비법 적용

In the 1980s and '90s, some conservationists predicted that orangutans would go extinct in the wild within 20 or 30 years. Fortunately that didn't happen. Many thousands more orangutans are now known to exist than were recognized at the turn of the millennium.

☞ 오랑우탄이 20~30년 안에 멸종할 것이라는 예상과 다르게 많은 오랑우탄이 현존하고 있다고 말하고 있다.

(A) In fact, the overall population of orangutans has fallen by at least 80 percent in the past 75 years. It's indicative of the difficulty of orangutan research that scientist Erik Meijaard is willing to say only that between 40,000 and 100,000 live on Borneo. Conservationists on Sumatra estimate that only 14,000 survive there.

☞ (in fact) 연결사 'in fact' 뒤에서 오랑우탄의 인구가 80퍼센트 감소했다는 구체적인 사실을 말하고 있다. 'in fact'는 앞내용을 구체적으로 말할 때 주로 사용된다. (in fact에 역접의 의미가 있기는 하지만, 여기서는 구체적인 사실을 언급하기 위해 사용됨.)

(B) This doesn't mean that all is well in the orangutans' world. The higher figures come thanks to improved survey methods and the discovery of previously unknown populations, not because the actual numbers have increased.

☞ (this) '오랑우탄의 세계가 모두 좋다는 의미는 아니다'라는 부정적인 의미로 진술하고 있으므로, 'this'는 오랑우탄에 대한 긍정적인 진술임을 예상할 수 있다.

☞ 'the 명사' 형태인 '더 높은 수치(The higher figures)'를 통해 '수가 많다'는 내용이 (B) 앞에 먼저 언급되어야 함을 알 수 있다.

(C) Much of this loss has been driven by habitat destruction from logging and the rapid spread of vast plantations of oil palm, the fruit of which is sold to make oil used in cooking and in many food products.
☞ (this loss) 앞에서 '이 손실(this loss)'에 해당하는 '감소, 손실' 등에 대한 언급이 (C) 앞에 나와야 한다.

오답의 모든 것

(1) 첫 번째 문단 찾기

▶ **주어진 글의 '오랑우탄의 수가 많다'는 점 뒤에서 '이것(this)'이 '오랑우탄의 세계에 아무 문제가 없다는 것은 아니다'라는 문제점을 지적하는 (B)가 정답**

▶ 주어진 글의 오랑우탄의 수가 많다는 말 뒤에서 '수가 적다'라는 내용이 나오는 것은 어색하므로 (A)는 오답

▶ 주어진 글의 오랑우탄의 수가 많다는 말 뒤에서 'loss'가 나오는 것은 어색하므로 (C)는 오답

(2) 두 번째 문단 찾기

▶ **첫 번째 문단인 (B)에서 언급된 향상된 기법이나 새롭게 발견된 오랑우탄에 대한 구체적인 사례가 들어있는 (A)가 두 번째 문단으로 오기에 자연스러우므로 정답**

▶ (C)에서 말하는 '이러한 감소의 상당 부분(much of this loss)'이 (B)에서 직접적으로 언급되지 않았으므로 (C)는 오답

(3) 세 번째 문단 찾기

▶ **(A)에서 급격하게 '감소한(has fallen)' 오랑우탄의 수를 의미하는 내용이 (C)의 '이러한 감소의 상당 부분(much of this loss)'과 어울리므로 (A) 뒤에 (C)가 정답**

주요 어휘 및 표현

conservationist	보호론자	go extinct	멸종하다
millennium	천 년	indicative	보여주는, 시사하는
figure	수치	habitat destruction	서식지 파괴
vast	거대한	plantation	대농장

본문 107쪽

2. 정답 [②]

해석

기원전 5세기에, 그리스의 철학자 Protagoras는 "인간이 만물의 척도이다."라고 선언했다. 다시 말해서, 우리는 세상을 향해 "당신은 무슨 쓸모가 있는가?"라고 물어볼 자격이 있다고 느낀다. (B) 우리는 우리가 세상의 기준이라고, 즉 모든 것이 우리와 비교되어야 한다고 추정한다. 그런 추정은 우리로 하여금 많은 것을 간과하게 한다. (A) '우리를 인간답게 만들어

준다고' 일컬어지는 능력들, 즉 공감, 의사소통, 슬픔, 도구 만들기 등은 모두 우리와 세상을 공유하는 다른 지력을 지닌 존재들에게도 다양한 정도로 존재한다. 척추동물(어류, 양서류, 파충류, 조류, 포유류)은 모두 동일한 기본 골격, 장기, 신경계, 호르몬, 행동을 공유한다. (C) 다양한 자동차의 모델들이 각각 엔진, 동력 전달 체계, 네 바퀴, 문, 좌석을 가지고 있는 것과 마찬가지로, 우리는 주로 우리의 외부 윤곽과 몇 가지 내부적인 조정 면에서 다르다. 하지만 순진한 자동차 구매자들처럼, 대부분의 사람들은 오직 동물들의 다양한 겉모습만을 본다.

비법 적용

In the fifth century B.C.E., the Greek philosopher Protagoras pronounced, "Man is the measure of all things." In other words, we feel entitled to ask the world, "What good are you?"
☞ '인간은 만물의 척도이다'라는 프로타고라스의 말을 소개하고 있다.

(A) Abilities said to "make us human" — empathy, communication, grief, toolmaking, and so on — all exist to varying degrees among other minds sharing the world with us. Animals with backbones (fishes, amphibians, reptiles, birds, and mammals) all share the same basic skeleton, organs, nervous systems, hormones, and behaviors.
☞ '우리를 인간으로 만들어주는 능력들(Abilities said to "make us human")'이 사실은 다른 동물들에게도 있다고 이야기한다. 이는 주어진 글의 '인간은 만물의 척도다'라는 말과 상반된 내용이며, (B)에서 많은 것을 '간과(overlook)'하게 한다는 내용과 일맥상통한다.
☞ 모든 척추동물들이 공유하는 기본 골격, 장기, 신경 시스템, 호르몬, 행동 등의 공통적 속성에 대해 말하고 있다.

(B) We assume that we are the world's standard, that all things should be compared to us. Such an assumption makes us overlook a lot.
☞ 주어진 글에서 이야기한 '인간은 만물의 척도이다(Man is the measure of all things)'라는 말을 'we are the world's standard'로 다시 한번 언급하였다. 주어진 글 마지막 문장의 'we feel'과 (B)의 'We assume'의 주어가 동일하게 표현되어, 우리의 일반적인 생각을 의미하고 있다.
☞ (B)의 마지막 문장에서 이러한 생각이 잘못 되었다고 하는 것으로 보아, (B) 뒤에서 '인간이 만물의 척도'라는 것과 상반된 내용이 나올 것이라 예상해 볼 수 있다.

(C) Just as different models of automobiles each have an engine, drive train, four wheels, doors, and seats, we differ mainly in terms of our outside contours and a few internal tweaks. But like naive car buyers, most people see only animals' varied exteriors.
☞ 자동차의 기본적 속성이 동일하지만, 이를 간과하고 외관의 차이만 보고 자동차를 구매하는 순진한 자동차 구매자의 예를 설명하고 있다. 다양한 자동차 모델들의 기본적인 속성이 동일하듯이, 우리 인간과 동물들은 '외관과 몇 가지 내부 속성 면에서만 차이가 있다(we differ mainly in terms of our outside contours and a few internal tweaks)'고 말하고 있다. 즉, 서로 다른 몇 가지 특성만 보고 인간이 만물의 척도이며, 세상의 중심이라고 하는 것은 잘못된 생각임을 (overlook)을 말하고 있다.

오답의 모든 것

(1) 첫 번째 문단 찾기

▶ **주어진 글의 '인간이 만물의 척도'라는 말을 '인간이 세상의 기준이다'라고 다시 한번 같은 말로 표현한 (B)가 정답**

▶ 인간을 인간으로 만들어주는 능력이 동물들에게도 있다는 내용은 주어진 글과 반대의 의미이므로 (A)는 오답

▶ 자동차의 비유를 들어 우리가 작은 차이만 있을 뿐 동일하다는 내용은 주어진 글과 반대의 의미이므로 (C)는 오답

(2) 두 번째 문단 찾기

▶ **(B)에서 이러한 생각이 많은 것을 간과하게 한다고 한 뒤에 이를 구체화하여 인간에게 고유하다고 생각한 능력들이 다른 동물들에게도 존재한다고 말하는 (A)가 정답**

▶ (B)에서 말하는 우리가 간과한 것이 무엇인지에 대한 구체적 설명 없이, 곧바로 사례를 들어 설명하는 것이 어색하므로 (C)는 오답

(3) 세 번째 문단 찾기

▶ **(A)에서 모든 척추동물이 공유하는 공통적인 특성에 대해 이를 자동차에 빗대어 설명함. 공통적 속성은 동일하나 외관과 몇 가지 내부만 다를 뿐임을 의미하는 (C)가 정답**

주요 어휘 및 표현

pronounce	선언하다	measure	척도
entitled to	~할 자격이 있는	empathy	공감
grief	슬픔	amphibian	양서류
reptile	파충류	mammal	포유류
skeleton	골격	organ	장기
overlook	간과하다	drive train	동력 전달 체계
naive	순진한	exterior	겉모습

본문 108쪽

3. 정답 [④]

해석

고대 그리스 역사가인 책략가 Aeneas는 문서의 언뜻 보기에 평범한 페이지에 있는 특정한 글자 밑에 작은 구멍을 내서 비밀 메시지를 전달할 것을 제안했다. 그러한 글자는 철자를 표시해 비밀 메시지를 나타내고, 의도된 수신자는 그것을 쉽게 읽을 것이다. 그러나 그 페이지를 유심히 쳐다보는 어떤 다른 사람도 아마 핀으로 찌른 작은 구멍들을 눈치채지 못할 것이고, 그 결과 비밀 메시지를 눈치채지 못할 것이다. 2천 년 후에 영국에서 편지 쓰는 사람들은 비밀 유지를 달성하기 위해서가 아니라 과도한 우편 요금 지불을 피하기 위해 정확히

같은 방법을 사용했다. 1800년대 중반 우편 요금 체계가 확립되기 이전에는 편지를 부치는 데 100마일 당 약 1실링의 비용이 들었는데, 이는 대부분 사람들의 재력을 넘어서는 것이었다. 그러나 신문은 무료로 우송될 수 있어서 이것은 검소한 빅토리아 시대 사람들에게 빠져나갈 구멍을 제공했다. 편지를 써서 부치는 대신, 사람들은 핀으로 찌른 작은 구멍들을 사용하여 신문의 제1면에 철자를 표시해 메시지를 나타내기 시작했다. 그런 다음에 그들은 한 푼도 지불할 필요 없이 우편으로 신문을 보낼 수 있었다.

비법 적용

However, newspapers could be posted free of charge, and this provided a loophole for thrifty Victorians.

☞ (역접) 역접의 연결사로 앞・뒤 내용을 예상한다.

☞ 주어진 문장에서 신문은 무료라고 한 것으로 보아, 앞에 오는 내용은 무료가 아니거나 신문 이외의 다른 수단에 대한 것을, 뒤에 오는 내용은 신문에 대한 추가 내용이 언급될 것을 예상해 볼 수 있다.

The ancient Greek historian Aeneas the Tactician suggested conveying a secret message by pricking tiny holes under particular letters in an apparently ordinary page of text. Those letters would spell out a secret message, easily read by the intended receiver.

☞ 글자 밑에 구멍을 내어 비밀 메시지를 전달하는 방법에 대해 소개하고 있다.

① However, any other person who stared at the page would probably be unaware of pinpricks and thus the secret message.

☞ (역접) 역접의 연결사가 사용되었으므로 의도된 수신자는 비밀 메시지의 내용을 이해하지만(앞내용), 그 이외의 사람은 알아채지 못한다는 내용이 이어지는 것이 자연스럽다.

② Two thousand years later, British letter writers used exactly the same method, not to achieve secrecy but to avoid paying excessive postage costs.

☞ (the same+명사) 'the same method'를 통해 앞내용과 동일한 '비밀 메시지 전달' 방법을 다른 목적으로 사용하였다고 말하고 있다.

③ Before the establishment of the postage system in the mid1800s, sending a letter cost about a shilling for every hundred miles, beyond the means of most people.

☞ 1800년대 중반의 과다한 우편 요금에 대해 설명하고 있다.

④ Instead of writing and sending letters, people began to use pinpricks to spell out a message on the front page of a newspaper.

☞ (instead) '편지'를 대신하여 신문을 사용한다고 하였으므로, 편지를 신문으로 대체할 만한 근거가 먼저 소개되었어야 한다.

⑤ They could then send the newspaper through the post without having to pay a penny.

☞ (they) 'They'가 신문을 보냈다는 것으로 보아 사람을 가리키며 앞 문장의 'people'을 의미함을 알 수 있다.

오답의 모든 것

① However, any other person who stared at the page would probably be unaware of pinpricks and thus the secret message.

▶ 역접의 연결사 뒤에서 의도된 사람 이외에는 비밀 메시지를 알아채지 못하다는 내용이 앞내용 뒤에서 흐름상 자연스러우므로 오답

② Two thousand years later, British letter writers used exactly the same method, not to achieve secrecy but to avoid paying excessive postage costs.

▶ 같은 방법을 사용하긴 했으나 그 목적이 달라진다는 내용으로 흐름상 내용이 자연스러운 오답

③ Before the establishment of the postage system in the mid1800s, sending a letter cost about a shilling for every hundred miles, beyond the means of most people.

▶ 앞에서 언급된 과도한 비용에 대한 구체적인 설명이 자연스럽게 연결되고 있으므로 오답

④ Instead of writing and sending letters, people began to use pinpricks to spell out a message on the front page of a newspaper.

▶ 우편 요금이 비싸다는 말 뒤에서, 아무 근거 없이 편지 대신 신문을 이용했다는 내용이 흐름상 어색하므로 정답

⑤ They could then send the newspaper through the post without having to pay a penny.

▶ 'They'가 가리키는 사람들이 앞 문장의 'people'을 의미하고 신문을 이용해 무료로 우편을 보냈다는 내용이 앞내용과 자연스럽게 이어지므로 오답

주요 어휘 및 표현

post	발송하다, 게시하다; 우편	free of charge	무료로
thrifty	검소한	convey	전달하다
apparently	언뜻 보기에	ordinary	평범한
spell out	철자를 표시하다	intended	의도된
receiver	수신자	stare at	~을 유심히 쳐다보다
unaware of	~을 눈치채지 못하는	pinprick	핀으로 찌른 작은 구멍
secrecy	비밀 유지	excessive	과도한
postage	우편 (요금)	establishment	확립
shilling	실링(영국의 옛 화폐 단위)	means	재력

4. 정답 [⑤]

해석

우리는 항상 다음 휴일, 물건 사기, 또는 음식 체험이 있는지 살피면서 기분을 좋게 해주는 경험을 찾아낸다. 행복에 대한 이런 접근은 비교적 최근의 것인데, 그것은 우리의 삶을 물질적으로 즐거움을 주는 것으로 채워 넣기도 하고 우리의 고통을 우리가 제어할 수 있다고 느끼기도 하는 우리의 능력에 좌우된다. 오늘날 우리가 알고 있는 진통제는 비교적 최근의 발명품이며, 물질적 안락에 대한 접근은 이제 훨씬 더 큰 비율의 전 세계 사람들의 손이 닿는 곳에 있다. 이런 과학 기술과 경제 발전은 상당한 문화적 영향을 미쳐서 우리가 우리의 부정적인 경험을 문제로 간주하게 하고 그 해결책으로 우리의 긍정적인 경험을 극대화하게 하였다. 하지만 이를 통해 우리는 인생에서 행복한 것이 단지 즐거움에 관련된 것만은 아니라는 것을 잊게 되었다. 안락감, 만족감 그리고 충족감이 행복의 특효약이었던 적은 한 번도 없었다. 오히려, 행복은 우리가 가장 상처받기 쉽거나 혼자이거나 고통을 겪는 그런 순간에 자주 발견된다. 행복은 거기, 이런 경험의 가장자리에 있고, 우리가 '그런' 종류의 행복을 언뜻 보게 될 때, 그것은 강력하고 뛰어나며 강렬하다.

비법 적용

Rather, happiness is often found in those moments we are most vulnerable, alone or in pain.

☞ (rather) 연결사 'Rather'로 앞내용을 예상할 수 있으며, '행복은 ~에서 발견되는 것이 아니다'라는 내용이 먼저 언급되어야 한다.

☞ 주어진 문장에서 행복이 발견되는 순간을 나타내고 있으므로, 뒤에 올 내용 역시 이와 유사한 내용일 것이라 예상할 수 있다.

We seek out feel-good experiences, always on the lookout for the next holiday, purchase or culinary experience. This approach to happiness is relatively recent; it depends on our capacity both to pad our lives with material pleasures and to feel that we can control our suffering.

☞ 행복에 대한 최근의 접근 방식에 대해 언급하고 있다.

① Painkillers, as we know them today, are a relatively recent invention and access to material comfort is now within reach of a much larger proportion of the world's population.

☞ 앞 문장에 제시된 행복에 대한 최근의 접근법에 대한 구체적인 예로 '진통제(painkillers)'와 '물질적 안락(material comfort)'에 대해 소개하고 있다.

② These technological and economic advances have had significant cultural implications, leading us to see our negative experiences as a problem and maximizing our positive experiences as the answer.

☞ (these+명사) 앞에서 말한 진통제와 물질적인 안락을 'these+명사'로 받아 부연 설명을 하고 있다.

③ Yet, through this we have forgotten that being happy in life is not just about pleasure.
☞ (yet, this) 역접의 연결사 'Yet' 뒤에서 앞 문장과 상반되는 의미의 '행복이 기쁨에 관한 것만은 아니다'라고 말하고 있다. 'this'는 앞 문장에 언급된 부정적 경험을 문제로 여기고 긍정적 경험의 극대화를 해답으로 여긴다는 것을 의미한다.

④ Comfort, contentment and satisfaction have never been the elixir of happiness.
☞ 'Comfort, contentment and satisfaction'은 앞 문장의 'pleasure'에 해당되는 내용이며, 이들이 행복의 특효약이 아니라고 말하고 있다.

⑤ Happiness is there, on the edges of these experiences, and when we get a glimpse of that kind of happiness it is powerful, transcendent and compelling.
☞ (there, these+명사, that+명사) 앞내용에서 행복이 '안락감, 만족감 그리고 충족감(Comfort, contentment and satisfaction)'에 있지 않다고 하였는데 '거기에(there)', '이러한 경험들(these experiences)의 가장자리에 행복이 있다고 하는 부분이 문맥상 어색하다. 앞에서 행복이 존재하는 구체적인 곳을 언급해줄 필요가 있다.

오답의 모든 것

① Painkillers, as we know them today, are a relatively recent invention and access to material comfort is now within reach of a much larger proportion of the world's population.
▶ 앞에서 언급된 행복에 대한 최신의 접근법에 대한 구체적인 사례가 나오므로 내용상 자연스럽게 이어지는 오답

② These technological and economic advances have had significant cultural implications, leading us to see our negative experiences as a problem and maximizing our positive experiences as the answer.
▶ 'These technological and economic advances'가 가리키는 내용이 앞 문장의 'painkillers'와 'material comfort'를 가리키며 의미상 유사하게 전개되고 있으므로 흐름이 자연스러운 오답

③ Yet, through this we have forgotten that being happy in life is not just about pleasure.
▶ 'Yet'과 'this'가 적절하게 사용되어 앞 문장의 내용과 흐름상 자연스럽게 연결되고 있으므로 오답

④ Comfort, contentment and satisfaction have never been the elixir of happiness.
▶ 'Comfort, contentment and satisfaction'은 앞 문장의 'pleasure'와 같은 의미로 동일한 내용이 이어지고 있어 논리상 오류가 없는 오답

⑤ Happiness is there, on the edges of these experiences, and when we get a glimpse of that kind of happiness it is powerful, transcendent and compelling.
▶ 진정한 행복을 찾을 수 있는 '거기(there)'에 해당하는 곳이 구체적으로 언급되지 않아 논리적으로 어색하므로 정답

주요 어휘 및 표현

vulnerable	상처받기 쉬운, 연약한	on the lookout for	~이 있는지 살피는
pad	채워 넣다, 메워 넣다	painkiller	진통제
proportion	비율	implication	영향, 함축
contentment	만족(감)	edge	가장자리
get a glimpse of	~을 언뜻 보다	compelling	강렬한, 설득력 있는

본문 110쪽

5. 정답 [①]

해석

농업을 습득하는 것과 그 후의 폐기는 지난 10,000년 동안에 걸쳐 반복적으로 일어났을지도 모르는 지역 상황에 대한 적응 전략으로 점차 인식되고 있다. 예를 들어, 태국 북부 출신의 현대 수렵채집 집단인 Mlabri에 대한 최근 연구에서, 이 사람들은 이전에는 농부였지만, 약 500년 전에 농업을 포기한 것으로 밝혀졌다. 이것은 감소 중인 현대의 수렵채집 문화 집단들 중 얼마나 많은 수가 실제로는 아마도 흉작, 식량 부족 또는 기후 변화로부터 시달린 후에야 더욱 유익한 생활양식으로서 이차적으로 수렵채집을 다시 채택했던 농부들의 후손이었는가에 대해 흥미로운 문제를 제기한다. 그러므로, 인간 사회의 '농업화'라고 불릴 수 있는 것의 과정은 적어도 국지적인 차원에서 보면 반드시 되돌릴 수 없는 것은 아니었다. 중서부 아메리카 원주민들로부터 아프리카 칼라하리의 !Kung족(族)에 이르기까지 전 세계의 수렵채집 문화는 풍부한 사냥감, 기후 변화 등과 같은 요인에 대응하여 농업을 아마도 역사상 여러 차례 채택하고 그 후에 폐기했을 것이다.

비법 적용

〈빈칸에서 묻는 말 파악하기〉

Therefore, the process of what may be termed the 'agriculturalization' of human societies was ______________________, at least on a local level.

☞ 빈칸에서 인간 사회에서 농업화의 과정이 어떠했는지 묻고 있으므로 농업화의 과정에 집중하여 읽도록 한다.

☞ 연결사 'Therefore' 뒤에서 앞내용에 대한 결과, 혹은 전체 주제를 요약하는 부분이 빈칸에 들어가야 한다.

Both the acquisition and subsequent rejection of agriculture are becoming increasingly recognized as adaptive strategies to local conditions that may have occurred repeatedly over the past ten millennia.

☞ 반복적으로 발생하는 지역 상황에 대한 적응 전략으로 '농업의 획득과 폐기(Both the acquisition and subsequent rejection of agriculture)'라는 전략에 대해 설명하고 있다.

For example, in a recent study of the Mlabri, a modern huntergatherer group from northern Thailand, it was found that these people had previously been farmers, but had abandoned agriculture about 500 years ago.

☞ 농업의 획득과 폐기에 관한 구체적인 사례를 들고 있다.

This raises the interesting question as to how many of the diminishing band of contemporary huntergatherer cultures are in fact the descendents of farmers who have only secondarily readopted huntergathering as a more useful lifestyle, perhaps after suffering from crop failures, dietary deficiencies, or climatic changes.

☞ '이것(This)'은 앞 문장의 '농업의 획득과 폐기'를 가리키며, 수렵채집을 선택한 이들이 사실은 농부의 후손이었다는 '농업의 획득과 폐기'의 과정에 대해 언급하고 있다.

Therefore, the process of what may be termed the 'agriculturalization' of human societies was________________ , at least on a local level.

☞ 빈칸은 '인간 사회의 '농업화'라고 불릴 수 있는 것의 과정(the process of what may be termed the 'agriculturalization' of human societies)' 즉, 지금까지 언급한 '농업의 획득과 폐기'의 과정에 대해 묻고 있다. 인과의 연결사 앞·뒤에는 동일한 맥락의 내용으로 이루어져야 하므로, 농업을 폐기하고 수렵채집을 선택한 사람들은 다시 '농업을 획득'할 수도 있을 거라 추론할 수 있다.

Huntergatherer cultures across the world, from midwestern Amerindians to !Kung in the African Kalahari, have adopted and subsequently discarded agriculture, possibly on several occasions over their history, in response to factors such as game abundance, climatic change, and so on.

☞ '농업의 획득과 폐기'에 대한 추가 사례가 제시되고 있다.

오답의 모든 것

① 반드시 되돌릴 수 없는 것은 아니었다

▶ **농업의 폐기와 습득에 관한 글로 앞에서 농업을 폐기한 사람들이 다시 '습득'할 수도 있다(되돌릴 수도 있다)는 의미가 완성되므로 정답 ('not necessarily'는 '반드시 ~한 것은 아니다'라는 부분 부정의 의미이며 'irreversible'의 부정의 의미와 결합하여 이중 부정, 즉 긍정의 의미로 사용되었음.)**

② 저항에 거의 부딪히지 않았다

▶ 영양소 부족, 기후 변화, 농업실패 등과 같은 이유 때문에 농업화를 폐기하였다고 하였으므로 저항 없이 충족되었다는 것은 오답

③ 적응에 필수적이었다
▶ 농업화가 적절하지 않았던 사례들이 제시되고 있으므로 적응에 필수적이라는 표현은 오답

④ 순수한 우연에 의해 시작되었다
▶ 순수한 우연으로 시작되었다는 내용은 언급되지 않았으므로 오답

⑤ 재고려의 대상이 되는 경우가 드물었다
▶ 농업의 습득과 폐기라는 것은 농업을 다시 고려했다는 의미가 포함되기 때문에 오답('rarely'는 부정의 의미임.)

주요 어휘 및 표현

acquisition	획득	subsequent	결과적인
rejection	거부, 거절	millenia	천 년
diminish	감소하는	contemporary	현대의
hunter-gatherer	수렵채집가	dietary deficiency	영양부족
agriculturalization	농업화	game	사냥감
abundance	풍부	irreversible	돌이킬 수 없는

본문 111쪽

6. 정답 [③]

해석

때때로 '그런데 이것이 예술인가?'라는 질문을 불러일으키지 않는다면 현대 예술이 제 역할을 하지 못하는 것처럼 보인다. 나는 그 질문이 물어볼 가치가 있는지 잘 모르겠다. 나에게는 예술과 예술이 아닌 것 간의 경계가 결코 뚜렷한 것이 될 수 없을 것이라고 생각된다. 설상가상으로 시, 희곡, 조각, 회화, 소설, 용, 기타 등등의 다양한 예술 형식은 매우 달라서, 나는 왜 우리가 그것들의 다양함을 표현할 수 있는 단 하나의 정의를 생각해낼 수 있다고 기대해야 하는지 잘 모르겠다. 예술은 비트겐슈타인의 '가족 유사성' 개념의 전형적인 예시인 것처럼 보인다. 무언가가 예술로서 자격을 갖추기 위한 필요충분조건을 명시하려고 노력해보라, 그러면 여러분은 여러분의 기준에 있어서의 하나의 예외를 항상 발견할 것이다. 만약 철학이 어떠한 예술의 변치 않는 본질을 찾아내는 데 있어서 실패를 인정한다면, 그것은 시도의 부재 때문일 리는 거의 없다. 거의 틀림없이 우리는 이것이 사상의 역사에 있어서 가장 부질없는 시도 중 하나였을 것이라고 생각할 충분한 이유가 있다.

비법 적용

〈빈칸에서 묻는 말 파악하기〉

Worse, as the various art forms–poetry, drama, sculpture, painting, fiction, dance, etc.– are so different, I'm not sure why we should expect to be able to come up with ____________________.

☞ 예술이 너무나 다르기 때문에(as–원인) 그 결과 빈칸의 것을 기대하기 어렵다고 있다.

☞ 'Worse'를 통해 앞내용보다 더 심각한 점을 언급하고 있다. 빈칸 앞에 있는 'not'에 주의하여 주제의 반대 의미가 되도록 빈칸을 완성해야 한다.

Sometimes it seems that contemporary art isn't doing its job unless it provokes the question, 'But is it art?' I'm not sure the question is worth asking. It seems to me that the line between art and notart is never going to be a sharp one.

☞ 예술과 예술이 아닌 것의 경계가 모호하여, 현대의 예술에서 '예술이란 무엇인가'라는 질문은 가치가 없다는 필자의 생각이 드러나 있다.

Worse, as the various art forms–poetry, drama, sculpture, painting, fiction, dance, etc.–are so different, I'm not sure why we should expect to be able to come up with ____________________.

☞ 앞에서 예술과 예술이 아닌 것의 경계가 모호하다고 언급하였고, 빈칸 문장에서는 예술의 형태가 매우 다양하다고 이야기하고 있으므로 빈칸에는 이와 관련된 결론이 들어가야 한다.

☞ 뒤에 이어지는 문장에서 구체적인 예시를 언급하고 있으므로 예시를 일반화한 문장이 빈칸에 들어갈 말이 된다.

Art seems to be a paradigmatic example of a Wittgensteinian 'family resemblance' concept. Try to specify the necessary and sufficient condition for something qualifying as art and you'll always find an exception to your criteria.

☞ 예술을 비트켄슈타인의 '가족 유사성'에 빗대어 설명하고 있다. 즉, 예술의 필요충분조건을 규정하려고 할 때 그 기준에 대한 예외 사항이 항상 존재한다고 말하고 있는데, 이는 예술의 경계가 '모호하다', '다양하다'는 앞내용과 유사하다.

If philosophy were to admit defeat in its search for some immutable essence of art, it is hardly through lack of trying. Arguably, we have very good reasons for thinking that this has been one of the biggest wild goose chases in the history of ideas.

☞ 철학의 사례를 들어 같은 말을 반복하고 있다. '예술의 변하지 않는 본질(예술의 정의)'을 찾지 못했다는 것은 그 본질을 찾으려는 시도를 하지 않아서가 아니며, 시도할 의미조차 없을 만큼 예술의 정의를 내리는 것이 어렵기 때문이라고 말하고 있다.

오답의 모든 것

① 예술의 기원을 추적할 세부적인 안내

▶ 예술의 기원을 찾아가는 내용은 관련이 없으므로 오답

② 예술을 통해 현실을 받아들일 새로운 방법

▶ 예술을 통해 현실을 인식하는 것은 관련이 없으므로 오답

③ 그것들의 다양함을 표현할 수 있는 단 하나의 정의

▶ 빈칸이 포함된 문장의 'not'과 해당 표현을 결합하면, 예술이 다양하고 항상 예외가 존재하여 정의를 내리기 어렵다는 본문의 내용과 일치하므로 정답

④ 다양한 예술적인 스타일을 섞을 수 있는 장르
▶ 다양한 예술 스타일을 혼합하는 것과 관련이 없으므로 오답

⑤ 존재하는 예술 형태에 도전할 수 있는 급진적인 아이디어
▶ 존재하는 예술의 형태에 도전하는 것이 아니라, 단지 예술의 본질이 무엇인지 규정하고자 하는 일이 어렵다는 내용이므로 오답

주요 어휘 및 표현

contemporary	현대의	provoke	불러일으키다
paradigmatic	전형적인	resemblance	유사성
specify	규정하다	qualify	자격을 부여하다
defeat	패배	immutable	변치 않는
essence	본질	wild goose chase	부질없는 시도

본문 112쪽

7. 정답 [③]

해석

신기술은 그것이 우리의 기존 습관을 얼마나 많이 바꾸겠다고 약속하는지와 이러한 습관의 강도 둘 다에 기초한 도전에 직면한다. ① 지속적인 행동 변화는 기존 습관을 바꾸려는 시도보다는 기존 습관을 통해 일어나야 한다. ② 전자계산기가 수학적인 계산을 더 빠르게 만든 것과 마찬가지로, 사람들은 기존 습관을 없애기보다 개선할 경우에만 혁신을 받아들일 것이다. ③ 전자 제품의 성공은 그것의 전자 처리 과정과 주요 부품 둘 다의 혁신적인 기술적 설계와 연관이 있다. ④ 따라서 공공 정책은 가장 덜 고착화된 습관을 목표로 함으로써 행동 변화를 장려해야 한다. ⑤ 예를 들어, 개발 도상국은 새로운 형태의 고단백 식품보다는 새로운 고단백 음료를 제공함으로써 단백질 섭취 증가를 촉진할 수 있었다.

비법 적용

New technologies encounter challenges based on both how many of our existing habits they promise to alter and the strength of these habits.
☞ 글의 주제 : 기존의 습관을 바꿀 때 고려할 점
글의 핵심 소재 : new technologies, existing habits

① Lasting behavioral change must occur through existing habits rather than attempts to alter them.

☞ 핵심 소재인 기존 습관이 언급되고 있으며 지속적인 행동의 변화는 이러한 기존의 습관을 통해 일어나야 한다고 말하고 있다.

② People are likely to adopt innovations only if they improve rather than destroy their existing habits, in the same way that electronic calculators made mathematical computations faster.

☞ 사람들은 기존 습관을 없애는 것이 아닌 습관을 개선해 줄 때에만 혁신(신기술, 행동의 변화)을 받아들인다는 점을 계산기에 비유하여 말하고 있다. 전자 계산기는 앞에서 언급된 '신기술'의 사례이며, 계산기가 계산을 더 빠르게 할 수 있도록 개선해주었기 때문에 사람들은 이를 받아들였다.

③ The success of an electronics product is linked to the innovative technological design both of its electronic processes and of its major components.

☞ 비법1, 2 오류) 핵심 소재인 습관에 관한 언급이 없으며 전자제품의 성공이 무엇에 달려있는가에 대한 주제와 관련 없는 내용을 다루고 있다.

④ Thus, public policy should encourage behavioral change by targeting the least fixed habits.

☞ '가장 덜 고착화된 습관(the least fixed habits)'을 목표로 행동 변화를 장려한다는 것은 기존의 습관을 개선한다는 앞내용과 유사한 맥락을 유지하고 있다.

⑤ For example, developing countries could encourage increased protein consumption by offering new high-protein beverages rather than new types of highprotein foods.

☞ 앞내용의 구체적 사례를 언급하고 있다. '단백질 섭취 증가(increased protein consumption)'는 앞내용의 행동의 변화를 꾀하는 '공공 정책(public policy)'의 예시이며, '새로운 단백질 음료(new highprotein beverages)'는 '가장 덜 고착화된 습관(the least fixed habits)'을 개선하려는 혁신을 의미한다.

오답의 모든 것

① Lasting behavioral change must occur through existing habits rather than attempts to alter them.

▶ 핵심 소재가 주제에 맞게 서술되고 있는 오답

② People are likely to adopt innovations only if they improve rather than destroy their existing habits, in the same way that electronic calculators made mathematical computations faster.

▶ 핵심 소재가 주제에 맞게 서술되고 있는 오답

③ The success of an electronics product is linked to the innovative technological design both of its electronic processes and of its major components.

▶ 앞에서 언급된 계산기를 이용하여 혼란을 유도하고 있으며, 전자제품의 성공 여부라는 주제와는 무관한 내용이므로 정답

④ Thus, public policy should encourage behavioral change by targeting the least fixed habits.
▶ 기존의 습관을 개선하여 행동의 변화를 유도한다는 내용이 일관성을 유지하므로 오답

⑤ For example, developing countries could encourage increased protein consumption by offering new highprotein beverages rather than new types of highprotein foods.
▶ 주제에 대한 구체적인 예를 다루고 있는 문장으로 오답 (핵심 소재를 비유적인 표현으로 나타내었기 때문에 핵심 소재가 없다고 생각하여 선택하지 않도록 주의)

주요 어휘 및 표현

encounter	직면하다	existing	기존의
alter	바꾸다, 변경하다	lasting	지속적인
adopt	받아들이다, 채택하다	innovation	혁신
improve	개선하다	computation	계산
component	부품	public policy	공공 정책
encourage	장려하다, 촉진하다	developing country	개발 도상국
target	목표로 하다	consumption	섭취, 소비
beverage	음료	protein	단백질

본문 113쪽

8. 정답 [④]

해석

우리가 매일 하는 일의 많은 부분은 자동적이고 습관에 의해 좌우되며, 의식적인 인식을 거의 필요로 하지 않는데, 그것은 나쁜 것이 아니다. Duhigg의 설명에 따르면, 우리의 습관은 꼭 필요한 정신 에너지 절약 장치이다. ① 우리는 새로운 문제가 발생할 때 그것을 해결할 수 있도록 의식적인 마음의 부담을 덜어주어야 한다. ② 예를 들어, 사교댄스를 추는 방법에 대한 문제를 해결하고 나면, 우리는 그것을 습관적으로 할 수 있어서 정신적으로 자유로워져, (춤에 집중하는) 대신에 춤을 추는 동안 대화에 집중할 수 있다. ③ 하지만 탱고를 처음 배울 때 말을 하려고 해보면 그것은 엉망진창이 되며, 우리는 스텝에 집중하기 위해 의식적인 주의가 필요하다. ④ 탱고 음악가는 다양한 배경에서 더 다양한 청중을 끌어 모으기 위해 각기 다른 장르의 음악을 한데 모은다. ⑤ 만약 우리가 모든 행동, 예를 들어 우리가 딛는 모든 스텝에서 발을 어디에 두어야 할지에 의식적으로 초점을 맞추어야 한다면 우리가 성취할 수 있는 것이 얼마나 적을지 상상해 보라.

비법 적용

Much of what we do each day is automatic and guided by habit, requiring little conscious awareness, and that's not a bad thing. As Duhigg explains, our habits are necessary mental energy savers.

☞ 글의 주제 : 정신적 에너지 절약을 위한 습관의 유용성
글의 핵심 소재 : habit, mental energy savers

① We need to relieve our conscious minds so we can solve new problems as they come up.

☞ 'relieve our conscious minds'는 앞 문장의 'requiring little conscious awareness'를 의미하며, 정신적 에너지 절약과 관련된 말이다.

② Once we've solved the puzzle of how to ballroom dance, for example, we can do it by habit, and so be mentally freed to focus on a conversation while dancing instead.

☞ 사교댄스를 배우는 과정을 예로 들고 있다. 춤을 배우고 나면, 습관적으로 춤을 출 수 있게 되고, 이는 정신적인 에너지를 절약하게 해주어 춤을 추면서 다른 일을 할 수 있게 해준다.

③ But try to talk when first learning to dance the tango, and it's a disaster – we need our conscious attention to focus on the steps.

☞ 역접 연결사 뒤에서 춤에 대한 습관 형성이 되기 전에 말을 하게 되면 엉망진창이 될 수있기 때문에, 초기에는 스텝에 집중하기 위한 노력이 필요하다고 말하고 있다. 즉, 습관이 되기 전에는 정신적 에너지가 필요함을 의미한다.

④ Tango musicians bring different genres of music together to attract a more diverse audience from varying backgrounds.

☞ 비법1, 2 오류) 글의 핵심 소재인 습관이 등장하지 않으며 탱고 음악가가 더 많은 청중을 끌기 위해서 다양한 배경 음악을 모으는 방법의 소개는 주제와 관련성이 없는 문장이다.

⑤ Imagine how little we'd accomplish if we had to focus consciously on every behavior – e.g., on where to place our feet for each step we take.

☞ ③번 문장에서 언급한 'our conscious attention'에 이어지는 내용으로 매사에 의식적으로 무엇인가를 집중하면 성취할 수 있는 것이 적다고 말하고 있다. 습관으로 인해 정신 에너지를 절약하면, 춤을 추면서 대화를 하는 식으로 더 많은 일을 할 수 있게 될 것이다.

오답의 모든 것

① We need to relieve our conscious minds so we can solve new problems as they come up.

▶핵심 소재인 습관이 정신적 에너지를 절약해준다는 내용이 드러나는 오답

② Once we've solved the puzzle of how to ballroom dance, for example, we can do it by habit, and so be mentally freed to focus on a conversation while dancing instead.

▶ 사교댄스를 배우는 사례를 들어 핵심 소재인 습관을 통해 정신적인 에너지를 줄여준다는 주제와의 일관성을 유지하는 오답

③ But try to talk when first learning to dance the tango, and it's a disaster – we need our conscious attention to focus on the steps.
▶ 습관이 형성되지 않은 배움의 초기에는 스텝에 더 많은 의식적인 집중력이 필요하다는 주제와 관련된 오답

④ Tango musicians bring different genres of music together to attract a more diverse audience from varying backgrounds.
▶ **앞에서 언급한 탱고를 이용하여 주제와 관련 없는 무관한 내용을 언급하고 있으므로 정답**

⑤ Imagine how little we'd accomplish if we had to focus consciously on every behavior – e.g., on where to place our feet for each step we take.
▶ ③번의 내용에 이어지는 내용으로 습관이 아닌 의식적으로 집중해야 할 때에는 성취할 수 있는 것이 적다고 하는 주제와 관련된 오답

주요 어휘 및 표현

conscious	의식적인	awareness	의식, 인식
ballroom dance	사교 댄스	disaster	재앙, 큰 실패
accomplish	성취하다	alert	경계하는
saver	절약 장치	beneficial	유익한, 이로운

본문 114쪽

9. 정답 [④]

해석

많은 산악 지역에서, 물을 이용할 권리가 토지의 소유와 연관되어 있는데, 예를 들어, 최근까지 안데스 산맥에서는 토지와 물 권리가 결합되어 토지와 함께 물 권리가 이전되었다. 그러나 주(州) 토지 개혁과 추가 공급원의 개발을 통해 물 권리가 토지와 분리되어 경매에 부쳐질 수도 있다. 그러므로 이것은 지역 사회의 모든 사람에게 이용할 권리를 보장하기보다는, 비용을 지불할 수 있는 사람에게 유리하다. 따라서 물이 없는 땅을 개인이 보유할 수도 있는 상황이 생긴다. 페루에서는, 정부가 토지와는 별도로 지역 사회에 물을 주고, 그것을 분배하는 것은 공동체의 몫이다. 예멘에서도 마찬가지로, 전통적인 분배는 100'립나'의 토지에 1척(타사)의 물이었다. 이것은 유수(流水), 우물 등의 전통적인 관개(灌漑) 공급에만 적용되었다. 갑작스럽게 불어난 물을 억류해서 얻어진 물은 불확실한 수원(水源)이 되는 것으로 여겨지기 때문에 이슬람 율법의 영향을 받지 않고, 따라서 그 물을 모아서 사용할 수 있는 사람들에게는 무료이다. 그러나 토지 단위에 따라 하는 이 전통적인 분배는 부분적으로는 새로운 공급의 개발에 의해서 뿐만 아니라, 경제적으로 상당히 중요한 작물의 재배 감소(→ 증가)에 의해서도 회피되었다. 이 작물은 일 년 내내 수확되고, 따라서 적정한 몫의 물 그 이상을 필요로 한다. 그 작물의 경제적 지위는 생계형 작물로부터 물 권리를 사거나 매수할 수 있도록 보장한다.

비법 적용

In many mountain regions, rights of access to water are associated with the possession of land – until recently in the Andes, for example, land and water rights were ① combined so water rights were transferred with the land.

☞ (병렬,예시) 예시문과 예시 앞에 제시된 문장은 유사한 의미가 되어야 한다. 예시 앞에서 '물의 이용 권리는 토지 소유와 연관되어 있다(rights of access to water are associated with the possession of land)'와 예시문인 '토지와 물 권리가 결합되어 있다(land and water rights were combined)'의 의미가 서로 동일한지 확인한다.

However, through state land reforms and the development of additional sources of supply, water rights have become separated from land, and may be sold at auction.

☞ (역접) 역접 뒤에서 앞에 나온 진술을 뒤집어 '물 사용 권리는 토지와 분리되어 경매로 판매된다'고 말하고 있다.

This therefore ② favours those who can pay, rather than ensuring access to all in the community.

☞ (인과) 'This'는 앞 문장(원인)을 의미하며, 'therefore'의 뒤는 앞내용에 대한 결과의 의미를 갖는다. 앞에서 경매로 판매된다고 하였으므로 돈을 지불할 수 있는 사람에게 '유리한' 상황이 되었다.

The situation arises, therefore, where individuals may hold land with no water. In Peru, the government grants water to communities separately from land, and it is up to the community to allocate it. Likewise in Yemen, the traditional allocation was one measure (tasah) of water to one hundred 'libnah' of land.

☞ (인과, 병렬) 돈으로 물 사용권 구매한다면 돈이 없는 사람들은 물을 얻지 못할 것이며, 그로 인한 결과를 'therefore'을 이용해 제시하고 있다. 'the situation'은 관계부사 'where'의 수식을 받아 '물이 없는 땅을 소유한 사람들'의 상황을 의미한다(주어를 수식하는 관계사절은 수식을 받아 길어질 경우 종종 문장 뒤로 도치된다). 'Likewise'는 앞내용과 유사한 상황을 추가로 제시할 때 사용하며, 여기서는 물 사용 권리가 토지와 분리된 페루와 예멘의 유사한 사례를 언급하고 있다.

This applied only to traditional irrigation supplies – from runoff, wells, etc., where a supply was ③ guaranteed. Water derived from the capture of flash floods is not subject to Islamic law as this constitutes an uncertain source, and is therefore free for those able to collect and use it.

☞ (부연 설명) 'traditional irrigation supplies(전통적인 관개 공급)'에 관해 관계부사의 계속적 용법으로 설명하고 있다. '전통적인 관개 공급'은 유수와 우물 등으로부터 공급이 '보장되는(guaranteed)' 곳이다.

However, this traditional allocation per unit of land has been bypassed, partly by the development of new supplies, but also by the ④ decrease in cultivation of a crop of substantial economic importance.

☞ (병렬) 'partly A but also B'는 'not only A but also B(A뿐만 아니라 B도)'와 유사한 의미를 갖는 표현이다. 그러므로 A와 B는 서로 병렬 관계로 유사한 맥락의 어휘가 들어가야 한다. A에 해당하는 표현인 '새로운 공급의 개발(by the development of new supplies)'은 긍정의 뉘앙스를 지니고 있기 때문에 B도 유사한 의미가 되려면 '경제적으로 상당히 중요한 작물의 재배(cultivation of a crop of substantial economic importance)'가 '증가(increase)'되어야 할 것이다. 새로운 작물 개발 등으로 인해 전통적인 물 공급 방식이 회피되고 있다는 내용을 언급하고 있다.

This crop is harvested throughout the year and thus requires more than its fair share of water. The economic status of the crop ⑤ ensures that water rights can be bought or bribed away from subsistence crops.

☞ (부연 설명) '그 작물의 경제적 지위(The economic status of the crop)'에 관한 설명이다. '그 작물(the crop)'은 앞에서 언급된 '경제적으로 중요하고 일 년 내내 수확되기 때문에 적정한 몫 이상의 물을 필요로 하는 작물'을 의미하므로 반드시 물의 권리를 구매해야 한다는 내용이 오는 것이 적절하다.

오답의 모든 것

① combined

▶ 예시를 이용해 앞내용과 동일한 의미로 적절히 사용되었기에 적절히 쓰인 오답

② favours

▶ 인과 관계의 문장에서 경매에서 물 권리를 구매하려면 지불 능력이 있는 사람에게 유리한 구조이므로 적절히 쓰인 오답

③ guaranteed

▶ 전통 관개 공급에 대한 설명으로, 이것은 유수와 우물로부터 공급이 보장되는 것이기에 바르게 쓰인 오답

④ decrease

▶ **병렬 구조를 활용해 출제된 것으로 'partly A but also B'가 'not only A but also B(A뿐만 아니라 B도)'와 같은 의미의 구조임. 따라서 앞·뒤가 유사한 맥락으로 제시되어야 하기에 적절하지 않은 정답 (전통적인 물 공급 방식을 회피하는 이유는 경제적으로 중요한 작물의 재배가 증가하였기 때문에 직접적인 물 사용권리가 필요했을 것임.)**

⑤ ensures

▶ 'the crop'은 '경제적으로 중요하고 일 년 내내 수확되기 때문에 적정한 몫 이상의 물을 필요로 하는 작물'이므로 이는 물공급이 보장되어야 가능할 것이기에 적절히 쓰인 오답

주요 어휘 및 표현

transfer	이전하다	reform	개혁
auction	경매	grant	주다, 수여하다
allocate	분배하다, 할당하다	runoff	유수(流水)
well	우물	guarantee	보장하다
derived from	~에서 얻은	flash flood	갑작스럽게 불어난 물
be subject to	~의 영향을 받다	cultivation	재배
bypass	회피하다, 무시하다, 우회하다	constitute	~이 되는 것으로 여겨지다, 구성하다
crop	작물	substantial	상당한

본문 115쪽

10. 정답 [⑤]

해석

아리스토텔레스는 모든 인간이 정치 활동을 하도록 허용되어야 한다고 생각하지 않았다. 즉 그의 체계에서 여자, 노예, 그리고 외국인은 자신 및 다른 사람을 다스릴 권리로부터 명백히 배제되었다. 그럼에도 불구하고, 정치는 어떤 공동의 목표와 목적을 향한 독특한 집단 활동이라는 그의 기본적인 생각은 오늘날에도 여전히 울려 퍼지고 있다. 하지만 어느 목적인가? 고대 세계 이후의 많은 사상가와 정계 인사들이 정치가 이룰 수 있거나 이루어야 하는 목표에 관해 각기 다른 생각을 발달시켰다. 이런 접근법은 정치적 도덕주의라고 알려져 있다.

도덕주의자들에게 정치적 삶은 윤리 혹은 도덕 철학의 한 분야여서 도덕주의적 정치 사상가 집단에 많은 철학자가 있는 것은 놀랄 일이 아니다. 정치적 도덕주의자들은 정치란 실질적인 목표를 이루는 쪽으로 향해야 한다고, 즉 정치적인 처리 방식은 어떤 것을 보호하기 위해 체계화되어야 한다고 주장한다. 이런 것들 중에는 정의, 평등, 자유, 행복, 동포애, 또는 민족 사결권과 같은 정치적 가치가 있다. 가장 근본적인 입장에서 도덕주의는, 1516년에 출간되었고 이상 국가를 상상했던, 영국 정치가이자 철학자인 Thomas More의 책 'Utopia'에서 이름을 딴, 유토피아로 알려진 이상적인 정치 사회에 대해 묘사한다. 유토피아적 정치사상은 고대 그리스 철학자인 플라톤의 책 '국가론'으로 거슬러 올라가는데, 그것은 Robert Nozick과 같은 현대 사상가에 의해 아이디어를 탐구하기 위해 여전히 사용된다. 일부 이론가는 유토피아적 정치사상은 유망한(→위험한)일이라고 여기는데, 그것이 지금까지 전체주의적인 폭력의 정당화로 이어졌기 때문이다. 그러나 최선의 상태에서 유토피아적 사상은 더 나은 사회를 향해 노력하는 과정의 일부이며, 많은 사상가는 추구되거나 보호되어야 할 가치를 제안하기 위해 그것을 사용한다.

비법 적용

Aristotle did not think that all human beings should be allowed to engage in political activity: in his system, women, slaves, and foreigners were explicitly ① excluded from the right to rule themselves and others.

☞ (부연 설명) '콜론(:)'을 활용하여 출제된 문제이다. 콜론 앞·뒤의 내용은 서로 유사한 의미를 갖는다. 따라서 첫 문장의 '모든 인간이 정치 활동을 허용 받아야 하는 것은 아니다'라는 말 뒤에서 정치 활동에서 배제된 사람들에 대한 설명이 이어지는 것은 적절하다.

Nevertheless, his basic idea that politics is a unique collective activity that is directed at certain ② common goals and ends still resonates today. But which ends? Many thinkers and political figures since the ancient world have developed different ideas about the goals that politics can or should achieve. This approach is known as political moralism.

☞ (부연 설명) 관계대명사 'that' 뒤에서 '독특한 집단 활동(a unique collective activity)'에 대해 설명하는 부분이다. 집단 활동은 공동의 목표를 향하고 있으며, 역접 뒤에서 모두가 정치활동을 허용 받는 것은 아니지만 공동의 목표를 향한 집단 활동이 바로 정치라고 말하고 있다.

For moralists, political life is a branch of ethics – or moral philosophy – so it is ③ unsurprising that there are many philosophers in the group of moralistic political thinkers.

☞ (인과) 인과 관계의 'so' 앞에서 정치적 삶은 윤리 혹은 도덕철학의 한 분야(원인)라고 하였기에, '도덕주의적 정치 사상가 집단에 많은 철학자가 있는(many philosophers in the group of moralistic political thinkers)' 것은 당연한 일일 것이다.

Political moralists argue that politics should be directed toward achieving substantial goals, or that political arrangements should be organized to ④ protect certain things.

☞ (병렬) 컴마 뒤에 'or'가 있으면, 동격의 의미를 갖게 되어 'or' 앞·뒤에 있는 두 개의 'that'절이 서로 유사한 의미를 지니게 된다. 따라서 정치란 '실질적인 목표를 이루는 쪽으로 향해야 한다(directed toward achieving substantial goals)'와, '어떤 것을 보호하기 위해 체계화되어야 한다(organized to ④ protect certain things)'가 서로 유사한 의미인지 확인할 수 있다.

Some theorists consider Utopian political thinking to be a ⑤ promising undertaking, since it has led in the past to justifications of totalitarian violence. However, at its best, Utopian thinking is part of a process of striving toward a better society, and many thinkers use it to suggest values to be pursued or protected.

☞ (인과) 인과 관계의 구조가 쓰였으므로 'since' 앞·뒤의 내용이 유사한 맥락을 지니는지 확인한다. 'since' 뒤의 원인 부분에서 유토피아적 정치사상이 '전체주의적인 폭력의 정당화(justifications of totalitarian violence)'로 이어진다고 하였으므로, 이는 유망하다기보다는 '위험한(dangerous)' 일로 여겨질 것이다.

오답의 모든 것

① excluded
▶ 부연설명을 하는 콜론(:)을 이용한 문장으로 '모든 사람이 정치 활동을 허용 받는 것은 아니다'와 '여성, 노예 등은 배제되었다'가 동일한 의미이므로 오답

② common
▶ 독특한 '집단' 활동에 대한 부연 설명으로 집단 활동이 '공동의' 목표를 향한다는 내용은 적절히 쓰인 오답

③ unsurprising
▶ 정치적 삶이 윤리나 도덕적 철학의 한 분야이기에 도덕주의적 정치 사상가 집단에 많은 철학자가 있다는 사실은 자연스러운 인과 관계이므로 적절히 쓰인 오답

④ protect
▶ 동격의 구조를 활용하여 앞·뒤의 내용이 '실질적인 목표를 이뤄야 한다'는 유사한 의미로 적절히 쓰인 오답

⑤ promising
▶ **유토피아적인 정치사상이 지금까지 전체주의적인 폭력의 정당화로 이어졌기 때문에(원인) 위험한 일로 여긴다는 맥락이므로 정답 (promising을 '위험한'과 같은 의미를 지닌 'dangerous' 정도의 단어로 바꿔 써야 함.)**

주요 어휘 및 표현

engage in	~에 종사하다	explicitly	명백히
exclude	배제하다	collective	집단적인
common	공동의	end	목적
political figure	정계 인사	moralism	도덕주의
unsurprising	놀랍지 않은	substantial	실질적인
arrangements	처리 방식	protect	보호하다
national self-determination	민족 자결권	radical	근본적인, 급진적인
undertaking	일, 사업	justification	정당화
totalitarian	전체주의적인	strive	노력하다

11. 정답 [③]

해석

수학 연습과 담화는 모든 학생이 수학 학습자로서 긍정적인 정체성을 발달시키는 문화적 맥락, 학생 관심사, 그리고 실생활 상황 안에 위치해야 한다. 수학 기술을 고립적으로 그리고 학생들의 이해와 정체성이 결여된 채 지도하는 것은 그들이 명시적 교수로 이익을 얻는 데 무력하게 만든다. 따라서 우리는 명시적 교수가 학생들에게 유익하다는 데에는 동의하지만, 문화적으로 적합한 교수법과 학습 및 숙달을 촉진하는 비 학습 영역에 대한 고려를 포함하는 것이 수학 교수에서 명시적 교수를 필연적으로 강화한다고 제안한다. 나아가 교사는 교실에서의 담화와 연습을 통해 학생의 정체성, 주체성, 그리고 독립심을 장려하는 환경을 개발하는 데 중요한 역할을 한다. 맥락화된 학습 과정에 적극적으로 참여하는 학생들은 학습 과정을 통제하고 있고 과거 학습 경험과 연계를 맺어 더 깊고 더 의미 있는 학습을 촉진할 수 있다.

비법 적용

Thus, we agree that explicit instruction benefits students but propose that incorporating culturally relevant pedagogy and consideration of nonacademic factors that ③ promoting learning and mastery must enhance explicit instruction in mathematics instruction.

☞ 준동사 vs 동사) 'factors'를 수식하는 관계 대명사 'that' 뒤에 동사가 없으므로, 동사 'promote'로 바꿔야 한다.

오답의 모든 것

Mathematical practices and discourses should be situated within cultural contexts, student interests, and reallife situations ① where all students develop positive identities as mathematics learners.

▶ 관계대명사 vs 관계부사) 뒤 문장이 완전한 구조이며 선행사인 'situations'을 수식하는 'where'은 적절히 쓰인 오답

Instruction in mathematics skills in isolation and devoid of student understandings and identities renders them ② helpless to benefit from explicit instruction.

▶ 형용사 vs 부사) 'render+목적어+보어' 의 구조에서 목적어인 'them'을 설명하는 형용사 'helpless'는 적절히 쓰인 오답

Furthermore, teachers play a critical role in developing environments ④ that encourage student identities, agency, and independence through discourses and practices in the classroom.

▶ 관계대명사 vs 접속사) 뒤 문장의 주어가 없는 불완전한 구조이며 선행사인 'environments'를 수식하는 관계사 'that'은 적절히 쓰인 오답

Students who are actively engaged in a contextualized learning process are in control of the learning process and are able to make connections with past learning experiences ⑤ to foster deeper and more meaningful learning.

▶ to부정사 vs 동사원형) 뒤 문장의 구조가 완전한 상태에서 to부정사의 부사적용법 중 결과적 의미(~해서…하다)로 쓰인 'to foster'는 적절하게 쓰인 오답

주요 어휘 및 표현

be situated	~에 위치하다	isolation	고립
render	주다, ~하게 만들다	helpless	무기력한
explicit	명백한	relevant	적절한, 적합한
pedagogy	교육학	foster	촉진하다, 기르다

본문 117쪽

12. 정답 [②]

해석

'기념비적'이라는 말은 이집트 예술의 기본적인 특징을 표현하는 데 매우 근접하는 단어이다. 그 전에도 그 이후에도, 기념비성이라는 특성이 이집트에서처럼 완전히 달성된 적은 한 번도 없었다. 이에 대한 이유는 그들 작품의 외적 크기와 거대함이 아니다–비록 이집트인들이 이 점에 있어서 몇 가지 대단한 업적을 달성했다는 것이 인정되지만, 많은 현대 구조물은 순전히 물리적인 크기의 면에서는 이집트의 구조물들을 능가한다. 그러나 거대함은 기념비성과는 아무 관련이 없다. 예를 들어, 겨우 사람 손 크기의 이집트의 조각이 Leipzig의 전쟁 기념비를 구성하는 그 거대한 돌무더기보다 더 기념비적이다. 기념비성은 외적 무게의 문제가 아니라 '내적 무게'의 문제이다. 이 내적 무게가 이집트 예술이 지닌 특성인데, 이집트 예술은 그 안에 있는 모든 작품이 단지 폭이 몇 인치에 불과하거나 나무에 새겨져 있을지라도, 마치 산맥처럼 원시 시대의 돌로 만들어진 것처럼 보일 정도이다.

비법 적용

Never before and never since has the quality of monumentality been achieved as fully as it ② did in Egypt.

☞ 대동사) 'as' 뒤에서 자주 쓰이는 대동사 형태로 'did' 이외에 다른 동사가 없기 때문에 대동사로 쓰였음을 확인할 수 있다. 앞에 나온 동사가 'has been achieved'이며, 문맥상 과거의 상황에 비교하고 있기 때문에 과거 시제를 사용하여 did가 아닌 'was achieved'의 'was'로 바꿔야 한다. 문두에 'never'로 시작하는 부정어 도치가 쓰여 '부정어 have S p.p.'형태로 쓰였다.

오답의 모든 것

"Monumental" is a word that comes very close to ① expressing the basic characteristic of Egyptian art.

▶ 동사 vs 준동사) that절 안에 동사 'comes'가 있고, 'close to'가 전치사로서 동명사를 목적어로 받기 때문에 밑줄 친 'expressing'은 적절히 쓰인 오답

Many modern structures exceed ③ those of Egypt in terms of purely physical size.

▶ 대명사의 수일치) 대명사'those'가 지칭하는 명사가 앞의 비교 대상인 'structures'를 지칭하므로 복수인 'those'는 적절히 쓰인 오답

An Egyptian sculpture no bigger than a person's hand is more monumental than that gigantic pile of stones ④ that constitutes the war memorial in Leipzig, for instance.

▶ 관계대명사 vs 접속사) 'that' 뒤의 문장은 주어가 없는 불완전한 구조이며, 선행사인 'that gigantic pile of stones'을 수식하므로 관계대명사 'that'은 적절히 쓰인 오답

This inner weight is the quality which Egyptian art possesses to such a degree that everything in it seems to be made of primeval stone, like a mountain range, even if it is only a few inches across or ⑤ carved in wood.

▶ 분사, 병렬) 'or' 뒤에서 반복된 표현인 'it is'가 생략된 구조이며, 주어 'it'이 '새기는' 것이 아니라 '새겨지는'의 수동의 의미를 갖기 때문에 과거분사 'carved'는 적절히 쓰인 오답

주요 어휘 및 표현

monumental	기념비적인	external	외부의
massiveness	거대함	admittedly	인정하건대
exceed	능가하다	carve	새기다

망설이는 순간

너만 아싸된다!